The Power to Die

The Power to Die

Slavery and Suicide in British North America

TERRI L. SNYDER

The University of Chicago Press
Chicago and London

The University of Chicago Press, Chicago 60637
The University of Chicago Press, Ltd., London

Published 2015
Paperback edition 2026
Printed in the United States of America

35 34 33 32 31 30 29 28 27 26   1 2 3 4 5

ISBN-13: 978-0-226-28056-1 (cloth)
ISBN-13: 978-0-226-85457-1 (paper)
ISBN-13: 978-0-226-28073-8 (e-book)
DOI: https://doi.org/10.7208/chicago/9780226280738.001.0001

Library of Congress Cataloging-in-Publication Data
Snyder, Terri L., 1956– author.
The power to die : slavery and suicide in British North America / Terri L. Snyder.
pages cm
Includes bibliographical references and index.
ISBN 978-0-226-28056-1 (cloth : alk. paper)—ISBN 978-0-226-28073-8 (e-book) 1. Slaves—Suicidal behavior—North America. 2. Slavery—North America—History. 3. Suicide—United States—History. I. Title.
E443.S594 2015
306.3′62097—dc23

2015012390

♾ This paper meets the requirements of ANSI/NISO Z39.48-1992 (Permanence of Paper).

Authorized Representative for EU General Product Safety Regulation (GPSR) queries: **Easy Access System Europe**—Mustamäe tee 50, 10621 Tallinn, Estonia, gpsr.requests@easproject.com

For Jesse

CONTENTS

FIGURES

ACKNOWLEDGMENTS

This book has been long in the making and has had many influences, and it is a pleasure to express my gratitude to those who helped to shape its final form. First thanks go to the anonymous readers for the University of Chicago Press. As models of scholarly review—frank in their criticism, sincere in their praise—they pushed me to rethink the arguments and structure of the manuscript. I am also indebted to my editors at Chicago. Robert Devens saw promise in the project, and Tim Mennel graciously worked with me through its conclusion. Thanks as well to Russ Damian and Nora Devlin for editorial assistance and to Michael Koplow for expert copyediting.

I am also grateful to those individuals who commented on previously published portions of the manuscript. In particular, Vincent Brown, Edward Linenthal, and Mark M. Smith offered perceptive observations on the article that preceded the book; I thank the *Journal of American History* for permission to repurpose that material here. I presented parts of this project across and outside of the United States and benefited from thoughtful commentary by Trevor Burnard, Edward Countryman, John Demos, Susan E. Gray, Margaret Newell, and James Sidbury and profited from the observations of audiences at meetings of the European Early American Studies Association in Venice; the Omohundro Institute of Early American History and Culture in Quebec City; the Western Association of Women Historians in Tuscon; the Ohio Seminar for Early American History at the University of Ohio in Columbus; the Making Books, Shaping Readers Project at University College, Cork, Ireland; the California American Studies Association at Soka University, Alisa Viejo; and the American Studies Graduate Student-Faculty Colloquium at California State University, Fullerton.

I have been fortunate to have enjoyed generous institutional support that helped me bring this project to completion. A Faculty Award from the

National Endowment for the Humanities provided me with a year to devote to research and writing this book. Fellowships from the Huntington Library, the Library Company of Philadelphia, and the Virginia Historical Society allowed me to conduct research in their rich collections, while College of Humanities and Social Sciences Dean's Summer Research Stipends and Faculty Research Grants from California State University, Fullerton, facilitated travel to state archives and supported summer writing. I am also grateful to Roy Ritchie and Steven Hindle, respectively the former and current W. M. Keck Foundation Director of Research at the Huntington Library, for generously providing me with an office refuge in which to work out my thoughts and plans for this book.

Librarians and archivists were generous in discussing their collections with me and pointing me in useful directions. I owe hearty thanks to Jackie Brown at the British Library; to Connie King, Nicole Joniec, and Phil Lapansky at the Library Company of Philadelphia; to Minor Weisiger and Sandy Treadway at the Library of Virginia; to Frances Pollard and Jamison Davis at the Virginia Historical Society; to Bryan Collars at the Department of Archives and History in South Carolina; to Leslie Hall of the Wellcome Institute; to Matthew A. Harris at the Special Collections Library at the University of Kentucky; and to the staff at the State Archives of North Carolina, the South Caroliniana Library, and the South Carolina Historical Society. More locally, I owe a huge thanks to Juan Gomez, Leslie Jobsky, Brian Moeller, Frank Osen, Jaeda Snow, and Catherine Wehrey at the Huntington Library. I am also grateful for the tireless efforts on my behalf by the staff of CSUF's Pollak Library. Stacy Caron patiently filled my numerous interlibrary loan requests, while near the end of this project, when an earthquake had closed the upper stacks of the library, David Duncan, Long Lammy, Kevin Phillips, and Christopher Salomone cheerfully and quickly paged many book requests for me.

This project has been greatly enriched by conversations with fellow scholars and generous colleagues. On this score, I am indebted to Rick Bell, Sharon Block, Holly Brewer, Kathy Brown, Thomas E. Buckley, S.J., Kevin Dawson, Nina Dayton, Shannon Doyle, Richard Godbeer, Sarah Hand-Meacham, Alison Kibler, Isabell Klaiber, Mary Helen McMurran, Simon Newman, Mary Beth Norton, Charles Romney, David Silkenat, Diane Miller Sommerville, and Roxann Wheeler. K. Dian Kriz, Katherine M. Smith, and Farid Leonardo Suárez were extraordinary in helping me parse some of the visual materials used in this book. At California State University, Fullerton, I am lucky to have enriching and discerning colleagues, both within and beyond the Department of American Studies, in Dustin Abnet, Mitch Avila,

Allan Axerad, the late Gordon Bakken, Erica Ball, Jesse Battan, Renae Bredin, April Bullock, Angela Della Volpe, Nancy Fitch, Sheryl Fontaine, Margaret Garber, Stephanie George, Adam Golub, Joe Gonzalez, Wayne Hobson, John Ibson, Carrie Lane, Elaine Lewinnek, Karen Lystra, Craig McConnell, Mike Norton, Andrea Patterson, Michael Steiner, Pamela Steinle, Susie Woo, and Leila Zenderland. Special thanks as well to Karla Arellano and Liz Ortiz for their administrative expertise and for their many acts of assistance on my behalf. I have benefited tremendously from conversations with my students, especially Melissa Anderson, Jamal Batts, Adriana Ruvalcaba, John Carlos Marquez, and Allison Wanger, and take great pleasure not only in thanking them, but also in watching their futures unfold, both within and outside of the academy.

Several individuals deserve special mention and allow me to reflect on my good fortune in life. Erica Ball, Jeannine DeLombard, Ann Plane, and James Spady graciously stepped up to read and comment on portions of the manuscript and guided me through some of its more harrowing moments. Their suggestions and insights—as well as their own scholarship—markedly improved this project. April Bullock traveled with me on research trips and generously contributed her time as well as her sound historical sense; she also probably learned more about South Carolina coroner's reports than she ever wanted to know. Rowan Bullock-Vaughan and Joe Vaughan deserve special mention as well for their enlivening presence. Heidi Brayman-Hackel is a paragon of unparalleled insight. As my officemate at the Huntington, she not only endured the audible groans inspired by revisions, she offered astute advice at crucial moments. I am lucky to count Linda Kerber among my staunchest of friends and allies; as a model of scholarly engagement, she has long inspired me. Kathy Jellison makes me laugh like no one else and has always been a loyal friend; she accompanied me to St. Simon's Island so that I could visit and photograph Ebos Landing. Hikes with Susanah Shaw Romney were intellectually stimulating and physically restorative; substantial bits of this book got worked out on the Beaudry Loop. Over dinner at Church and State in Los Angeles, Fredrika Teute helped me work out the precise focus for the book, and much later offered wise counsel that enabled me to complete it. Sharon Wood has always been among my first and best sounding boards, and I treasure our annual summer writing week in Maine.

Outside of the academy, friends and family deserve to be recognized since they, too, lived through the vicissitudes of this project. Jean Hagen has been a steadfast listener throughout the process of writing this book and has provided me with welcome respites from it. Steve Harrison has long been an ideal friend to me and to this book; I thank him for hanging in there through its completion and look forward to enjoying with him the newest phase of his life. I also thank Sharon Hobson for introducing me to midcoast Maine and inviting me to her camp; I am very lucky to count her as a wise and generous friend. Sue Winter did not live to see this book completed, and when she passed on, a great light of my life went dark. Her legacy to me, however, was the best of gifts, and by any reckoning, I am lucky indeed to count myself a member of the Lyons and Taylor clans. Thank you Sydney, Greg, Hannah, and Kate as well as Jordan, Laura, and Adelaide, for welcoming me into your families and for all of the many things you do for me and bring to my life. To my mother and father, Pat and Carol Snyder, as well as to my brothers, Michael and Patrick, I thank you, once again, for teaching me about what matters.

It seems perhaps ironic to dedicate a book whose subject is death to the person who has brought the greatest joy to my life. Yet in the final summing up, Jesse Battan has made all things possible for me. This book is for him.

PROLOGUE

Anna's Leap

—but I did not want to go, and I jump'd out of the window—

—Anna, *A Portraiture of Domestic Slavery*, 1817[1]

Her name was Anna. An enslaved woman confined to the attic in George Miller's three-story brick tavern on F Street in the District of Columbia, she was part of a coffle of slaves destined for Georgia in 1815. She awaited transport with two of her children; her Maryland owner had sold them to a "Georgia man," a slave trader, but had retained ownership of Anna's husband and refused to let her see him before she left. Desperate over the separation of her family and uncertain about the future, in the early morning hours of December 19, Anna leapt from the garret window of her attic room into the empty street below. She survived the fall. Afterward, she recollected that she was so confused and distracted—"I did'nt know hardly what I was about"—that she leapt out the window rather than parting with her family and enduring enslavement in the Deep South (figure 00.1).[2]

Anna's leap did not go unnoticed. Reports of her attempt at self-destruction echoed beyond the hushed square in the nation's capital, carrying a variety of political messages and occasioning outright debate. The Washington mayor, James Heighe Blake, and his wife, Elizabeth Holdsworth Blake, resided near Miller's tavern. She was roused by the sound of Anna's fall and subsequent groans, a detail that suggests the gendered conscience of antislavery sentiment; the distress of the enslaved mother's distinctive plight stirred the empathy of the free woman, herself the mother of five children. The mayor, trained as a physician, was called to the scene to treat Anna's wounds, an act that was emblematic of his need to address the ongoing injuries of slavery—and the wrongs endured by enslaved people—in the city that he governed.[3]

00.1. "Asking her what was the cause of her doing such a frantic act as that, she replied, *'They brought me away with two of my children, and would'nt let me see my husband—they did'nt sell my husband, and I did'nt want to go;—I was so confus'd and [d]'istracted, that I did'nt know hardly what I was about—but I did'nt want to go, and I jumped out the window;—but I am sorry now that I did it;—they have carried my children off with 'em to Carolina.'*" Source: Jesse Torrey, *A Portraiture of Domestic Slavery* (Philadelphia, 1817). This item is reproduced by permission of The Huntington Library, San Marino, California.

Anna's leap also awakened discord over slavery in the early United States. In April 1816, four months after she jumped out the window, hers was one of several reports of slave suicide that inspired an investigation into human trafficking in the District of Columbia. One year later, her story was chronicled in Jesse Torrey's *Portraiture of Domestic Slavery in the United States*, and when Miller's tavern burned in 1819, at least one citizen refused to join the bucket brigade, preferring instead that the structure that had confined Anna and other enslaved people burn to the ground. One early twentieth-century historian claimed that the controversy generated by Anna's leap made the site one of the more historic places in the nation's capital. While her suicide attempt became an immediate political example for antislavery activists, Anna survived to become a local legend and was sought out for interviews well into the 1830s.[4]

An engraving made by German immigrant artist Alexander Rider accompanied Anna's story and captured the essential details of the scene. In it, Anna's figure exists in sharp relief against the shadowy courtyard. The startling appearance of her body, seemingly suspended in air, stands out against the planes of domestic urban architecture. Alternating rectangles of dark and light—windowpanes, door panels, brick courses, cobblestones—accentuate the shuttered vacancy of the neighborhood as the eye travels toward the horizon. Every structure is dark; every door is closed; each window is fastened. At this moment of seemingly impending death, she is the only living person in sight.[5]

Anna is arrested in midfall, posing contradictions for the viewer to consider. The whiteness of her dress signals her purity, even as it hugs her breasts and thighs and exposes her bare arms, décolletage, and feet. As the instrument of her own destruction, she is simultaneously a sexualized object. Beneath a smudge of clouds, she is illuminated by moonlight, while at the edge of the square, cedarlike trees, traditional sentries of burial grounds, bear witness to her descent. While suicide was a crime in many jurisdictions at the time and some churches refused to offer rites to or inter those who killed themselves, the light underscores the innocence of her motives and the trees mark this as hallowed space. This seeming suicide, while tragic, sprang from pure intentions: Anna's impending self-destruction, driven by grief and unmarked by intentionality—"but I did not want to go"—is not sensationalized as the result of sexual seduction, romantic melancholy, or excess debauchery, typical themes in popular culture depictions of suicide at the time.[6] Anna's leap may have been an act of compulsion, but her words testify that the prospect of separation from her family propelled her out of the garret window. The blame for this act is assigned to agents of the domestic slave trade, including viewers of this image who tolerated its existence, even in the nation's capital.

Anna's leap, like other acts of suicide by enslaved people before and after her, exemplified the contradictions of slavery that had arisen in early North America. Perhaps foremost among these is that suicide, an anguished assertion of personhood, undermined the human commodification—the chattel principle—that was fundamental to enslavement.[7] Once dead, a slave ceased being an object of property, an entity to be traded, or a subject from which to extract labor. In this sense, self-destruction by enslaved people was often viewed as an act of power, a visceral rejection of enslavement as well as a visible statement of personhood. Yet there was a fatal cost in asserting the power to die, of course. Death by suicide was not always, consistently, or even typically an unequivocal, unambiguous, or intentional act. For instance, when Anna declared, "I did not want to go," she meant that she did not want to leave her family and travel with the coffle of slaves to the Deep South; indirectly, her statement also referred to her self-destructive leap out of the window. Afterwards, she reflected, "I am sorry now that I did it." She felt remorse because her disabling fall ensured that her children went south without her; whatever their fate, in retrospect she would have preferred to face it with them.[8]

Accounts of self-destruction by enslaved people can be found across a variety of early Anglo-American institutions and, even before the rise of antislavery activism in Revolutionary-era America, they were powerful vehicles for exposing the contradictions of slavery. Long before Anna's leap focused the debate on slave trafficking in the early national District of Columbia, the paradoxes of enslaved people's acts of suicide were evident across the slave societies of colonial British North America. They were visible in the transatlantic slave trade, as well as during the early years of seasoning and settlement, and apparent in law, periodicals, newspapers, and literature. Beginning in the 1770s, the earliest expressions of Anglo-American antislavery activism drew directly on the many contradictions revealed by the suicides of enslaved men and women in order to illustrate the wrongs of slavery. In their accounts, antislavery activists remade self-destruction, traditionally the most reviled of deaths, into a justifiable response to enslavement and, therefore, a moral way of dying.

Anna's story used suicide to initiate and sustain a dialogue about the injustices of the domestic slave trade in the early United States. In Rider's illustration, her body casts a shadow on Miller's tavern, and for good reason. That establishment and the surrounding blocks bore witness to the grim history of slavery and suicide in Washington. One enslaved woman,

00.2. After hearing an account of Anna and believing her to be dead, Jesse Torrey went to Miller's tavern to view her body. Surprised to find her alive, he questioned her about her reasons for jumping out the window. In this illustration, he is the central and tallest person in the engraving, both typical visual tropes used to depict racial superiority. He is also the most illuminated figure in the scene, a detail that conveys the moral force of his antislavery work. Anna is shown here as he reported "on entering the room, I observed her lying upon a bed on the floor." He faces away from her, interviewing one of three kidnapped free blacks who were confined with her in the garret. Source: Jesse Torrey, *A Portraiture of Domestic Slavery* (Philadelphia, 1817). This item is reproduced by permission of The Huntington Library, San Marino, California.

on her way to Miller's, cut her throat and died in the hack that transported her.[9] When Anna jumped, she left in the upper rooms of the tavern her two children and three kidnapped free blacks destined for the southern slave market.[10] Those closed doors and shuttered windows were not simply the artist's conceit: in the words of one observer, Miller's tavern was a "Negro Bastille" in the midst of the nation's capital, a place where enslaved and free blacks were incarcerated after having been "torn from their connections and the affections of their lives" (figure 00.2).[11]

Suspended between brick and sky, death and life, Anna's figure asks viewers to consider why this moment arose and what should be done about it. Beyond her descending body and the square, there is only a void of uncertainty. Anna could not imagine that she could endure the trip south or separation from her family: she leapt out of the window because death in the present was an imaginable alternative to the inconceivable prospect of separation and sale. In parallel fashion, those who viewed this image or heard her story could not see beyond this shuttered block into the future of slavery in the United States. Anna's leap, made in the country's capital and memorialized in Rider's etching, posed a central political question for the nation. Could Americans conceive of a future without slavery and the domestic slave trade? Anna's attempted suicide conveyed a powerful, if deeply tragic, political force because it exposed the contradictions of slavery that were central to the unfolding of the early United States, the legacy of which continues to shape national dialogue today.

The suicides of enslaved people in early America have a history that both preceded and followed Anna's near-fatal early-morning jump from the garret window of George Miller's tavern in the District of Columbia in 1815. Beginning with the Atlantic trade and the emergence of slave societies in colonial British North America, to the formation of the United States in the wake of the American Revolution, and up through the eve of the Civil War, the suicides of enslaved people were visible and significant features of slavery in America. Anna's story, then, emerges as only one of many possible points from which to chart the implications of those deaths. It is the extensive, entangled, and evolving history of suicide by enslaved people in early North America that is chronicled in these pages.

INTRODUCTION

The Problem of Suicide in North American Slavery

> Brought to the Work-House. December 12, 1758. A young Mandingo negro man, who calls himself CAESAR, and says he belongs to William Godfrey, Gordon, or Goddard at Pedee, has lost a tooth in the upper and lower jaw, and has on an old white negro cloth jacket and breeches. Says his master had a negro that killed himself, and his being ordered to cut the dead negro's head off was the occasion of his running away.
>
> —*South Carolina Gazette*, 1759[1]

In December 1758, an escaped slave named Caesar was picked up by patrollers and delivered to the workhouse in Charleston, South Carolina. The initial notice of his capture, which included a physical description and approximations of his master's surname, appeared periodically in the *South Carolina Gazette* over the next three months. When Caesar remained unclaimed in early May 1759, the notice was amended, perhaps in an effort to stir his owner's memory, to include the reason for Caesar's flight. The paper's altered version, given in the epigraph above, offered up a rare, if not singular, explanation in the printed genre of runaway advertisements. As Caesar reportedly put the matter, one of his fellow slaves had killed himself, and, to punish this act of suicide, Caesar's owner had commanded him to "cut the dead negro's head off." Caesar's refusal of this order was the "occasion" or reason for his running away.[2]

Few of those who read or heard Caesar's story at the time were strangers to acts of self-destruction by either enslaved or free persons. Most South Carolinians of European extraction would have considered intentional suicide—that is, a purposeful act of self-destruction by a mentally sound person—to be a grievous offense against church, state, and community.

BROUGHT to the WORK-HOUSE,
December 12, 1758. A young Mandingo negro man, who calls himself CAESAR, and says he belongs to one William Godfrey, Gordon, or Goddard, at Pedee; has lost a tooth in the upper and lower jaw, and has on an old white negro cloth jacket and breeches. Says his master had a negro that killed himself, and his being ordered to cut the dead negro's head off was the occasion of his running away.

For more new ADVERTISEMENTS see the SUPPLEMENT.

0.1. Advertisement for Caesar. Source: *South Carolina Gazette,* 5 May 1759. This item is reproduced by permission of The South Caroliniana Library, Columbia.

Of all of the ways to die, suicide was surely one of the worst. Throughout Christendom, self-destruction was understood to be the vilest of sins: it violated the sixth commandment's prohibition against killing, and because despair was to be endured rather than escaped, those who chose self-murder had surrendered to the Devil's instigation. In addition to indicating weakness and wickedness, self-murder also exemplified a willful rejection of the fate assigned by God. Suicide was self-indulgent; anguish imposed by the Almighty was a test to be borne.[3] As English clergyman and theologian Henry Hammond explained in *A Practical Catechism,* first published in 1644, Christians were expected to submit to "providence, and to wait, though it be in the most miserable, painful, wearisome life" until God was pleased to offer "manumission and deliverance" from existence.[4]

Suicide also robbed the state of a subject, making it one of the worst possible felonies against the Crown. "Self-murder," the legal term, captured its essential transgression: an intentional suicide was a felon of the self or *felo de se*. In contrast, suicide as the result of insanity, delirium caused by illness, or mental disability—that is, by anyone *non compos mentis,* or not of "sound mind"—was considered to be unintentional and therefore not a felony. As Michael Dalton wrote in *Countrey Justice,* a popular legal manual used by local magistrates throughout England and colonial British America, because willful suicide was an "offence against God, against the King, and against Nature," it was in fact a "great[er] offense" than killing another person.[5] As was the case for any early modern felony, suicide was penalized: the personal estates of self-murderers were subjected to confiscation and forfeited to the Crown's authorities. Suicide also defied the law of nature, which compelled individuals to "preserve and cherish" the self.[6] Punishments could extend beyond forfeiture to public ignominies, including irregular burials and postmortem desecration of suicides' corpses.[7] It is difficult to know how common the latter was in early modern Europe—it clearly occurred, but may have not been routine—but internment within the churchyard accompanied by Christian rites was generally proscribed for those who died by suicide, in order to signal their separation from the community of the living and the dead.[8] In Virginia in 1819, a private burial was arranged for a man who died by suicide; and in 1832 another young man who killed himself was buried in the evening.[9] It is difficult to know, however, whether these were typical burial practices for *felo de se* verdicts.

Whether Caesar's owner absolutely condemned all acts of self-destruction in all these ways is impossible to guess, but he certainly objected to the suicide of this unnamed enslaved man. When Caesar's owner ordered him to be the agent of punishment, the former meant not only to demonstrate his power over dead slaves, but also to frighten living ones away from self-destructive inclinations. For many European settlers in the slave societies of colonial America, a suicidal slave was the worst of rebels, akin to those who engaged in armed revolt against their captors and masters.[10] Self-inflicted death by enslaved people defied their very ownership and deprived their masters of property. Slave owners also reviled suicide because they feared that the act was contagious and attributed it to particular African ethnic groups who appeared to prefer self-inflicted death to slavery. Perhaps above all, suicide by enslaved people not only challenged European beliefs about good and bad deaths, it also shattered their pretentions of power over bondpeople.

Caesar's beliefs about suicide are more difficult to pin down. In mid-eighteenth-century South Carolina, enslaved Africans were a multiethnic, polyglot assemblage of people with origins in countries that, according to mostly European onlookers, exhibited considerable variance in their views toward suicide. Among the early modern Yoruba and Ashanti, for instance, suicide was deemed a praiseworthy and honorable response to peril, disgrace, and a life that had become burdensome. In other nations, the act was condemned; in still others, murderers were expected to hang themselves for their crimes.[11] Despite any preexisting cultural prohibitions, however, the horrors of capture and enslavement as well as the brutalities of transport and sale may have rendered suicide both more easily imaginable and more acceptable for forcibly transported Africans regardless of their origins. From the beginnings of the Atlantic trade, for instance, as Michael

Gomez has demonstrated, both the Igbo (variously, Ebo or Ibo) and the Akan gained reputations for a propensity for suicide and appear to have viewed self-destruction as a permissible response to enslavement.[12] Similar views can be found in the earliest slave narratives published in the 1700s, and suicide remained a recurring theme in nineteenth-century examples of the genre as well; in their narratives, a range of slave protagonists discussed self-destruction without condemning the act, viewing it as a tragic but reasonable, if not morally imperative, alternative to slavery.[13] In addition, for those individuals who believed in reincarnation, as some Africans did, suicide extinguished only the physical self.[14] Death, however achieved, was a medium of transformation and rebirth: it was a conduit for the spirit to rejoin families and ancestors and a channel for the soul to return home to Africa.

If we cannot know precisely how Caesar regarded suicide, his actions speak volumes about his reasons for fleeing. Caesar risked the hazards of running away—he was picked up about sixty miles from Charleston—and endured the hardships of the workhouse, the disciplinary terrors of which were reportedly equal to those of the harshest plantations, rather than obey his master's order.[15] The command to dismember a fellow slave—or to decapitate anyone—may have horrified him. Possibly, he objected to it for spiritual reasons. Proscriptions against interfering with the bodies of the dead were shared widely across much of the early modern world, not least because those who endured violent deaths were believed to possess the capacity to haunt the living. Just as Europeans staked the bodies of suicides at crossroads to prevent their ghostly risings, some Africans as well avoided the graves of those who died violently. Both cases reflect the belief that, if aroused, the dead could harm the living.[16] Whatever Caesar's beliefs about the task assigned to him—horror, fear, or loyalty—he expected to be punished for refusing the order, and so he ran away. Of the many things we cannot know about Caesar, we do know this telling detail: he preferred the risks of flight and the likelihood of a flogging if apprehended to carrying out his master's order.[17]

Why does Caesar's story matter? For many people, suicide, both past and present, is unfathomable. In the contemporary United States, specialists typically link suicide to psychological and emotional distress and often attribute it to depression, anger, or hopelessness. Communities extend sympathy to the families of those who die by suicide, and public and private funds support hotlines and suicide-prevention measures. News organizations report spikes in suicide rates with alarm. Surging numbers of suicides among

Gulf and Iraq War veterans and US military servicewomen and -men, for instance, are viewed as an urgent national problem for which Americans seek explanations and demand solutions.[18] These modern responses to suicide only emerged, however, beginning in the mid-eighteenth century, when self-destruction began to be attributed to emotional hardship and psychological distress, often defined as a product of mental diseases, such as melancholy or mania. The rise of medical explanations for suicide surfaced alongside philosophical and religious debates over the right to suicide, the terms of which were publicly argued both in specialized treatises and common newspapers. Some of those who supported the decriminalization of suicide, including Thomas Jefferson, viewed the act as a disease; others regarded it as within the compass of rational free will exercised by individuals. Furthermore, arguments for the decriminalization of suicide were not solely issued from the pens of Enlightenment *philosophes* and political leaders: over the course of the eighteenth century, local juries in England and British America increasingly declined the *felo de se* verdicts that would have punished suicide with criminal penalties and instead favored *non compos mentis* rulings. Together, the debates of intellectuals and clerics as well as the practices of local legal actors combined to level a challenge to traditional attitudes toward suicide, and in many states criminal sanctions were removed in the wake of the American Revolution.[19] Still, divided views of suicide persist in American law and culture. [20] Self-destruction still carries religious and cultural stigma, and it remains a profoundly unsettling act for families, communities, and nations. Despite our comparative humanitarianism today, acts of suicide, as can be seen most clearly in debates over assisted suicide, continue to challenge our understanding of the divide between private will and public interest.

As Caesar's story illustrates, suicide carried far different meanings in the context of early modern British American slavery. His account, along with the many other reports of enslaved people's suicides that are the subject of this book—evidence found in ship logs and surgeons' journals, judicial and legislative records, across a range of newspapers, periodicals, novels, and plays, and drawn from abolitionist print culture and slave narratives—is meaningful because it illustrates the significance of death by suicide in the slave societies of colonial British America and, later, the United States. Stories like Caesar's matter because they illuminate the intimate circumstances, cultural meanings, and political consequences of enslaved people's acts of self-destruction in the context of early American slavery.[21] Suicide reflected the struggles between enslaved men and women and their traders and owners; self-destruction by enslaved people was an ongoing aspect of the culture of colonization that shaped understandings of race and gender in early America. In literary and popular culture, representations of slave suicide were vehicles for considering the character of enslaved people and reflecting on the imperial and national implications of Anglo-American slavery. Acts of suicide by slaves also highlighted tensions in understandings of property and personhood that were fundamental to the legalities and commerce of slavery. Whether or not they intended it, slaves' self-inflicted deaths shaped criticisms of slavery: when the earliest abolitionist literature emerged in the late eighteenth-century Anglo-Atlantic, it used occasions and images of slave suicide to denounce the institution. In short, suicide was central to the history and culture of slavery and antislavery efforts in early British America and the United States. In these pages, I consider the suicides of enslaved people in eighteenth-century America from several perspectives.

First, this book explores the circumstances that fostered enslaved people's acts of self-destruction and examines the meanings of their choices to die by suicide. Slaves chose suicide for many reasons: self-destruction could be impulsive or premeditated; a defensive response to brutality, trauma, or alienation; a deliberate escape from punishment, transport, or sale; a conduit to spiritual or ancestral reunion; or a means of cheating the gallows. Whatever slaves' reasons, however, their traders, transporters, and owners, like Caesar's master, considered suicide dangerous and treasonous. For them, preventing suicide was central to the social order of slavery: like forestalling insurrection, suicide prevention was crucial to maintaining control of ships, coffles, and plantations.

Second, accounts of enslaved people's suicides challenged European beliefs about suicide. In colonial North America, Indians, Africans, and Europeans judged one another by their deathways. Cultural arbiters often expressed recognition at familiar death practices or surprise at their strangeness.[22] However, European responses to *slave* suicide did not always fall on the same side of this neat divide; sometimes their reactions betrayed a grudging admiration for enslaved people's acts of self-destruction, a fascination that paralleled their observations of Indian suicide as well. In addition, Europeans divorced slave suicide from the processes of enslavement. Rather than link suicide to slavery, instead they reported that slaves killed themselves because they were ethnically predisposed to suicide, superstitious and fearful, or temperamental and stubborn. Representations in literature and popular culture often sustained these connections, using acts of suicide to examine, quite admiringly at times, enslaved people's codes of honor while simultaneously demonstrating their fitness for slavery. As Europeans grafted distinct motives and methods of suicide onto their assumptions about Africans and African Americans, they forged connections among race, gender, and temperamental differences.[23] They used suicide to brand slaves as commodities; self-destruction illustrated the qualities of tractability or aggression in order to make certain ethnicities more or less saleable.[24]

Third, this study analyzes the legal and cultural ramifications of enslaved people's suicides in the slave societies of eighteenth-century British North America. As we see in Caesar's story, suicide was an affront to plantation hierarchies. At the same time, acts of self-destruction by slaves mattered to emerging slave codes, local courts, and colonial and state legislatures as well. The law may have simultaneously defined slaves as human beings and chattel properties, but in the very act of killing themselves, slaves became criminally culpable persons under the law. Criminal acts, including suicide, were the outcome of *mens rea* or intention, and suicide, ironically, erased the civil death that was slavery. [25] Yet because slaves were also chattel, colonial legislatures fashioned laws that, under certain circumstances, allowed masters to recover from government coffers the monetary value of slaves who died by their own hands. In addition, plantation owners singled out suicidal slaves for exceptional punishments. Privately and publicly, traders and masters subjected slave suicides to the worst manner of physical retribution: their bodies were burned, hung, gibbeted, decapitated, dismembered, and left to rot in full view.[26] By the mid-eighteenth century, these sanctions for suicide in British America were, as far as I have been able to ascertain, routinely visited only on the bodies of enslaved people.

Fourth, the contradictions posed by slave suicide led to fundamental changes in the way that Americans and Europeans viewed slavery. Every choice to die by suicide could be politically construed as fundamentally, even if unintentionally, an antislavery act, a resounding criticism of the institution. Enslaved people's deaths by suicide unsettled the question of slavery in colonial courtrooms, legislatures, plantations, and cities as well as in newspapers, periodicals, novels, and plays decades before antislavery activists used accounts of slave suicide to exemplify the wrongs of slavery. Like resistance to sale or running away, slave suicide created a heightened public awareness of the violence and power of slavery.[27] The earliest expressions of these contradictions were not lost on those who objected to the peculiar institution: the first generation of antislavery activists used these paradoxes to alter the international dialogue about the legalities of slavery. Drawing on allegedly true instances of slave suicide, antislavery poems like Thomas Day's *The Dying Negro* (1773) used self-destruction to challenge England's role in international slave trafficking as well as British colonials' reliance on and acceptance of slavery. After the American Revolution, slaves and abolitionists alike recounted stories of slaves who self-inflicted death in response to labor regimes, domestic sale, and physical and sexual violence.[28] In relating these stories of self-destruction, antislavery activists, including former slaves, aimed for nothing less than changing the imperial and, later, the national discussion of slavery. Each generation and constituency of antislavery activists found a distinct target: the earliest abolitionists focused on eradicating the international slave trade; after its cessation, attention shifted to the domestic trade, gradual emancipation, and colonization schemes; antebellum activists took full aim at the institution of slavery itself. Among all of these groups, suicide remained a persistent image of the injustice of slavery.

Finally, slave self-destruction remained a changing and contested part of American cultural memory well after the Emancipation Proclamation ended slavery in the United States.[29] Among African Americans, suicide by enslaved persons was the subject of fiction, as well as a touchstone in Works Progress Administration (WPA) interviews of ex-slaves in the 1930s.[30] Stories of suicide in slavery found perhaps their fullest flowering in the regional folklore of the flying Africans that originated in the Sea Islands of South Carolina and Georgia; these were tales of slaves who possessed the magical power of flight to leave their labors in North America and return home to Africa. Well after slavery ended, former slaves and their descendants, along with African American writers, reshaped stories of slave suicide into a powerful regional folklore and an enduring literary motif. These cultural expressions reflect the ways in which memory transfigured the tragedy of self-destruction in slavery and reveal the perseverance and relevance of both slavery and suicide as historical subjects. Considering the memory of slave suicide suggests the ways in which generations of Americans have grappled with its meanings and reshaped its implications not only for individuals, but also for families, communities, and, eventually, for the nation as well.

The Power to Die is largely focused on the slave societies of eighteenth-century British North America, particularly Virginia, Maryland, and North and South Carolina, although some evidence is also drawn from the Caribbean. Because the history of suicide in slavery begins in an imperial context and ends in a national one, I make use of sources that originated in and circulated throughout England, colonial British America, and the United States. This is not to say that acts of suicide by enslaved people were everywhere the same in British America or unchanging over time. Like slavery itself, self-destruction varied by region, and this study is attentive to these differences. With the onset of both the American Revolution and Anglo-American abolitionism in the 1770s, however, my focus narrows to consider the meaning of slave suicide in antislavery activism in the early national and antebellum United States.

I use a broad base of evidence, both out of necessity and design. Anyone who studies enslaved people in eighteenth-century North America must grapple with a profound scarcity of primary source materials; that lack is even more pronounced for those who study the period before the American Revolution. Indeed, that dearth is one of slavery's legacies. Despite the relative lack of sources by enslaved people, however, slave suicide was evident across a range of Anglo-American institutions from the seventeenth through the nineteenth centuries. For this reason, the sources employed here include commercial accounts (captains and surgeons' logs, traders' correspondence); legal documents (court orders, litigation, petitions); legislative records, including investigations into the slave trade; newspapers, periodicals, and fiction; and antislavery visual and print culture, including slaves' narratives. In short, it includes any material that circulated among an Anglo-American readership or depicted slave suicide in early America. Many but not all of these sources reflect actual instances of self-destruction by enslaved people. However, no matter how imaginative, these materials reflect the circulation of ideas and representations about slave suicide. These accounts do not all agree: some existed to support slavery while others were used to contest it. Yet their diversity attests to the far-reaching cultural and political implications of enslaved people's suicides throughout the settlement of British America and formation of the United States.

Historians of early American slavery have mostly overlooked the systematic study of suicide and slavery, and *The Power to Die* is the first attempt at a full-length study of the subject. In the historiography of slavery, suicide is often used anecdotally, to illustrate the cruelty of the institution or the strength of slave resistance. Seldom has slave self-destruction been the sole focus of investigation, and certainly this is its first book-length study. Historians who have considered slave suicide in depth have been most likely to show, as do John Thornton, Daniel Walker, and Michael Gomez, that enslaved people's attitudes toward suicide were linked to African ethnicity, culture, and religion and were altered by the rise of the slave trade.[31] Slave suicide has also been studied as an aspect of national identity, as Louis A. Pérez, Jr.'s, work on Cuba has demonstrated.[32] Historians Mark S. Schantz and Richard Bell have examined slave suicide in the context of abolitionist reform, while David Silkenat and Diane Miller Sommerville use suicide as a lens into race and death in Civil War America. Until the last decade, historians who study suicide, rather than slavery, have not even considered slave suicide as part of their evidence, but recent scholarship on early national and antebellum suicide, particularly by the scholars cited above, offers much-needed correctives to this long-standing omission.[33]

If historians have not looked deeply at enslaved people's acts of self-destruction, in part it is because suicide is an intricate historical problem to study; in the context of slavery, it is doubly difficult. For the most part, slaves did not leave suicide notes, so we appear to lack direct written evidence of their intentions. For the pre-Revolutionary period, we have almost no accounts of slave suicide from the viewpoint of other enslaved people. Popularly circulating sources, like the newspaper account of Caesar, for instance, also appear to give little insight into slave subjectivity. By the mid- to late-eighteenth century, legislative petitions and sporadic coroners' inquests begin to report slave suicide, but these terse documents tend to focus mostly on how and when some slaves killed themselves, leaving unanswered the question of why they did so. Only with the rise of antislavery literature in the nineteenth century do African American writers, many of them ex-slaves, discuss suicidal ideation or relate episodes of self-destruction. Despite the fact that slave narratives are politically purposeful accounts, they still offer a window into the personal subjectivity of enslaved men and women. In doing so, they provide an accounting of "what it felt like to suffer, and what it cost to endure" the suffering of slavery.[34]

Despite these limitations, however, the documents are not completely opaque; meaning can be derived from these fragments if we can learn to read the how and the when for reflections on the why. Moreover, reports of slave suicide are addressed in early modern traders' letters, masters' diaries, travelers' accounts, and printed discussions of slavery across and beyond the Anglo-Atlantic. In part, the reemergence of death as a category of historical analysis, as illustrated by the work of Vincent Brown, Drew Faust, Karla FC Holloway, and Erik R. Seeman, has offered key insights, methods, and theories—mortuary politics, the centrality of deathways to colonization—that have importantly shaped the directions of this study.[35]

Studying suicide raises questions about slave resistance and agency, two of the most fraught terms in the historiography of slavery. Is suicide the ultimate act of resistance, as some antislavery activists and, later, some historians argue? Is it only a purposeful expression of the individual and, on occasion, the collective power to reject slavery?[36] While surely at times it was so, it is also necessary to penetrate the rhetoric of abolitionism and push beyond the model of resistance in order to grasp the complexities of suicide in slavery. Often, the power of enslaved people's suicides, intentionally or not, lay in the way self-destruction directly exposed the contradictions of slavery and implicitly called into question the institution's pretensions to paternalism. That is a very different thing from viewing any suicide by any slave as an unequivocal act of resistance or a clear reflection of agency, two terms that are used cautiously in these pages. Some enslaved men and women carefully planned their suicides; these acts might be understood as resistant, although they were not necessarily intended to express that broad power. Others lost their minds. According to mariners along the Middle Passage, a few slaves who killed themselves "showed every sign of being mad," making "great" noises and displaying uncontrolled emotions and physical convulsions.[37] Still other slaves killed themselves impulsively and impetuously, rather than deliberately. Caesar's fellow slave lies silent on this issue, but Anna describes her leap as the result of panic and compulsion rather than forethought; she does not in fact ever refer to her jump as an attempt at suicide and expresses regret over having done it.[38]

Viewing self-destruction by enslaved people only or even primarily as an act of resistance, moreover, obscures the finer grains of its political and personal significance. To understand self-destruction as one slave resisting one master risks losing sight of the meanings of those deaths for the immediate slave community, the slave trade and plantation system, and for Anglo-American culture and politics more broadly. Moreover, to see slave suicide as resistance suggests that self-destruction was a freely made choice; to the extent that suicide was conscious and deliberate, it was selected from an egregiously narrow range of possibilities. Suicide resulted in the death of the subject; this factor alone should temper any unqualified sense of triumph. Jennifer Morgan argues that resistance to enslavement was routine: many actions by the enslaved, ranging from the quotidian to the extraordinary, reflect this truth. Yet to assume a kind of "perpetual resistance" is to enter an interpretative vacuum that can erase the physical pain and suffering as well as the emotional and psychical wounds of slavery.[39] Similarly, Walter Johnson argues that using agency as the defining issue in the history of slavery can forestall important considerations of the intricacies of human activity. Agency is a concept upon which the history of slavery ought to be predicated; to view it as an outcome of the evidence obliterates the complexity of slavery.[40] In the case of suicide, to say that slaves, ironically, chose it in order to die autonomously or to argue that slave self-destruction was an index of their humanity ignores both the chillingly fatal cost of slaves' self-destructive acts—they died—and the meanings of those deaths. Instead, I focus on the forces that propelled enslaved people to that moment of self-harm as well as the legal, political, and cultural ramifications of those fatal acts as essential features of early American slavery.

Stepping outside of the resistance model allows us to better comprehend the history, implications, and politics of slave self-destruction. The suicides of enslaved men and women in early America were predicated on a complex range of material, emotional, and physical circumstances. In addition, those deaths conveyed a host of cultural and political paradoxes and contradictions. To reduce all suicide by slaves to resistance, after all, is to consider only the masters' (e.g., slave suicide resists the owner's authority) or the abolitionists' (e.g., slave suicide resists the slave trade or the institution of slavery) point of view. In order to offset these oppositions, as much as possible I also consider the perspectives of the enslaved—admittedly often imperfectly surmised from a close reading of the evidence—and by drawing from slave narratives, ex-slave interviews, and memories of suicide in slavery.

Beyond resistance, suicide is also difficult to study because the act is not as easily defined and straightforward as it first would appear. Europeans had legal definitions of suicide that were specific and hinged on intentionality. While this may appear to be a clear-cut determination, in reality the application of legal standards varied with region and changed over time. For those relatively few instances for which a coroner's report for slave suicide exists—mostly from the late eighteenth and early nineteenth centuries—the act was almost always determined to be a criminal *felo de se*. Sometimes, juries noted if slaves possessed "goods or chattels, lands or tenements" to be forfeited, although this was even more rare.[41]

Yet intention is not only an issue to be judged through the eyes of eighteenth-century empowered actors; it poses a lingering question for the historian as well. I do not rely solely on European assessments of intentionality. If an enslaved woman was surrounded by patrollers and was shot when she refused to surrender, was her death a homicide or a suicide? If an enslaved man ran into a pond to escape an imminent beating and drowned because he would not come out and could not swim, was his death a suicide? In 1828, a Virginia jury ruled that it was so. An enslaved man named James, "being alarmed by information of there being patrolling," ran into the Staunton River and attempted to cross; the jurors determined that he was "voluntarily and feloniously a felon of himself."[42] Legal onlookers did not always agree on these matters, however. In 1770, for instance, a North Carolina coroner's jury ruled that Quamey had accidentally drowned trying to escape from patrollers. An agent for his master, however, testified that Quamey had run away, but when he was about to be retaken, he "jumped into the North East river and drowned himself."[43] Masters and patrollers routinely found slaves dead in the woods with no apparent marks of violence. Were self-starvation and deliberate exposure to the elements forms of suicide or part of what Karla FC Holloway describes as "suicide-like" behaviors?[44] Sometimes these actions were clearly understood or intended to produce death. In 1813, for instance, a South Carolina jury found that the enslaved Rose came to her death by "starving in the woods with hunger and cold."[45] In 1823, another jury similarly ruled that Booker, an enslaved man, was an "[accessary] to his own death by drinking too much spirits and being exposed to the inclemency of the weather."[46] In 1866, former slave Matty J. Jackson reported that her grandfather "in deep despair and overwhelmed with grief . . . made his escape to the woods, determined to put an end to his sorrows by perishing with cold and hunger."[47] In legislative petitions, court records, and newspaper accounts, direct evidence of suicide is often ambiguous. Some slaves were simply listed as "found dead" and may have ended their lives through poison or starvation. Others died apparently inexplicably while awaiting trial; some reportedly "set fire to" their jails; still others appear to have courted or sought death quite deliberately. Suicidal inclinations can be understood to encompass some of these kinds of acts as well: that is, those that suggest self-destructive behaviors.

However, it cannot be too strongly stated that all of these data from legal records must be treated with great caution. Patrollers' reports, masters' claims that their slaves killed themselves, and verdicts of suicide from coroners' inquests potentially mask homicidal violence against slaves. Similarly, deaths that might be legally ruled as accidental may have been homicides or suicides; on occasion, for instance, juries determined that slaves had accidentally hanged themselves or unintentionally died by accidentally stabbing themselves.[48] Some inquests were no doubt held at the request of masters who suspected foul play and wanted to sue for damages. Finally, and perhaps significantly, both in the past and present, suicide is underreported. This may have been especially true in slave societies because enslaved people's suicides damaged owners' reputations and spoiled the illusion that plantations were pastoral idylls. In order to protect their names and standing in the community, some masters appear to have concealed evidence of slave suicide.[49]

All of these qualifications suggest the ways in which counting suicide, a difficult and rather inconclusive task even today, is extraordinarily problematic in early modern North America. I offer no absolute measures of suicide by enslaved people and cannot say with certainty whether it was frequent or rare. One British lieutenant and West Indian slave owner testified in 1790 that slave suicide was "not uncommon" among newly imported, unseasoned slaves, a charge that was widely echoed in a parliamentary investigation into the slave trade. Those observers were hardly disinterested.[50] Yet we simply lack consistent statistics on which to draw. Captains and surgeons kept logs for insurers and investors and were required to account for their profits and losses. These provide some measures of shipboard suicide, but studies using them exhibit a wide variation. In his sample of eighty-six slave ship surgeons' journals from 1788–1797, Marcus Rediker finds that twenty-five of eighty-six ships, or nearly one-third, witnessed suicide by captive cargo. This estimate does not tell us how many slaves may have resorted to suicide, but Rediker describes this rate of reporting as a "serious understatement."[51] On the other hand, in his study of ninety-two slave ship surgeons' logs for the five-year stretch of 1792–1796, David Eltis calculates that 7.2% of slave deaths during loading on the African coast and on the Middle Passage were attributed to suicide.[52] If we cannot say for certain that suicide by enslaved people was rare or frequent, it seems clear enough that it was visible and notable.

In addition, numerical estimates of slave suicide date from late eighteenth-century England, after several key legal decisions ruled that losses due to suicide aboard slavers were uninsurable. For instance, the 1785 *Jones v. Small* decision established new guidelines for insurers of slave ships. The issue in the case was an insurrection in which six slaves were killed or drowned and an additional fifty-five died of injuries. Losses to this cargo of slaves had been insured against mutiny, but the court ruled that the deaths of slaves who jumped into the sea or starved themselves after the insurrection were not insured. In effect, that meant that any suicide that occurred aboard ship in the absence of an insurrection was not considered in and of itself a form of mutiny; such a death was therefore uninsured.[53] The legal decision gave captains and surgeons incentives to conceal evidence of self-destruction. For instance, some ship logs report but do not directly attribute to suicide slaves who died "suddenly" or from "sulkiness"; those who were "drowned" or went "missing"; or for whom no reason was given.[54] In British North America and the United States, coroners' inquests on dead slaves were erratic and irregular, as has been noted; there was no legal requirement that inquests be held on slaves, and usually this was done only if owners planned to sue for damages. Masters could petition the legislature for compensation for suicidal slaves, but this would be guaranteed only if the slaves were already charged with felonies. Therefore, these numbers, too, undercount actual suicides. All of this means that any attempt to reckon the numbers of suicides by enslaved people will be incomplete, and attempts to count them will likely render underestimates.[55] Ultimately, then, if the question of how many slaves killed themselves in the early modern Anglo-Atlantic and British North America is unanswerable, a more expressly qualitative and complex history of suicide and slavery can be found in a surprising array of sources. Indeed, seen in this light, the numbers may be the least revealing of the evidentiary foundations of understanding the history of suicide by enslaved people in early America.

Despite the fragmentary evidence and sponginess of the numbers, however, the history of suicide in slavery is not only knowable; it is very much worth knowing. Suicide by enslaved people was evident in the transatlantic slave trade and apparent as slave societies developed in colonial British North America. With the onset of the American Revolution, slave suicide continued to convey political, cultural, and social significance throughout the early United States. Enslaved people's acts of self-destruction occurred on rural plantations and urban centers, generated legal change and literary representations, and inspired the earliest antislavery activism as well as an expressive African American folklore. Suicide by enslaved people shaped relations between masters and slaves and ideas about gender and racial identity, fashioned and challenged the legalities that were central to slavery, and became a foundational political metaphor for abolitionism. Self-destruction by enslaved people conveyed a constellation of meanings across time and space that were at once local and transnational, personal and political.

The Power to Die proceeds thematically, with most of the chapters focused on the eighteenth century. Chapter 1 discusses suicide in the Anglo-Atlantic slave trade, examining the patterns of suicide among enslaved Africans and charting the responses of mariners, owners, and traders to slaves' acts of self-destruction. Chapter 2 follows the story onto dry land, exploring the contradictory and complex meanings of suicide that emerged as enslaved people endured seasoning in pre-Revolutionary British America. Chapter 3 explores cultural understandings of slave suicide in colonial North America and compares suicide among enslaved, indigenous, indentured, and free individuals. Chapter 4 considers the emergence of public (criminal) and private (plantation) justice systems, examining legal codes and slave owners' petitions for compensation in cases of slave suicide. Chapter 5 investigates the politics of suicide in transatlantic Anglo-American popular print and drama. Chapter 6, which bears the chronological thrust of the book, moves the story onto the national stage by charting the emergence of suicide as a key image in Revolutionary-era antislavery literature and examining its persistence into the early national and antebellum periods. It evaluates the continuing and changing meanings of self-destruction in slave narratives and ex-slave interviews. Finally, the epilogue considers the memory of self-destruction in slavery and the continuing power of suicide in slavery to preoccupy the living.

Caesar's story played out against a backdrop of tradition and transformation. The suicide of his fellow slave—as well as Caesar's response—illustrate the ways in which the global forces of the slave trade and the dynamics of power between slave and owner collided in local contexts in British North America. The meanings of suicide in slavery were neither stable nor static. Instead, they reverberated through print and law and eventually became a powerful force in antislavery activism in the early United States; long after slavery ended, suicide lingered on in African American memory and folklore. Suicide is a privately encumbered, culturally laden, and politically meaningful act; any act of self-destruction casts a value judgment on life.[56] The self-inflicted deaths of enslaved people exposed fundamental contradictions in the institution of slavery and communicated cultural meanings and political effects throughout the early modern Anglo-Atlantic, across colonial British America, and into the early United States. Those deaths continue to speak to historians today.

ONE

Suicide and the Transatlantic Slave Trade

These blacks in general regard death very stoically . . . . This is what makes them, without caution but with steadfastness, rush into the most dangerous circumstances. The women have the same spirit and the same resolution. On my 1679 voyage, a black woman of Aquambou, being unable, as she wished, to nurse a small child which she had, and having further got it into her head that we were taking her and her child to eat, threw herself one day, unnoticed, into the sea, leaving her child on the mast-strut. . . . a canoe was sent to her rescue. . . . she gave us to understand that she had done everything she could to make herself drown, but that she had not been able to succeed in this, nature obstructing her destruction and making her, in spite of herself, employ the swimming ability and buoyancy she had acquired [earlier in life].

—Jean Barbot, *Description of the Coasts of Guinea*, 1688[1]

On ships crossing the Atlantic, from the African coast to American ports, captive Africans leapt into the ocean or refused to eat. They strangled and hanged themselves. They tore open their throats. Once in the New World, they ate dirt and stones, hurled themselves down hills and off ledges, ran into burning buildings, ingested poison, and dashed their heads against rocks. From the beginning to the end of the slave trade, from the African interior to its littoral, spanning the Atlantic passage to dispersal throughout the Americas, Africans responded to enslavement by destroying themselves. Often, with little else save their own bodies and stolen moments of opportunity, they chose death over slavery. That they did so made suicide a visible feature of the early modern trade in human beings from its earliest beginnings.

Despite the best efforts of captains and crews to prevent human cargoes from destroying themselves, the struggle over death was unceasing throughout the transatlantic trade. In order to maximize investors' revenues and ship profits, mariners had to arrive in American ports with as full a shipment of slaves as possible. Doing so meant that crews not only needed to manage disease outbreaks and thwart revolts, they also had to stop captive Africans from destroying themselves. The concern for shipboard suicide was so pronounced, in fact, that slavers shared advice about and practiced suicide prevention.[2] Surgeons, captains, and traders kept logs, wrote manuals, published journals, and corresponded with one another. Their observations generated a commercial working knowledge about the African trade and suicide, one that revealed as much about the enslavers as it did about their human cargoes. This lore was at once capacious and tenacious. It arose on the African coast, accompanied slave ships across the Middle Passage, and persisted as slaves were offloaded, sold, and scattered across the eighteenth- and nineteenth-century Americas.

Some of the most common early modern beliefs about enslaved people's suicides that were generated by the pens of Europeans are visible in the anecdote of the unnamed enslaved woman given above. The author of the report, Jean Barbot (1655–1712), accompanied French slave ships as a commercial agent and provided some of the earliest descriptions of slaving to appear in print.[3] In his brief but detailed anecdote, he first linked suicide to African ethnicity: "these blacks" was a specific reference to Akan-speaking people, native to present-day Ghana, where he traveled. The Akan, like all people of the Gold Coast, he continued, were fearless, resolved, and headstrong in their commitment to death: "without caution," he noted, they "rush into the most dangerous circumstances."[4] This fearlessness of death knew no gender: women had "the same spirit and same resolution" as did the men. Some of these particulars would have been familiar to a European readership who understood self-destruction as a passionate and stubborn act and sometimes linked it to national character.[5] Other specifics likely challenged their attitudes. Europeans understood suicide to be a sinful felony rather than an exemplification of heroism, and many believed that men and women considered suicide for distinct reasons; for instance, men killed themselves in the face of financial ruin while women did so in response to sexual transgressions. Europeans also believed that women were less likely to possess the resolve necessary for successfully carrying out suicide.[6] Thus, this anecdote of an attempted suicide reflected that beliefs about race, gender, and self-destruction operated as reference points for the recognition of cultural similarity and difference.[7]

Beyond these initial assessments of their fearlessness of death, Barbot also offered evidence of particular anxieties that fostered self-destruction in captive Africans. Slaves' fears of cannibalism, regardless of sex, were frequently featured in slave traders' repertoires. Yet, enslavement also gave men and women different motives for suicide. According to Barbot, both the unnamed woman's fear of being eaten and her inability to nurse her child were factors that propelled her leap overboard. In a revealing dovetailing, both of these reasons centered on sustenance; the Middle Passage engendered a heightened and symbolic anxiety about the body that centered on nourishment—or the lack thereof. Moreover, while the Akan mother's inability to nurse, easily imaginable as a product of the trauma and conditions of captivity, in part led to her suicide attempt, she left her child to survive, suggesting that she did not wish to take the child's life as well. In addition to giving specific reasons for her leap from the ship, Barbot also described her suicide attempt in terms of her temperament: she had "got it into her head" that she was going to be eaten, he tells us, and she was unable to nurse her child "as she wished." Her stubbornness and irrationality, for him, also explained her attempt to die. The anecdote illustrates how the encounter between the French mariner and the enslaved Akan woman generated knowledge about suicide, gender, and ethnicity in the Atlantic slave trade.

The significance of shipboard suicide by captive Africans, like the attempt of the unnamed Akan-speaking woman in Barbot's account, comes into sharper relief by comparing the perspectives of both slaves and their enslavers. Africans and Europeans carried competing and changing ideas of good and bad deaths with them through the Middle Passage, and these concepts shaped their views of self-destruction. In addition, the patterns of captive Africans' suicides and mariners' responses to those deaths expose the mortal struggles of power aboard ship. Those conflicts—African against European, commodification versus personhood, and, for some, life and death—visibly defined the physical, emotional, and psychological experience of the slave ship. The reports of enslaved people's suicides come from the hands of the enslavers, whose records are imperfect and fragmentary. Enslaved people did not leave suicide notes, but when, like the Akan woman described by Barbot, they jumped overboard or refused food, they telegraphed intention and meaning to other slaves as well as to the officers and crew.[8] Those accounts, used carefully, can yield insights into African subjectivities aboard ship and provide a corrective to the predominantly European archive of those who controlled the trade.

The patterns of Africans' shipboard suicides partly reflected the physical, emotional, and psychological experiences of captivity. For instance, enslaved people killed themselves in response to the conditions of the slave ship. In the face of high mortality and disease epidemics, dying by their own hands seemed to be a reasonable alternative to painful and sometimes lingering deaths from dysentery, smallpox, typhoid, fevers, and fluxes, all diseases that were exacerbated by inadequate provisioning, overcrowded holds, and seafaring catastrophes. In addition, enslaved people also died by suicide in response to the unfamiliar discipline of shipboard regimes, during attempts at insurrections, or in the aftermath of rape, sexual violence, and physical brutality.[9] Their physical experiences of captivity were, of course, accompanied by interior traumas that were intensified by the unknown, unfamiliar, and unpredictable nature of the slave ship. The unnamed Akan woman, for instance, conceivably suffered psychologically from her inability to nurse her child; uncertain what more the future might bring, she leapt from the ship.

Still other emotional and spiritual reasons became common reference points for explaining enslaved people's attempts to end their lives. Barbot cited slaves' fears of cannibalism as a factor in their suicides; other observers of the trade, particularly those from the late eighteenth century, influenced by the language of sentimentalism and antislavery politics, cited melancholy, despondency, despair, and nostalgia as reasons for slave self-destruction.[10] Africans aboard ships killed themselves because they could not or would not recover from the psychological and emotional ravages of captivity, punishment, and the fracturing of community, familial, and parental relationships. Enslaved people, observers noted, adamantly wished to die in response to all that they had endured. Perhaps most subversive to the slave trade was the belief held by some Africans that suicide, in the context of the slave trade, was an acceptable, if not more precisely a desirable, way of dying.

African shipboard suicides also shaped the conduct of mariners. For captains, surgeons, and crews, preventing slave suicide was essential to controlling shipboard order. What is more, their observations of slave death practices also deepened their conceptions of the racial differences between Europeans and Africans. Mariners and traders rarely viewed slave suicide in traditional Western terms. They did not interpret it as a sin or the product of diabolical inspiration, although they sometimes attributed it to mental unsoundness, the routine categories used in European explanations of suicide in the early modern era. Instead, Europeans more often used a modern secular and remarkably commercial argot to describe self-destruction by enslaved people aboard ships. Writing about the seventeenth century, for instance, Barbot attributes suicide to fear or sadness, rather than to sin or diabolical inspiration.[11] In the mid-eighteenth century, South Carolina merchant Henry Laurens described a "poor, pining" woman who hanged herself with a small vine; her ability to do so led him to a stark assessment of her low value, observing that "her carcass was not very weighty." He also wrote to a Liverpool ship owner and slave trader that "stout healthy fellows sell to the most advantage" regardless of their country of origin, unless they were Igbo or Callabar who were "quite out of repute from numbers in every Cargo . . . destroying themselves." Based on their propensity for suicide, on another occasion he wrote that "Callabar slaves won't go down when others can be had in plenty."[12] In 1790, a planter from South Carolina similarly testified that Igbo Africans were "remarkably high spirited" and did not "brook slavery so well as those from several other countries."[13] As mariners and traders assessed their human cargoes' propensities for self-destruction, they effectively branded slaves according to ethnicity and temperament, qualities that made them more or less saleable commodities. These descriptions underscored the idea that slave suicide was endemic to certain types of human cargoes, specific ethnicities of Africans, rather than to the system of enslavement itself.

Acts of suicide by captive Africans were ubiquitous aboard slave ships crossing from Africa to the Americas. Although eighteenth-century British America is the focus of this study, slave suicide is evident in the records left by a range of European mariners from the seventeenth through the nineteenth centuries, including after 1807, when Britain and the United States abolished the Atlantic slave trade.[14] This is the case because self-destruction was the choice of individuals ranging across all groups of ethnic Africans subjected to the trade, and it was witnessed and reported by all European nations that made their fortunes through slaving. Individual captives identified as Akan, Angolan, Asante, Fante, Igbo, Kongo, and Mina found ways to end their lives. Their choices were evident to the Danish, Dutch, English, French, Portuguese, and Spanish traders and mariners who transported their human cargo to outposts and, later, settlements in North, Central, and South America, including the Caribbean. Beginning in the 1770s, ex-slaves and abolitionists would use accounts of slave suicide to contest the very legitimacy of the slave trade itself. Until that moment, however, aboard ship, the suicides of enslaved cargoes were themselves visible and powerful expressions of shipboard struggles in the trade that transported them from the African coast to British America.

The Atlantic trade brought together African and European ideas about good and bad deaths and set those beliefs against one another in the small confines of the slave ship. In many early modern cultures, but certainly not all of them, suicide was regarded as the apex of a bad death and the worst way of dying. Suicide was, in a word, abhorrent; intentional self-destruction carried legal and religious punishments and community condemnations. Philippe Ariès has observed that attitudes toward death change comparatively slowly, and indeed, after centuries of censure, views toward suicide slowly began to modernize in Europe and the Americas only toward the end of the eighteenth century.[15] Cataclysmic events do, however, have the potential to more quickly alter outlooks on death. War, trade, famine, and economic upheavals, like those caused by the acceleration of the transatlantic slave trade or the impact of European colonization of America, did transform views of death, including self-inflicted death.[16] These changing African and European beliefs about good and bad ways of dying collided with one another.

Although prohibitions against suicide appear to have existed across early modern Africa, they were not uniform. Africa was ethnically various, and different countries evidenced a range of perspectives on good and bad deaths. In West Africa, for instance, the Akan (modern Ghana) considered the suicides of war prisoners admirable.[17] In contrast, in Igboland (modern Nigeria), suicide was considered an "abomination": offenders were denied burial in ancestral grounds and families suffered social humiliation. Michael Gomez argues that, in most early modern African societies, suicide was "unthinkable."[18] In the twentieth century, anthropologist Melville Herskovits reported that in West Central Africa, suicide was not "looked upon with the horror" occasioned by other untimely deaths. Suicides were buried with clothes and gifts, but the funeral rites, he reported, were "quiet" and "small."[19] Similarly, other anthropologists have found that the bodies of African suicides were relegated to irregular burials. For instance, they might be placed in trenches, alongside the bodies of other cultural outsiders, such as those who had died from epidemics, had been convicted of crimes, or were understood to be witches.[20] These details suggest that the bodies of suicides were treated irregularly because they were feared, reviled, or perhaps both. Some archeologists have suggested that these practices continued in the Americas, where some evidence from Barbados indicates that those who had died in unusual ways, as through suicide, or possessed negative social traits, like witches, may have been buried face down, although it is not known whether this was done by order of the slave owner or the will of the slave community.[21]

Despite the evidence of cultural proscriptions against suicide, it is clear that, as the Atlantic slave trade advanced in the eighteenth century, West and West Central Africans responded to enslavement by killing themselves.

The depredations caused by the transatlantic slave trade altered traditional ethnic African attitudes toward suicide: self-destruction might have been regarded as a bad death in much of early modern Africa, but in those societies that were subjected to slave raids, traditional proscriptions against self-murder appear to have eroded.[22] This radical rethinking of self-inflicted death seems to have occurred in the early stages of captivity. On African rivers or coasts, slaves leapt out of ships. Some were attempting to escape by swimming, but others who had no such skills clearly risked their lives.[23] Along the Middle Passage, captives repeatedly attempted to die by suicide. Accounts of these acts by mariners, surgeons, and traders suggested that African captives deemed suicide to be not only imaginable and acceptable, but even in some cases laudable and admirable.[24]

Suicide appears to have carried spiritual meanings for some Africans as well. In parts of West Africa, for instance, the dead were "remote and powerful" spiritual figures. The living worshipped their departed forebears and believed that ancestors inhabited an afterlife where they influenced the living.[25] Kongolese buried the dead deep in the forest to give the soul maximum rest, and ceremonies honoring the dead included leaving food and drink at altars.[26] If West and West Central African attitudes toward suicide responded to the social and cultural depredations wrought by the commerce in slaves, as Michael Gomez so forcefully argues, then acceptance of suicide had a positive cultural function: self-inflicted death was a conduit for ancestral reunion.[27] Destroying the body did not necessarily encompass destroying the self. It is also possible that some acts of suicide by enslaved people reflected African concepts of law and custom; captives in the slave trade, of course, came from communities that had distinctive legalities. The Igbo, for instance, recognized two systems of law, one divine and one human-made. Both systems of jurisprudence, Sally E. Hadden argues, shaped "legal relations, conceptions of guilt and innocence, and presumptions about human nature." Violations of divine law carried the highest penalties. The Igbo expected murderers to hang themselves and assumed that other criminals would serve appropriate penance in order to restore the favor of the gods.[28] Additionally, if some Africans believed that enslavement was a punishment for violating spiritual law, perhaps suicide came to be viewed as an attempt to regain the favor of the divine. All of these details suggest that, for some Africans, suicide became an acceptable and perhaps admirable response to captivity and enslavement; others may have seen it as a duty according to their legal philosophy. Shipboard suicides were shaped by both corporal, emotional, and psychological experiences as well as by spiritual, cultural, and legal beliefs.

Whether suicide was a response to brutality and punishment, a product of fear or resignation, or sought because of the powerful spiritual prospect of ancestral reunion, surviving communities of enslaved people did not condemn the act. The 1789 narrative of Olaudah Equiano, for instance, chronicled his capture in the African interior and Middle Passage; he reported that he "envied" the dead their "freedom" and did not criticize the suicide attempts of captives aboard ship.[29] More to the point, other enslaved people well into the nineteenth century echoed his lack of condemnation of suicide. Accounts of slave suicide suggest that communities of enslaved people accepted and approved of the self-destructive acts of their peers. In mid-nineteenth-century Cuba, for instance, traveler Fredrika Bremer noted that other slaves revered the bodies of suicides, although this may have been more typical of enslaved people in Latin America or Cuba in particular.[30] While nineteenth-century North American ex-slave narratives do not address specific rituals honoring those slaves who died at their own hands, neither do they condemn self-destruction. Elizabeth Keckley, for instance, was matter of fact about the death of her uncle who hung himself from the branch of a willow tree: she condemns slavery's "dark side," but not his act of self-destruction.[31] Frederick Douglass warned enslaved men and women away from the "crime" of suicide, even as he acknowledged that self-destruction was a reasonable response to slavery.[32] Most explicitly, perhaps, Charles Ball argued that no one could "attach blame" to slaves who took their own lives, and he openly discussed his own suicidal ideation.[33] If the Atlantic trade and enslavement altered some Africans' attitudes toward self-inflicted death, those transformed beliefs persisted among enslaved men and women in North America up through the eve of the Civil War.

The perception that enslaved people regarded suicide as an acceptable, honorable, or even good way of dying directly contradicted the perspectives of Europeans. For them, slaves' acts of self-destruction acquired new and subversive meanings. Early modern European terminologies for suicide implied culpability: phrases like *self-murderer, self-slayer*, and *self-destroyer* reflected not simply the revulsion for suicide but the need for retributive justice obtained through punishing the suicide's fortune, family, and body. Of course, these attitudes were not static. The word "suicide" itself, coined in seventeenth-century England but not commonly used until the eighteenth century (when it spread to France, Spain, Italy, and Portugal), derived in a rather linguistically circuitous route from John Donne's phrase "self-homicide." The rising use of this comparatively milder neologism in the eighteenth century reflects changing attitudes toward suicide, as it was less damning of the perpetrator.[34]

Still, as we have seen, European religious, legal, and medical institutions consistently condemned intentional suicide. These denunciations eased over the course of the eighteenth century and were replaced by humanitarian understanding and medical explanations for suicide. However, slave traders, owners, and overseers did not extend this modern empathy to slaves; the commercial interest in slavery effectively countered any compassionate impulses. For Europeans, intentional suicide had long been linked to either diabolical inspiration or dispositional weakness that rendered individuals particularly ripe for the devil's temptations.[35] Suicide violated legal, religious, and communal values and engendered a response from church, state, and community. For Protestants as well as Catholics, suicide was a heinous sin, and church officials could and did refuse the bodies of suicides Christian rites and burial in consecrated grounds. Because intentional suicide was, as Puritan John Sym noted in his introduction to the earliest known English treatise on self-murder, a "horrible temptation" to sin, burial outside of the church in an unmarked grave signaled the suicide as permanently dismembered from the church.[36]

In English law, intentional suicide was, as jurist William Blackstone phrased it, a "peculiar species of felony.[37] A *felo de se*—or felon of the self—was punished through the forfeiture of his or her personal estate.[38] However, suicide was punished inconsistently. Those families with the most social capital were the least likely to suffer either official religious or legal penalties for the act. Perhaps no other felony existed in quite this position, and there is clear evidence that early modern English juries were ambivalent about declaring a suicide from the middling or upper classes to be a *felo de se*.[39] The family name would be associated with the unholy and illegal act far into the future, and juries were all too aware of the long-term material, emotional, and psychological impact of their decisions.

Self-murder provoked horror, demanded retribution, and inspired fear in European communities. European attitudes toward suicide were deeply ingrained with ideas of pollution: the body, weapon, site, and, to some extent, even the family were contaminated by the sin of suicide. Bodies could be buried upside down, without the benefit of the traditional funeral shroud or coffin, and often interred at night. Sometimes suicides were buried at a crossroads, their bodies staked to the ground to prevent ghostly rising and the possibility that they might haunt the living.[40] The corpse was segregated from the community because it was a symbol of spiritual and criminal pollution; this exclusion, then, would continue in perpetuity in a spot that was marked as unholy. In spiritual, legal, and social terms, Europeans viewed suicide as the epitome of a bad death.

The mariners, traders, and surgeons on board ships that carried captive Africans to the Americas found their own views of suicide often in profound conflict with those of their captive cargoes. Self-destruction by African captives was laden with spiritual and political meanings that mariners, traders, and, later, British American owners would attempt to dominate and diminish. For newly captive Africans, suicide had become more imaginable, conceivable, and perhaps even desirable, despite the reality that in some cases it violated the customs and laws of their countries of origin.[41] For some, suicide was a conduit into a spiritual realm, but for others it was an avenue away from the existential realities of captivity and enslavement. Mariners and traders typically viewed the suicides of African captives through a commercial, secular lens, but they subjected the bodies of those who killed themselves to grisly postmortem punishments and desecrations that echoed European understandings of suicide and treason. Self-destruction was an affront to the order of the ship, an unpredictability that destabilized the smooth operation of the trade and posed a threat to commercial ambitions. Mariners and traders, therefore, consigned African suicides to categories that were distinct from those of Europeans and, in doing so, deepened understandings of racial differences. Still, over the course of the eighteenth century, the visibility of suicides of enslaved Africans aboard ships had the potential to convey politically troubling messages to imperial observers of the trade.

From the onset of the transatlantic slave trade, Africans appeared to choose suicide over captivity, and their acts were the subject of both fascination and concern to the captains, surgeons, and crews who worked aboard slave ships. Mariners' observations circulated around common themes and offer insight into general and more specific circumstances surrounding Africans' suicides aboard ships. Observers cited rape, brutality, epidemics, and insurrection as reasons for self-destruction by enslaved people, and reported that Africans killed themselves because they feared cannibalism, rejected enslavement, and sought spiritual rebirth. Very late in the eighteenth century, sympathetic assessments, influenced by abolitionism, attributed self-destruction to the emotional and psychological damage of enslavement.

When mariners observed and attempted to forestall shipboard suicide by captive Africans, they unwittingly revealed their own anxieties about the nature of the slave ship. Those who ran the trade—European, Iberian, Scandinavian—were keenly concerned about slave suicide because it signaled their failure to keep a smoothly running craft. Disorder was always a danger on a confined vessel, and the need for order was doubly critical on slave ships: both crews and human cargo needed to be kept healthy and controlled. Additionally, the deaths of the enslaved diminished revenue margins in the trade; little could be done about natural mortality from diseases like dysentery and typhoid that swept through ships, but suicide was a preventable death. Slavers feared suicide because they quickly learned that Africans' acts of self-destruction were precipitated by many circumstances and that one suicide appeared to influence another.

Occasionally, the accounts of mariners or observers distinguished captive Africans' acts of self-destruction by gender. In his account of an attempted suicide in 1679 given at the outset of this chapter, Barbot marveled at the unnamed woman's swimming abilities and described her rescue; he linked her suicide attempt to her inability to nurse her child.[42] Similarly, other captive African mothers chose to destroy themselves and their children rather than face enslavement. In 1695, a nursing woman surmised that sale would take her to America, and so she "seized the child, and angrily threw him against a stone, and then grabbed some arrows from the hands of a man, and wrathfully used them to pierce her own breast."[43] Similarly, Dutch mariners reported that a woman "died of grief" after the death of her newborn, a clear indication of the ways in which enslavement fractured the parental bond—or perhaps more particularly, the ability to sustain their infants—in ways that impelled women toward suicide.[44]

Enslaved women also sought suicide after episodes of rape or sexual brutality, incidents which likely happened on every ship that crossed the Atlantic.[45] One mariner reported that the captain of the *Ruby* had a chosen "mistress," an enslaved "girl," who accidentally ripped his son's shirt. The officer beat her so severely that she "threw herself from him against the pumps," causing great self-harm in an attempt to defend herself. The same sailor related other instances of sexual abuse against the women aboard the same ship, and, although he did not directly connect their rapes to their attempts at suicide, the connection was tellingly implied. He noted, "It was the general practice with the captain, on the receipt of a woman slave, to send for her into [the captain's cabin]" in order that he might sleep with her; those who resisted his attempts were beaten and sent below. After relaying this information, the witness stated that three of the women aboard the *Ruby* had "threatened to throw themselves overboard."[46] The account, in this case occasioned by an inquiry into the slave trade, let the investigators draw their own conclusions, but the link between the rapes of enslaved women and their attempted suicides seems clear enough. Aside from issues of parenting and sexual abuse, which mariners principally related to enslaved women, they largely did not differentiate between enslaved women and men's shipboard suicides. Indeed, many observers remarked on suicide by enslaved people without commenting on their sex.

Along the Middle Passage, enslaved people appear to have killed themselves in response to disease epidemics and high shipboard mortality. Arriving in port with live slaves was essential to maximizing profits for investors, and the livelihoods of captain and crew depended on their ability to contain both sickness and the self-destruction that followed on the heels of epidemics. The sickness and death common to slave ships fostered disorder for the crew (some of whom also succumbed) and created opportunities for slaves to choose self-destruction. In 1824–25, an outbreak of dysentery proved fatal to about one-third of the slaves on the clandestine French brig *Le Jeune Louis*. Along with 115 enslaved men and women, the captain and 9 of the crew perished, another 9 slaves leapt overboard, and a tenth reportedly lost his mind.[47] Alexander Falconbridge reported that a flux swept through his ship, killing nearly half of the slaves on board.[48] In the face of such epidemics, crews separated the dead and the dying and pitched their bodies out the porthole or overboard; some surviving slaves who watched this unceremonious process were inclined to jump from the ship, too. For example, a young boy aboard a French ship reported that when two Africans died in the hold, the captain ordered the rest of the cargo to be brought up for inspection. As they reached the ship's side on the upper deck, "first one, then another, then a third sprang up the gunwale, and darted into the sea before the astonished sailors could tell what they were about."[49] Another surgeon reported that of the slaves who became ill, many lacked the will to recover, even when they were dosed with medicine.[50] The opportunity for suicide—as well as the desire to die—seems to have accompanied sickness and epidemics; great numbers of dead and dying slaves resulted in desperation aboard ships.

In addition, Africans' acts of suicide both precipitated insurrection and followed failed revolts. One captain who traded slaves illegally in the early years of the nineteenth century noted that a few days after the *Venus* left the African coast, one slave leapt overboard in a "fit of passion" and another choked himself during the night. Two suicides in twenty-four hours, he admitted, caused him much "uneasiness as in them I saw a germ of revolt."[51] Africans' self-inflicted deaths signaled a failure in the ship's order and an inability to control the human cargo aboard. The captain of the *Venus* was correct in his surmising, later noting that "every precaution was taken against a rising, but it finally took place when we least expected it."[52] If mariners understood suicide to be closely related to insurrection, did slaves as well?

Self-destruction by some of their numbers may have similarly signaled—or even deliberately precipitated—slippages in ship surveillance that could provide the opportunity for rebellion.

The suicides of captive Africans were themselves understood to be a form of revolt. When slaves were brought on deck on the *Le Rodeur* in 1819, three leapt over the side and "many more" made the attempt, unsuccessfully. Those who had successfully escaped "danc[ed] about" among the waves, singing a "song of triumph" in which they were joined by the remaining men and women on deck. When informed of the "revolt," the captain identified ringleaders, shot three of them and hanged another three "before the eyes of their comrades."[53]

If enslaved people's suicides precipitated insurrections and were understood as traitorous, individual revolts, it is also the case that slaves killed themselves in response to failed insurrections aboard ship. The English case of *Jones v. Small* (1785), for instance, recounted a failed revolt on a ship that was loaded with 255 captives off the coast of Africa in 1783. The uprising began when women seized the captain and attempted to throw him overboard; in the ensuing battle, six slaves were killed or drowned and another fifty-five died in consequence of "bruises, chagrin at disappointment, and abstinence." In other words, after the revolt failed, the slaves starved themselves. Evidence given in the trial referred to them as a cargo of "desperate" slaves, "gnawing their chains in despair"—a striking image of self-starvation—who "died not of a mutiny but of disappointment for a mutiny."[54] In this way, both insurrection and suicide were also tied to slave temperament through the use of descriptors like "chagrin," "despair," and "disappointment."

Africans' fears of cannibalism also accounted for shipboard suicides. Barbot, like many mariners, interpreted this fear literally; the belief that slavers were cannibals appears to have been widespread in the African interior and on the Middle Passage, where large kettles aboard ships stoked captives' fears of being eaten.[55] Yet this dread was not purely literal, as in slavers' reports that their captives believed that the red wine they were drinking was blood.[56] As John Thornton has shown, slaves' fears of being eaten had symbolic and political implications. For some Africans, a cannibal referred to any individual who embraced greed and avarice, an emblem that the captive slaves might have easily extended to their captors. After all, enslavement was a kind of devouring: Africans were seized, stripped, and, their captors hoped, forcibly remade into commodities. Moreover, enslavers were tantamount to witches—resonant and real entities for Europeans and Africans alike in the seventeenth century—who swallowed up the identities of their victims. In this sense, the unnamed woman from the Gold Coast may have viewed the cessation of milk production as the onset of a devouring, the first step in the stripping of her personhood. In viewing slavers as witches and cannibals, captive Africans relayed a kind of "radical folk ideology" that served as a critique of their enslavement.[57] To fear cannibalism was to fear the parasitism—that is, the literal and figurative feeding off the other—that was at the heart of enslavement. Mariners and traders ridiculed slaves' fears of cannibalism as evidence of African superstition, but in doing so, they missed the ways in which fears of being eaten reflected Africans' grasp of the physical realities and political symbolism of enslavement.

If Africans chose death by suicide in response to disease epidemics, insurrections, and anxieties over their fears of cannibalism, they also did so because death was preferable to the physical brutalities and psychological displacements of slavery. In 1730, *The Sea Surgeon*, a guide for medical officers on slave ships, warned that enslaved captives starved themselves. They would "never eat any thing by fair means, or foul, because they choose rather to dye, than be ill treated."[58] Slaves were often described as melancholy and despondent, gloomy and listless, weak and sickly; their physical and mental states were emblematic of one another. One surgeon testified that by the time his ship carrying 602 Africans reached the West Indies, 155 people had died. When queried further, he averred that the greater proportion of these deaths, two to one, could be attributed to "melancholy," a "gloomy pensiveness" caused by enslavement.[59] Pressed further, the surgeon testified that of the captives who had taken ill, those with melancholy died and those "who had not that melancholy" recovered. He added further that the enslaved themselves confirmed their despondency because he "heard them say in their language, that they wished to die." Or, as he rephrased, their deaths were "owing to their thinking so much of their situation."[60] Some slaves who were ill simply refused aid: one woman refused medicine, food, and wine; when asked what she wanted, she reportedly replied, "she wanted nothing but to die." And she did.[61]

All suicides compromised European control of slave ships, but enslaved people's embrace of the positive spiritual outcome of self-inflicted deaths stirred powerful anxieties for those who ran the trade. As early as 1693, Captain Thomas Phillips recorded that slaves drowned or starved themselves because they believed that upon death they would transmigrate to Africa and rejoin their ancestors.[62] As late as 1823, a Jamaican planter noted that the enslaved universally shared in this belief.[63] Such anecdotes accumulated over the course of the eighteenth century, and slavers could have had little doubt that many Africans were prepared to kill themselves rather than endure enslavement.

Captain and crew understood that slave self-destruction could be precipitated by circumstances (sickness, revolt, despair) that were common to all slave ships. In addition to these commonalities, the commanders of slave ships made idiosyncratic decisions that further fostered suicide by their enslaved cargo. In the notorious case of the English slaver, the *Zong* (1781), for instance, the captain, Luke Collingwood, carried a sickly cargo. Over 400 slaves were loaded on the ship in September; by November, 60 were dead, and nearly half of the original crew of 17 also had been killed by illness. In response, Collingwood ordered his remaining sailors to jettison 133 living Africans in order to recoup their value in insurance money. He had no claim if the slaves died naturally, but their value could be recovered by proving that the "peril of the seas"—in this case, the pretense that shifting winds had blown the ship off course and that water supplies were low—required him to jettison the sick in order to preserve the healthy. As the screams of the less valuable (to the ship captain) women and children who were tossed overboard first reached slaves below deck, one asked that the crew simply withhold from him food and water so that he could starve to death. Ten other slaves jumped into the ocean of their own accord.[64]

For all of these reasons, mariners feared Africans' acts of suicide aboard ship. Slavers, surgeons, and traders on their journeys from Africa to North and South American ports as well as those in Liverpool, Paris, and Copenhagen traded stories about slave self-destruction, creating a commercial lore across European empires. In the spaces of slave ships, Europeans, as Stephanie Smallwood has eloquently argued, needed to turn Africans into slaves. Chained and confined, "Africans revealed the boundaries of the middle ground between life and death where human commodification was possible."[65] Too much punishment, and slaves might kill themselves; too little, and they might revolt. What is more, if suicide was exacerbated by the all-too-common contexts of shipboard brutality, epidemics, contagions, and insurrections, slavers were more likely to lose the upper hand in controlling the struggle over life and death.

To allay these anxieties, the crews of slave ships employed some of the earliest technologies of suicide prevention. It is perhaps an irony of the slave trade—an institution that we associate with brutality and violence—that it fostered innovations in the prevention of suicide, if only for the purpose of turning captive Africans into fit commodities for the market. Slaves who would not eat were whipped or beaten, although such disciplinary measures

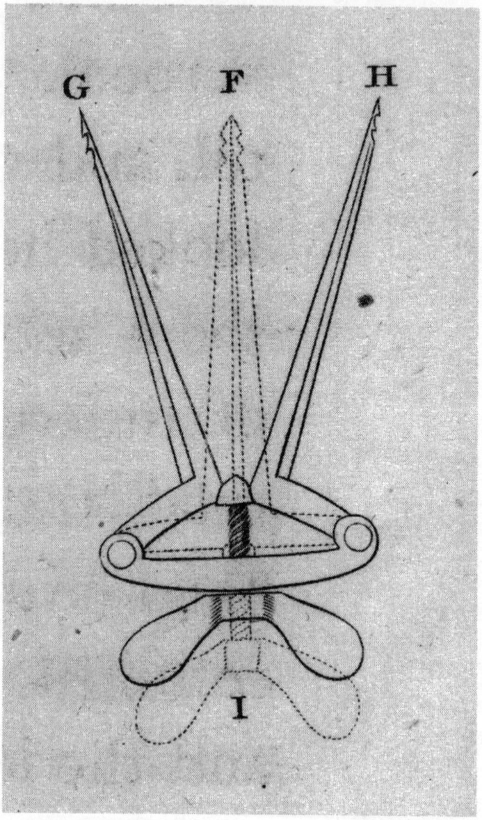

1.1. The *speculum oris*, used to forcibly feed slaves who refused food and water. Source: Thomas Clarkson, *An Essay on the Slavery and Commerce of the Human Species, Particularly the African* (1786). This item is reproduced by permission of The Huntington Library, San Marino, California.

had uneven results. A British surgeon reported that one woman who refused to eat was "repeatedly flogged" and subsequently forcibly fed. Nothing could convince her to swallow, however, and she soon died.[66] In order to keep slave cargoes alive and, ultimately, saleable, the crew used the *speculum oris*, an instrument that forced the jaws open, on enslaved persons who tried to starve themselves. A Dutch mariner noted that he attempted to force feed a slave, who "bit so hard on the 'mouth screw' that the teeth fell out." The slave, he reported, was so stubborn that "he would rather be dead than eat."[67] Portuguese mariners asserted that Africans from the Bijago archipelago were very prone to suicide, claiming that the latter killed themselves by refusing to eat, an act that the Europeans attributed to melancholy.[68]

On an English ship, one slave refused food and then attempted to cut his throat; after it was stitched, he removed the sutures and unsuccessfully repeated the attempt. Again he refused to eat or drink and died within ten days. Even children "t[ook] sulk" and refused sustenance.[69] Deprived of other weapons, slaves used their bodies as agents in their demise. Aboard ship, they could and did refuse to eat and drink.

Mariners were also scrupulous in removing from slave ships any material or instrument that might aid the enslaved in attempts to destroy themselves. One Danish medical officer remarked that slaves used "any and every opportunity . . . to kill themselves." One had to use the "greatest forethought," he continued, to prevent it. He also reported that captains on French ships were careful of strips of linen and string because slaves hanged themselves with these meager materials.[70] The logbook of the brig *Sally* noted only that a woman slave hanged herself between decks, while an English mariner reported that two women did the same with rope yarn that they had secreted below deck.[71] If the rails on deck were not high enough, mariners attached nets around the gunnels of slave ships to catch captives who might try to jump to their deaths. When that failed, they would lower boats and rescue those who had leaped.[72] One mariner reported that the nets were used to prevent slaves from accidently falling overboard, but that seems like an extreme measure, considering that slaves were typically shackled.[73]

If the crew could not always physically prevent suicide attempts, they instead struggled to manipulate the spiritual beliefs of their enslaved cargoes in order to prevent their suicides. Some enslaved people allegedly took their own lives in triumph. One man reportedly jumped overboard and, as he was drowning himself, put his head under water, lifted his hands up, and "thus went down as if exulting that he got away."[74] Like Captain Phillips of the *Hannibal,* many mariners believed that slaves killed themselves because doing so would allow them to "return home to their own country and friends again.[75] Attempting to control those beliefs was fundamental to suicide prevention aboard ship. When three Africans jumped overboard and were joined in their shouts of joy by those remaining on deck, the captain took six of them, hanged three, and shot three while forcing the others to watch.[76] Ship captains may have initiated the practice of mutilating the corpses of slaves who had killed themselves and appeared to draw on traditional European punishments for suicide and treason. One ship commander reported that he dismembered or beheaded the corpses of recalcitrant slaves as a way of terrorizing the remaining captives; he told them that the souls of dismembered or decapitated slaves could not return to Africa to rejoin their ancestors.[77]

1.2. "The slave-trader, and the captive chief, mutually recognized each other. On the same day, when the slave-trader was on board, it happened that the chief was permitted to walk on deck, without his fetters. No sooner had the captain and his friends sat down to dinner than a signal was given. The slaves rose to a man, knocked off each other's fetters, and, headed by the chief, attacked the barricade. But they failed. The guns were pointed at them, some were killed, many leaped into the sea, and the insurrection was quelled." Source: C. B. Wadstrom. *An Essay on Colonization, Particularly Applied to the Western Coast of Africa* (London, 1795), pp. 86-87. This item is reproduced by permission of The Library Company of Philadelphia.

Other captains ordered the bodies of suicides to be tossed to the sharks that followed ships across the Atlantic, forcing remaining captives to watch the grisly feeding as a means of discouraging any further contemplation of suicide. Some slavers essentially chummed the waters with African corpses, using those bodies as food for the swelling numbers of aggressive sharks who followed the slave ships.[78] The captain of the *Hannibal* noted that captives nonetheless leapt out of ships because they were loath to leave their own country, despite the fact that he and his crew had witnessed "divers[e] of them eaten by the sharks" that followed slavers from the coast of Africa to Barbados.[79]

Despite the physical technologies and spiritual threats employed to control captive Africans aboard ship, by all accounts their acts of self-destruction remained difficult to prevent. Suicide aboard ship was erratic and random; like epidemics and insurrection, it was a constant possible danger. Suicide taught traders that they were not in control of the trade: they could not cure sick slaves who had no will to live, enliven those overwhelmed with melancholy and despondency, or deter those who believed suicide would return them to their African homes. To put it another way, Africans' suicides gave slaves a fleeting, if fatal, leverage, and the specters of their self-inflicted deaths haunted the Atlantic trade. No matter what Europeans did to prevent suicide, they continued to chronicle the actions of enslaved cargoes who killed themselves by leaping overboard, strangulation, or refusing to eat.

The visibility of shipboard suicide illustrates that enslaved captives' acts of self-destruction shaped the dynamics of slave ships and the economics of the slave trade. If preventing suicide by enslaved people was necessary in order to maintain shipboard control, then each act of slave self-destruction highlighted the failure of mariners to achieve their aims. Enslavers' anxieties revolved around uncertainties: epidemic and contagion, insurrection and revolt, melancholy and refusal. The capital advanced by investors, limits of insurers, skills of captains, and remedies of surgeons were all imperiled if the crew could not thwart enslaved cargoes' repeated persistent attempts at self-destruction throughout the Atlantic trade.

The visibility of slave suicide in the Atlantic trade reflected the circumstances and beliefs that impelled enslaved people toward acts of self-destruction and revealed the concerns of mariners, investors, and traders. In contrast, the manner in which enslaved people killed themselves can reveal more about their subjectivities and intentions. For some modern suicidologists, for instance, the method of suicide proves to be just as enlightening as the reason behind it. At a basic level, suicide can be viewed as either a planned or an impulsive act.[80] As the argument goes, the more lethal the method of suicide—jumping from a precipice or using firearms, in which one is almost certain to die—the more likely that the suicide is a matter of impulse, a response to an acute crisis that could, given time, pass. Those who plan suicide are likely to choose less definitively lethal methods, such as poison or wrist cutting.[81] These basic insights can be useful in thinking about suicide by the enslaved. When a slave leapt off a ship "in a fit of passion," does the description reveal an unplanned, impulsive act of self-destruction or one that was more deliberate?[82]

If there are few clues into the precise state of mind of those captive Africans who chose to kill themselves aboard ship, we do know that many were willing to end their own lives in response to captivity. The enormous significance of this response—that one would truly risk one's life or engage in a purposeful act of self-destruction rather than face further enslavement—reflects the profoundly morbid despair that was occasioned by the transatlantic slave trade. Suicide was no doubt an index of the miserable conditions on the slave ship: it was a moveable prison that erased the aspects of existence in which individuals often take comfort—food, drink, sleep, sex, family, routine, work—and replaced them with a regime of terror in the form of physical brutality, bodily invasion, and emotional cruelty. This context transformed the unthinkable into the possible; some Africans responded by choosing death. On the slave ship, the power to die by self-inflicted means became for many Africans newly conceivable.

Despite shackles, confinement, and the vigilance of the crew in the Atlantic trade, slaves were resourceful in finding opportunities for suicide. When captains put up special netting around the ships to prevent slaves from leaping overboard, they climbed out of portholes or gun gratings.[83] At least some of the captives who leapt from ships were bent on self-destruction, although near the African coast, others seem to have been attempting to swim to shore.[84] Other slaves clearly intended to drown themselves, and leaping into the ocean may have carried personal implications since some Africans considered water a sacred space.[85] Consider again the West African woman of Barbot's account. Before she leapt from the ship, she left her child on the small platform that supported the mast strut. She could have taken the child with her; other mothers facing enslavement or who were already enslaved did kill their children before destroying themselves.[86] It may be that while suicide was an acceptable way of ending her own life, that choice did not encompass taking the life of her child, an act that itself was likely in her country to be punishable by death.[87] Perhaps her leap was born of impulse. Death through drowning—particularly when it entailed leaping from decks or masts or crawling through portholes—was the more opportunistic of suicides aboard slave ships.

Enslaved people also drowned themselves serially and collectively. Some captives jumped overboard in response to brutality: two women watched the crew lash slaves who refused to eat, and "folding themselves in each others arms," jumped overboard. The crew was "obliged to put all of the women immediately" in the hold because "most of them were preparing to follow their companions."[88] In the 1780s, nearly twenty slaves jumped overboard the *Enterprize*.[89] Equiano reports that two men who were chained together made it through the nettings and cast themselves into the sea. Another "dejected fellow" followed their example immediately; Equiano added that he believed that "many more would very soon have done the same if they had not been prevented by the crew."[90] Arriving in American ports could also inspire collective suicide. For instance, Captain Japhet Bird had released the slaves from their chains after his ship anchored off St. Kitts in April, 1737. Near sunset, "above an hundred men slaves jumped over board." His crew managed to retrieve about two-thirds of them. The rest, he reported, had "resolved to die" and, refusing to save themselves, "sunk directly down." For a hundred slaves to jump roughly together must have required some agreement and a signal or, perhaps in the chaos of the moment, one leap into the ocean quickly inspired another.[91]

Similarly, suicide by starvation required not just opportunity, but planning and resolve as well. Investigations into the slave trade noted that slaves' refusals to eat and drink occurred repeatedly. These deaths would be slow and excruciating, and success uncertain. However committed a slave might be to death, the premeditation and time required to achieve death by self-starvation left room for their attempts to be thwarted, particularly, as we have seen, by violent technological interventions by crews and masters. Yet when slaves stubbornly continued to refuse food and prevailed even over the *speculum oris*, their teeth were often broken and their mouths forced open with hot coals or molten lead. Such punishments appear, despite their brutality, to have strengthened rather than undermined the resolve of slaves.[92]

Some refusals of food and water also could have been caused by deprivation rather than intention. Some slaves suffered from advanced dehydration, which would have swollen their tongues and throats and rendered them physically incapable of chewing or swallowing food.[93] Some who leapt into the water may have been mistakenly impelled to do so, believing that the saltwater would quench their thirst.[94] Conditions commonly found in the slave hold—dysentery, seasickness, and high temperatures that induced profuse sweating—all potentially contributed to rapid and, in some cases, irreversible dehydration. Moreover, European remedies for dysentery included emetics, enemas, and limited water; all of which could weaken slaves or cause their deaths. At the same time, severe fluid loss could have shaped the temperamental responses of the enslaved. For instance, many were overtaken with "despair and lethargy" that led them to refuse all food and water."[95]

Other means of self-destruction lay somewhere between the impulsive leap into the ocean and the premeditation of self-starvation. Slaves used bits of clothing or even the rigging of ships to hang, strangle, or otherwise asphyxiate themselves. Lacking materials, slaves relied on their own physicality, using their hands to choke themselves, their weight to achieve strangulation, or their fingernails to tear their throats.[96] Strength and resolve were necessary for inflicting such levels of self-directed violence. Whether planned or impulsive, intentional or indirect, enslaved people's deaths by suicide appear to have been a fairly recurrent feature of the slave ship.

Aboard ship, enslaved people, like the unnamed Akan woman whose story began this chapter, sought to destroy themselves in conjunction with epidemics and insurrections and in response to physical assaults to their bodies and psychological assaults to their identities. They killed themselves in ways that reflected impulse and premeditation; they sought self-destruction individually, serially, and collectively. For Africans, the processes of captivity and enslavement reshaped the meaning of self-destruction. Suicide was not only conceivable, it had become an acceptable, if not a positive, response to enslavement. As we shall see, these patterns would prevail and evolve as enslaved cargoes were offloaded in New World ports and dispersed throughout the Americas.

Mariners worked to prevent material acts of self-destruction aboard ship, and at the same time, their observations disarticulated suicide from the processes of enslavement. Like Barbot, others in the trade attributed slave suicide to African ethnicity, fears of cannibalism, or temperament rather than to the processes and circumstances of enslavement. Barbot tells us that the unnamed Akan woman leapt overboard because she was afraid of being eaten and unable to nurse her child; he does not directly link her action with her captivity. Even sympathetic discussions of Africans' depressed emotional and psychological states attributed melancholy and despondency to nostalgia—as it was called in Latin America—or a kind of homesickness, rather than to the processes of enslavement. Later, in the mid-nineteenth century, a medical student who shipped aboard an illegal slaver claimed that Africans would squat down, place their chins on their knees, clasp their arms around their legs and, in a short time, expire. He believed that captives could hold their breath until death followed, a trait, he claimed, that reflected their barbaric nature, since among the "civilized races it is thought impossible to hold one's breath until death."[97] All of these assessments tied Africans' acts of self-destruction to racial character and persisted as African captives were discharged on American shores.

The inclination to disarticulate suicide from slavery—as Barbot does in his account of the unnamed Akan woman—accumulated in private diaries, plantation accounts, and print culture over the course of the eighteenth century. Rather than link slave suicide to the circumstances of captivity, enslavement, and sale, traders and owners instead pointed to the temperament and disposition of enslaved people as explanations for their acts of self-destruction. Indeed, the work of early antislavery activists was to reconstruct suicide as a product of the institution and system of slavery, rather than a problem rooted in enslaved people. In making that connection, abolitionists fought against the ways in which, from the earliest years of the Anglo-American slave trade forward, self-destruction had been naturalized as a product of temperament and race, while it was simultaneously disassociated from slavery. Yet long before the onset of organized Anglo-American abolitionism in the 1770s, suicide by enslaved people continued to be a visible feature of the emerging slave societies of British America, and slaves and their owners held divergent attitudes toward and explanations for self-destruction. The die was cast in the Atlantic trade, but the meanings of suicide in slavery would evolve as captive Africans arrived on American shores.

TWO

Suicide and Seasoning in British American Plantations

June 24. I . . . got home around 8 o'clock in the morning, where I found all well except that a negro woman and seven cattle were gone away. . . . I neglected to say my prayers and was out of humor extremely and had indifferent health and thoughts, but God send me better if it please his good will.
June 25. My people could not find the negro woman but found her hoe by the church land. I neglected to say my prayers but had indifferent health, humor, and thoughts; God send me better.
June 28. The negro woman was found again that they thought had drown herself. I said a short prayer and had good health, good thoughts, and good humor, thank God Almighty.

—William Byrd II, *Secret Diary*, 1710[1]

In the summer of 1710, an enslaved woman owned by Virginian William Byrd II escaped into the woods. Her fellow slaves reported to him, incorrectly as it turned out, that she had drowned herself. Other details suggest that she was recently imported, and like other newly arrived Africans in British America, was considered to be at an elevated risk for suicide.[2] She may have communicated her intention to die to other slaves, although it is also possible that their report to Byrd was devised to cover an escape attempt and forestall a search for her. In any case, he accepted their account without apparent question, indicating that their explanation of suicide was both convincing and credible. The threat of suicide by enslaved people was particularly acute during the initial years of enslavement, as they were discharged from ships, dispersed to plantations and cities, and confronted with New World labor regimes. Planters referred to this early period of acclimation and adjustment as "seasoning." According to English abolitionist Thomas

Clarkson, this phase of slavery lasted for about two years or "the amount of time an African must take to be so accustomed to the colony, as to be able to endure the common labour of a plantation."[3] Modern historians recognize that seasoning encompassed emotional and psychological adaptations as well.[4] Alexander X. Byrd, for instance, describes seasoning in Jamaica as a "gauntlet of disease, heartbreak, famine, exhaustion, and labor," an interval that renewed the chaos and confusion of initial enslavement.[5] In Virginia as well, as Brenda Stevenson has demonstrated, seasoning replayed the "harsh lessons" learned during the Middle Passage.[6] And as along that journey, suicide remained a constant hazard. One West Indian planter ranked suicide as one of the top six causes of slave mortality during seasoning; the period compounded the unimaginable assaults to personal, familial, and community identity that slaves had already suffered as a result of their initial captivity, sale, and transport to the Americas.[7] During this initial phase of enslavement on American ground, owners attempted to reconcile Africans to enslavement and transform them into laboring commodities.[8]

The temporary escape of the unnamed Virginia woman in 1710 illustrates that both enslaved people and their owners understood that self-destruction was a potential hazard of seasoning. When she was returned to Byrd's plantation, the unnamed woman continued to struggle against enslavement by running away repeatedly, sometimes days or weeks in succession. Over the course of six months, from June to November, she left the plantation at least nine times, repeatedly exhibiting an unwillingness to be reconciled to slavery.[9] After her last escape, she was found dead in the woods. She may have deliberately sought death through exposure and starvation; certainly other slaves did so. We do not know if the slave community or Byrd believed this death to be self-inflicted. However, their shared understanding of her self-destructive aims, alongside her repeated attempts to escape, make it possible to at least suggest that the plantation community believed that she had occasioned her own death.

To consider suicide by newly imported Africans in British America during the initial years of enslavement illustrates not only the circumstances under which slaves chose self-destruction, but also the intricacies of emerging power relations between enslaved people and their owners. Like seasoning itself, some of the conditions that fostered slave suicide were continuous with those of the Middle Passage. Once on American ground, however, other routine features of slavery—labor regimes, anomic isolation, the renewal of separation from shipmates, multiple sales, sexual coercion, corporal punishment, and even the English criminal justice system—also shaped enslaved people's deaths by suicide. In response to these circumstances, some newly imported enslaved Africans drowned or hanged themselves, while others achieved their deaths indirectly. Some slaves refused to follow orders when they knew that doing so would bring on further life-threatening punishments; some lay down and simply refused to rise when ordered to do so. In some of these instances, death appears to have been the aim of the enslaved. In addition, once in America some Africans continued to believe that death by suicide would return them to their homes, reunite them with their ancestors, or allow them to be reborn into their families. Just as processes of capture and enslavement made suicide more acceptable to captive Africans, the initial months after disembarkation appear to have sustained that sentiment among enslaved people, evidence of which can be found throughout the eighteenth century in British America. If not a good death, self-destruction was one of few possibilities for escaping slavery.

Owners viewed the suicides of newly acquired enslaved people as weaknesses in plantation order and failures of mastery. For instance, death—by whatever means—of his enslaved people mattered to men like William Byrd. Slaves were costly investments, of course, and losing them was financially significant.[10] More importantly, however, slave deaths reminded owners of the limits of their powers: episodes of sickness and mortality among the enslaved women and men who labored on Byrd's vast estates were a constant source of concern. His preoccupation extended even to the spiritual implications of slave deaths. On one occasion, for instance, he dreamt of a flaming sword in the sky; about a week later he witnessed a day vision of a "shining cloud" in the "shape of a dart" over his plantation. Both of these portents signaled misfortune that, as he related, later came to pass in the form of the "death of several of my negroes after a very unusual manner," although he left unstated the exact cause of their decease.[11] After relating the dream and vision, he wrote, "God avert his judgment from this poor country," a statement which further illustrates Byrd's acute anxiety over these deaths.[12] Slave deaths mattered not just to his plantation ledger, but also to his future spiritual accounting as well.

The deaths of enslaved people, especially when self-inflicted, inspired doubts, misgivings, and anger in owners and masters. Although he never explicitly says so, Byrd very likely viewed suicide by enslaved people as an inherently political act. Slave self-destruction compromised his power, perhaps because he understood that it positioned the beliefs of slaves above his own. In his magisterial natural history, *A Voyage to the Islands* (1707), Hans Sloane had written that slaves "regard death but little, imagining they shall change their condition by that means from servile to free" and "for this reason often cut their own throats."[13] Byrd had requested a copy of the book; he appears to have received it in 1711.[14] Slave suicide also ruptured the fantasy that the enslaved community of Westover—"my people," as he often referred to them—were in fact extensions of his own will and identity.[15] In death, ironically, the enslaved triumphed over their masters in the contest between personhood and ownership. This was, however, a pyrrhic victory in which the enslaved paid with their very selves and lives. Still, their actions carried a charged meaning that individuals like Byrd, as suggested by his anxieties about the seeming suicide of the unnamed enslaved women, did not fail to grasp; in this way, self-destruction by enslaved people was a part of the political seasoning of masters themselves.

For many slaves, particularly those in South Carolina and the West Indies, seasoning began with a scramble, a sale named for its chaotic nature. Before docking in New World ports, mariners raised food and water rations and cleaned and oiled the bodies of their captives. Upon arrival, ships were often quarantined for a week or ten days, but during this period, merchants sorted human cargoes according to their health and strength, set prices, and often allowed buyers on board to inspect prospective purchases.[16] On the sale day, upon signal, buyers were unleashed onto the ship or into slave pens and attempted to secure their purchases. Equiano describes a scramble in Barbados as full of a terrifying "noise and clamour."[17] According to a shipboard surgeon in 1790, scrambles had an "astonishing effect" upon slaves who cried out "with all the language of affliction" at being separated from their friends and family. Alexander Falconbridge explains that a gun was fired to open the sale, and purchasers ran on board to place tokens about the necks of the slaves; in one instance, "forty or fifty" enslaved people leapt into the sea in response.[18] Sales meant a renewal of dispersal that further fractured the surviving or nascent social bonds that had been formed on the slave ship. When a husband was separated from his wife in a scramble, he hung himself the next day.[19]

Seasoning varied according to region and master and, therefore, so did slave suicide. In the British West Indies throughout the early modern period, for instance, high mortality rates fostered suicide by slaves, just as shipboard epidemics had done on the Atlantic crossing. In 1698, Edward Littleton, one of the largest land and slave owners on Barbados, wrote that a Caribbean planter should plan to lose a full third of newly imported slaves "before they do him any service."[20] By the end of the eighteenth century, the situation was unchanged. According to the testimony of a West Indian planter in 1790, many of his counterparts still expected to lose at least one-third of their unseasoned slaves during their first year on the islands.[21]

Slave mortality rates in early to mid-eighteenth-century Virginia and South Carolina rivaled Littleton's estimates. Between a quarter of Africans died within the first year of arrival in Virginia, and the odds of death in the Lowcountry were even greater, with 30 percent of newly imported Africans dying within one year of disembarkation.[22] Such high rates of death produced grisly scenes. In 1769 in South Carolina, for instance, the bodies of slaves who died awaiting or during sale were thrown into the river and accumulated in the marsh opposite Charleston; by 1807 traders and owners in the harbor threw the bodies of dead slaves overboard to avoid paying burial fees.[23] Just as on ships, the "constant proximity" to the dead, overwhelming mortality, and evident disregard for ritual burials for transported slaves may have encouraged suicide among the survivors.[24] In addition to lamenting mortality rates in the seventeenth-century West Indies, for instance, Littleton implicitly associated high rates of slave death with self-destruction. He provided examples of mortality and disability that resulted from the "dangers" of the sugar trade—slaves fell into rum cisterns, were crushed in mills, or scalded with boiling sugar cane syrup. He subsequently remarked that slaves often ran away and were "never [to be] seen more" or that they "hang[ed] themselves, no creature knows why."[25] A century later, testimony from a House of Commons investigation into the slave trade still corroborated Littleton's assessment that unseasoned enslaved people killed themselves regularly. When asked if suicide was "common" among newly imported slaves, witness after witness answered affirmatively; some cited the Igbo or the Coromontee as having a particular propensity for suicide.[26] Similarly, in Virginia, during years of high imports, slave owners petitioned the House of Burgesses, seeking compensation for deceased slaves; in 40 percent of those petitions, enslaved people had died by suicide.[27]

Regardless of region, seasoning was a harrowing experience. Accounts by enslaved men and women who survived the early years can shed light on those who destroyed themselves soon after their arrival in the Americas. For instance, the story of 'Sibell, given near the end of her life in 1799, illustrates the multiple fracturing of social relations that often was fundamental to the experience of seasoning. 'Sibell recollected her kidnapping in Africa by her brother-in-law, who carried her all night and day away from her home. She arrived on the African coast, alone and became so frightened by the sound of the ocean that she thought that she would die.[28] Aboard ship, she was relieved to meet some people from her country—captive shipmates could become fictive kin as brothers and sisters—but when the ship docked in the West Indies, however, she was sold away from them.[29] Having found temporary respite in the companionship of familiar others was a source of comfort that was all too short lived. Her story ends abruptly here, as the trauma of separation ruptures the narrative: 'Sibell's account, Stephanie Smallwood argues, ends in dissolution.[30] 'Sibell's story of relationships repeatedly formed and lost is a theme that is echoed in accounts of slave suicide. One witness in the parliamentary investigation testified that newly imported Africans experienced "despondency" because they had been torn from their "friends, relations, and country."[31] In this context, as the enslaved Belinda's 1787 petition to the Massachusetts legislature illustrates, some bondpeople viewed death as an alternative to slavery. Enslaved as a young child and separated from her parents, she poignantly recounted her seasoning as an interval in which she "learned to catch the ideas, marked by the sounds of language, only to know that her doom was slavery, from which death alone was to emancipate her."[32] Belinda did not kill herself; rather, she equates liberty and death in order to plead for her freedom. She understood, however, as other slaves did, that death, by whatever means, would allow them to escape the psychic and physical damages of slavery.

If shattered ties of family and fictive kin quickened slaves' thoughts of death, bonds among slaves could hasten the path to death, too. Death by suicide was associated with the seasoning of newly imported Africans across British America, among whom there is evidence of collective suicide. This suggests that despite the renewed disorientation produced by seasoning, enslaved people demonstrated a "significant measure of camaraderie," even in seeking death.[33] For instance, an overseer left a group of recently purchased slaves on a small Caribbean island to plant cotton; when he returned, they were "all hanging together in the woods."[34] In 1740, a Virginia planter complained that seven of his slaves, likely newly imported individuals, ran away and were found shortly thereafter drowned in the Mattapony River.[35] Unseasoned enslaved people building canals in early nineteenth-century North Carolina also killed themselves collectively, as did a group of recently imported Igbos in Georgia in 1803.[36]

Among enslaved people, self-destruction during seasoning was not limited to either sex or any particular age group. Witnesses often did not indicate the gender or age of slaves who died by suicide; but when specific, gave examples of unseasoned men, women, and children alike who killed themselves soon after arrival on American plantations. In 1769, for instance, South Carolinian trader Henry Laurens described a group of nine recently imported "new negros" in which one woman hanged herself.[37] At the turn of the nineteenth century, another unseasoned enslaved man in Charleston was found by a jury to have hanged himself "in a fit of despair."[38] A few observers claimed that enslaved women adapted to seasoning more quickly than did their male counterparts, noting that the "despondency" that was associated with suicide continued "in general" for men but wore "out sooner with the women." One witness attributed this fact to his assessment that women were better treated in slavery than were men, although he did not offer any evidence for this conclusion.[39]

During seasoning, a lack of social cohesion, linguistic and cultural differences, regimes of labor, corporal punishment, sexual battery, and physical pain combined to foster self-destructive impulses in newly arrived Africans. In addition to these, observers noted that suicide was a generalized response to the status of slavery, rather than to specific circumstances of enslavement. Some enslaved men and women "destroyed themselves on their first arrival, when they understood that they were in a state of slavery."[40] One man explained that his counterparts chose self-destruction because "they would rather lose their lives than live in the situation they were in."[41]

Owners attempted to force or persuade enslaved people to at least outwardly adapt to slavery: some responded with suicide, while others resisted adjustment in ways that could result in death. For instance, the story of Tony, an enslaved man in mid-seventeenth-century Maryland, captures the ongoing struggle that lay at the heart of seasoning, a struggle that, perhaps as he intended, resulted in his death. The account suggests that Tony was not the Atlantic creole typical of the time and region; perhaps he was a refuse slave, one who was not immediately saleable because of perceived physical or temperamental characteristics. He was purchased by Symon Overzee, a St. Mary's City trader with ties to Amsterdam and, by 1656, had singled himself out as a troublesome slave to his master.[42] Tony lived as an outlaw, foraging in the woods and coming into houses for supplies when others were out in the fields. He lived in a "rival geography" outside the boundaries of his master's power.[43] While slightly more than half of unseasoned slaves in eighteenth-century Virginia and South Carolina absconded in pairs or other groups, Tony, in contrast, was a lone fugitive.[44] Because his truancy was proximate to the plantation, however, despite his isolation, he nonetheless consorted to greater and lesser degrees with other members of the Overzee household.

Tony consistently refused the terms of his seasoning; he not only ran away, he refused to prepare food, and rejected his labor assignments. In order to force him into compliance, his master used corporal punishment, routinely beating and torturing him. The struggle between master and slave came to a climax about six months after Tony arrived in Maryland, when his master chained him up by his wrists for unspecified misdemeanors. Mistress Overzee (when her husband was absent) released Tony and ordered him to go to work, but he declined. Instead, he "laid himself down and would not stir." When his master returned, he commanded increasingly severe punishments; Tony was first whipped, then doused with hot lard, and, finally, hoisted up by an Indian slave to hang by the wrists. Three hours later, Tony was dead. Legally speaking of course, this death was not a suicide; in fact, Overzee later was charged with manslaughter.[45] Tony's rejection of his seasoning, however, took several forms. He refused to make food, to work, to talk, and, finally, to move. All of these refusals can be understood as physical embodiments of emotional states that eventually, as he may have intended, beckoned death. According to onlookers, he refused his enslavement by maintaining his "stubbornness" and making "no signs of conforming himself to his master's will or command."[46] Although an indirect suicide, this death was anything but passive.

Testimony from others associated with the Overzee household also emphasized linguistic and cultural distances between themselves and Tony. Overzee's brother-in-law, Job Chandler, testified that of "all the human creatures that I ever saw" he had never seen such a "brute"; Chandler could not perceive "any speech or language" from Tony but only that which was "ugly yelling brute beast like." Communication with Tony was not, however, impossible, particularly if it was augmented with threats of a dog whip. Chandler testified that he and Tony "made signs" to one another. Tony "made signs that he would be gone" or run away; in response Chandler related that he "made signs to [Tony] to sit down again." When Chandler took a lash to Tony, the enslaved man came in the house, sat down, and "did not make more proffers to be gone."[47] Another servant in the household testified that Tony was "mute and stubborn" and prone to fits, although she described them as "feigned."[48] Did Tony suffer some form of epilepsy? Was he a refuse slave? We also have to consider his physical pain: according to Chandler, Tony had an infected finger that needed to be amputated; his hand and arm were similarly at risk.[49]

According to some of the testimony, the laborers in this household demonstrated little social cohesion; Tony's fellow workers included an enslaved Indian man, an African or African American woman, and at least one female British indentured servant. Yet details also suggest that Tony was not completely unaided. On an earlier occasion, a maidservant had come into the house to find Tony eating hominy; she notified her master, who bound Tony to the bars of the window, with the rope knotted behind his back, and asked her to watch Tony for the night. By morning, he had escaped. Job Chandler concluded that the "Devil" must have helped Tony untie the knot, but also noted that his maid did "not well" look after him.[50] In addition, of the unfree witnesses present on the day Tony died, Hannah Littleworth was the only one with the legal standing to offer testimony against her master, but only did so two years after Tony's demise, when she was freed from her indenture. She described a violent and fragmented household where the unfree aided one another cautiously. She watched mutely as Tony was punished, as he remained "in his stubbornness," and as he was hung to twist in the wind. The female slave on the plantation remained in a "quartering house" and "never stirred out" during these events.[51] No one attempted to intercede on Tony's behalf until the master and mistress of the house had departed. Only then, as it was clear that Tony was dying, did the maidservant ask her male counterparts to release Tony from his bonds, but they refused.[52]

Tony's experiences were not singular, and his story reflects the range of conditions endured by slaves during their early years in the Americas. He was isolated both by choice (absconding) and by circumstance (speech) from everyone else in the household. These were similar to details found in other accounts of direct suicide by enslaved people: those who "met with no other slave who could talk their dialect, and quiet their fears" hung themselves.[53] Other slaves also used their bodies—and specifically refused to rise—to signal their rejection of enslavement. One slave chained to a gang refused to rise even after being dragged; the overseer ordered a fire to be set around him and forced a smoldering iron between his teeth. Still he did not rise.[54] Self-destruction also occurred in response to imminent corporal punishment, material deprivation, and physical pain. In addition, as Tony was unable or unwilling to communicate beyond superficial exchanges with the others in his household, his existence alternated between foraging, imprisonment, and punishment; he was profoundly isolated. Tony's death can be interpreted in several ways: as murder, as indirect suicide through refusals that would only bring further violence from his enslaver, or, as the Maryland court essentially ruled, as an unfortunate but legitimate exercise of his master's authority. Tony's story also reflects the ways in which specific regimes of seasoning could foster suicidal behavior among enslaved people and cause them to rethink the acceptability of suicide during their early years in America.[55]

The accounts of British American planters reflect that the conditions that fostered slave suicide varied with region and master. In contrast to Tony's owner, other masters employed a combination of psychology, corporal punishment, and coercive technologies in attempts to season their slaves. In seventeenth-century Maryland, Overzee clearly attempted to govern by brute force. In Jamaica, the destination for the largest number of enslaved Africans transported in British ships during the eighteenth century, the circumstances of seasoning hardly differed from those aboard slavers and, just as aboard ships, a small number of whites wielded "extraordinary power" over enslaved Africans.[56] In the case of William Byrd's enslaved woman who repeatedly ran away, Byrd responded each time by attempting to discipline and reconcile her to slavery. Her death by suicide was likely indirect like Tony's, and the details of her experience in Virginia reflect those of other slaves. Byrd first attempted to discipline the unnamed woman by bestowing a name on her: he called her Betty.[57] This bestowal of a name demonstrated his authority over her and was an attempt to draw her into the paternal ranks of his great family, along with Jenny, Eugene, and Anaka, his other slaves. In naming her Betty, Byrd meant to discipline, comfort, and socialize her into slavery; his success as a master depended upon his doing so.[58]

Byrd, of course, could also discipline the enslaved woman through corporal means. After naming her, Byrd employed the bit—a common technology of enslavement—which, depending on which type he used, made eating, talking, moving, and resting extremely difficult. The use of the bit suggests that Byrd believed that Betty would repeat her attempt at suicide or flight. She did not disappoint him: five days later, she ran away with the bit in her mouth. She must have been recaptured immediately, for the very next day, Byrd wrote that she "ran away again with the [bit] in her mouth and my people could not find her." Less than a week passed before he reported that she "was found and tied but ran away again." She was not apprehended until the middle of the month, 15 July, and four days after that, she ran again, only to be immediately recaptured. Byrd portrayed himself as a dispassionate disciplinarian, but at her fourth attempt to escape, he lost his temper, although not with Betty. Rather, he wrote that he was "angry" with his overseer for "losing the screw of the [bit]."[59]

Despite her successive escapes and recaptures, Betty, like Tony, could not be reconciled to seasoning and slavery. In early November she ran away for the ninth time, and a week later she was found dead in the woods.[60] She probably did not starve to death in a week unless she had already been refusing food. Although it was November, Byrd had remarked in his diary that the weather was "very fine" and "not cold considering the time of year," so exposure did not necessarily cause her death.[61] Douglas Chambers argues that the Igbo imported into eighteenth-century Virginia had access to a number of poisonous substances that they were accused of using on each other as well as their owners; perhaps Betty used poison on herself.[62]

However Betty died, across eighteenth-century British North America and, later, the nineteenth-century South, the bodies of enslaved people were found in the woods, in rivers, and on roadsides, dead from unknown causes. In North Carolina in 1754, for example, a coroner's jury assembled around the body of a "negro wench late of [Craven County] then and there lying dead." Their verdict was that the woman had met her death by "mischance or willfully by her own act." Similarly, in 1759, the body of the enslaved woman Judith was found lying "dead on the ground in the woods and distant from any path," and her death was attributed to intoxication and the "hardness of the weather." Hannah, a suicide, was found to be an "accessory to her own death," when the jury viewed her body hanging from a dogwood tree.[63] Similarly in South Carolina, coroner's juries viewed slave bodies lying on riverbanks and hanging from trees; at least one man was found to have hung himself accidentally.[64] In 1866, former slave Matty J. Jackson reported that her grandfather "in deep despair and overwhelmed with grief . . . made his escape to the woods, determined to put an end to his sorrows by perishing with cold and hunger."[65] Like Jackson's grandfather, the reports of Betty's intention to drown and her repeated attempts to run away suggest that she fled to the woods in November with the intention of dying by whatever measures that she found near to hand.

If seasoning fostered the suicidal thoughts of some slaves, the transition from slave ships to American plantations also offered enslaved people access to a wider variety of methods and opportunities for self-destruction. In cities, slaves leapt from buildings into the streets; in the countryside, they threw themselves down hills and into millponds. In the woods, they fashioned nooses from vines and green branches. Confined to jails or attics, they hanged or strangled themselves. Outside of the close confines of the Middle Passage, slaves procured knives, poison, and very occasionally guns to use as weapons of self-destruction. Refusing to eat, hanging, and drowning remained the most readily available means of suicide, but they were no longer the only methods that enslaved people used.

On dry land, enslaved people also may have found greater opportunities to engage in ritual practices to accompany their suicides, and the association between slave self-destruction and spiritual transmigration became evident across British America. Many Africans believed that water and woods were sacred spaces. Water was a conduit to the spiritual world and a channel of "repatriation" to families, ancestors, and Africa. Souls of the dead were understood to pass over "broad waterscapes," and many believed "that the realm of the dead lay at the bottom of the ocean."[66] In addition, the woods, specifically, were associated with ancestors' spirits who might guide slaves' journeys to Africa, while water was viewed as a barrier that the dead needed to cross in order to rejoin families.[67] Drowning and hanging, therefore, were means of suicide that would "ease" enslaved people's "spirits to their homelands." In addition to choosing spiritually meaningful environments like forests and rivers, enslaved people accompanied their suicides with ritualistic elements necessary to their transmigration.[68] Some slaves put on all of their clothes; others placed food and water nearby; still others tied chains or bundles of food around their waists before they threw themselves into rivers.[69] An enslaved female domestic servant allegedly stole jewelry from her mistress, adorned herself with it, and then "applied the fatal chord." The writer of this account cast aspersions on this manner of dying, joking that the woman believed that she would be revived in Africa and made rich with the purloined jewels. More likely the use of jewelry was part of a custom.[70] Collective suicides in South and North Carolina involved ritual preparations that included singing and chanting.[71]

The belief that self-destruction began the processes of transmigration or reincarnation could be a powerfully positive inducement to suicide. In some cases, suicide was understood to destroy the body in order to preserve the soul.[72] That idea was, of course, anathema to those who profited from and owned slaves. Nonetheless, evidence of self-destruction during seasoning suggests that enslaved people's initial experiences in the American colonies intensified their beliefs in the transformational power of death, even when it was self-inflicted.[73] In New England in 1733, for instance, an enslaved woman cut open her stomach, saying that she was returning to her own country.[74] In 1707 naturalist and physician Hans Sloane briefly remarked that because of slaves' spiritual beliefs, they imagined that death would bring freedom and "for this reason often cut their own throats."[75] In the Dutch West Indies, a creole translation of this belief emerged, "mij dodte mij loppe in myn land" or "when I die, I shall return to my own land."[76] Suicide could also provide a resurrection of the self: one enslaved New England woman averred that once deceased, no matter how death occurred, an individual was reborn as the next child born into the family.[77] As late as 1823, a Jamaican planter noted that the enslaved people "all" expected that, "after death, they shall first return to their native country, and enjoy again the society of kindred and friends, from whom they have been torn away."

It was this idea, he continued, along with the terrors of seasoning that "used to prompt numbers, on their first arrival, to acts of suicide."[78]

As the eighteenth century wore on, enslaved persons' spiritual beliefs about suicide reverberated far beyond their immediate acts of self-destruction. In 1785, for instance, the *Pennsylvania Evening Herald* complained about increasing numbers of suicides among New Englanders. The paper blamed this surge on Africans and African Americans, claiming that New Englanders had adopted the African belief that death, even by suicide, brought a return to one's homeland. This idea, the newssheet scathingly noted, had been adopted from the "*refined* negroes."[79] Despite its tone, the remark exposed the ways in which the spiritual dimensions of self-destruction by enslaved people were commonly understood, as well as feared, across and outside of the slave societies of eighteenth-century British America.

In response to enslaved people's acts of self-destruction during seasoning, owners and traders, like mariners before them, redoubled their efforts at suicide prevention. They tortured those who resolved not to eat and beat those who refused to rise. Planters also continued their attempts to control suicide through a manipulation of slave religiosity. In order to frighten slaves away from contemplating the positive spiritual outcome of self-inflicted death, masters told their slaves that transmigration or reincarnation was impossible if the body was desecrated, dismembered, or decapitated. As had been the case aboard slave ships, owners used postmortem punishment in attempts to prevent suicide. For instance, masters in Saint-Domingue beheaded or defaced the first Igbo slave in a shipment to die, and in Cuba, the corpses of suicides were burned and their ashes scattered. Across the Americas, the heads of suicidal and rebellious slaves were struck from their bodies and displayed on pikes, which was consistent with the traditions of Europeans, who also used decapitation and dismemberment to punish traitors and some suicides.[80] Up through the end of the seventeenth century, at least, slaves were not the only individuals whose bodies were subjected to such desecration. By the end of the eighteenth century in British American slave societies, however, slaves were the only suicides who appear to have been routinely exposed to postmortem punishments.[81]

Planters had strategies that they believed would prevent slaves from committing suicide, but the extent to which slaves accepted or shared those beliefs is much less clear. No evidence suggests that slaves acquiesced to owners' attempts to shape their spiritual worldview or that these terrorizing methods of deterrence were effective. That is, slaves may not have always feared or been deterred from suicide by threats of beheading or dismemberment. William Pierson points out that "thousands" of individuals were beheaded in funeral sacrifices in West Africa so that they could serve the nobility in the afterlife. Moreover, West Africans who were killed away from their countries were sometimes dismembered, and a part of the body was returned home for burial.[82]

In some respects, the anxieties of owners and planters paralleled those of mariners in the Atlantic trade; slave suicide destabilized plantation order and diminished owners' capital investment in human labor. Owners differed from mariners, however, in at least one very telling respect: planters were much less forthcoming on the subject of slave self-destruction and appear to have suppressed evidence of its occurrence. In part, masters were anxious about their reputations. Mariners worried about slave suicide because it could spark insurrection and was contagious; it also was uninsurable and diminished profits. Masters' reticence on the subject, in contrast, was related to the politics of personal reputation. The suicides of enslaved people shattered masters' pretensions to gentility and revealed the violence of slavery. Planter paternalism is often associated with the antebellum era, but easily a century earlier, owners like William Byrd II distanced themselves from responsibility for their enslaved subjects' acts of self-destruction. As early as the mid-eighteenth century, the mask of gentility may well have necessitated a public denial of slave self-destruction.[83] When Teena, an enslaved woman from South Carolina, died from the "appearance of barbarity" and "severe and inhumane treatment" in 1796, for instance, her owner swore before the coroner that he had never mistreated any of his bondpeople and claimed instead that she had died from a cold.[84] As one slave recalled in the nineteenth century, when the corpse of a suicide was discovered, his owner admonished the slave community to never speak of it.[85]

Slave self-destruction exposed the institution of slavery in all its brutality. Outside of British North America, cruelty was cited as a factor in slave suicide and an occasion on which masters could collect monetary damages from the agents of cruelty. In 1741, for instance, a plaintiff in Louisiana sought damages for the death of Francois, an enslaved carpenter who cut his throat "in despair, whether for ill-treatment or for other causes."[86] Yet slave suicide rarely surfaced in planters' private writings: Byrd, a man exceedingly vocal on so many subjects, records two instances of possible slave suicide in his many diaries, but they are addressed indirectly and inconclusively. Similarly, Byrd's fellow planter, Landon Carter, did not discuss slave suicides in his own extensive diaries, although he gave brief mention to the self-inflicted death of a neighboring planter's slave.[87] Both of these men were active in Virginia governance during stretches of time when legislators received over one hundred petitions from slaveholders seeking compensation for deceased slaves, 40 percent of which referenced slave suicide.[88] As far as I can ascertain, neither man ever submitted any petitions for compensation. Of course, this could simply mean that none of their enslaved people ever died by suicide, were killed by patrollers, or were executed for committing a crime. Given that they owned above six hundred slaves between them, however, that seems unlikely. They may have privately punished and executed their slaves and kept them out of the way of the law. However, what seems more likely is that they avoided public disclosure of slave crimes and slave deaths, including death by suicide.

Similarly, in 1783, Virginian William Beverley, studying in London, testified in a House of Commons investigation into the slave trade. The committee directly asked him about the incidence of slave suicide in Virginia. Having taken evidence from sailors and planters about the repeated instances of slave suicide aboard ship and in the Caribbean, House members may have been surprised when Beverley testified that "never one" report of slave suicide had ever reached him. It is certainly possible that Beverley never gossiped over a coroner's inquest, consulted a neighbor about a petition to the burgesses, or, for that matter, visited any county court in the nearly twenty years that he lived in the colonies, but that seems unthinkable for a well-born Virginian who planned to enter the law.[89] As the member of one of the colony's wealthiest families—Beverley's father owned some five hundred slaves—his flat denial lacks credibility.[90] In a later investigation in 1790, one-time South Carolina planter George Baillie allowed that one of his slaves had hanged himself; however, Baillie averred that he was in no way responsible for the act. His slave had destroyed himself, Baillie claimed, not because of "harsh treatment" but rather because his disposition "could not brook the idea of slavery."[91] Slave temperament, rather than the nature of individual master-slave relations, he argued, accounted for suicides. These kinds of statements lay at the heart of the decoupling of suicide from slavery that was initiated by mariners in the transatlantic slave trade and sustained by slave owners during and after seasoning.

The reason that owners suppressed evidence of enslaved suicides ran deep. Slave self-destruction during seasoning brought into sharp relief the brutality of the entire enterprise of slavery and was inconsistent with depictions of plantations as bucolic refuges. Exposing cruelty as the essence of the slave trade and seasoning called into question the character of slave-owners. Men like Byrd and Carter in particular believed themselves to be enlightened patriarchs, and suicide by slaves potentially challenged their self-regard. As early as the mid-eighteenth century, the mask of gentility may well have necessitated a public denial of slave self-destruction. Because slave suicide exposed the paradoxes of slavery, masters like Byrd and Carter (privately in their diaries) and Baillie and Beverley (publicly in an investigation into the trade) affirmed their own humanity by denying outright or minimizing their possible role in slave self-destruction.

Like mariners and traders, owners' understandings of suicide also created social distance that defined slaves as beings beyond the scope of European understanding and distanced slave self-destruction from the processes of seasoning. Instead, they explained suicide with reference to African spiritual beliefs. They also branded African identities according to their association with suicide, revolt, or even propensities to labor. In 1734, for instance, mariner William Snelgrave connected suicide with the Coromontee, who "despised punishment and even death itself."[92] In 1755, South Carolina merchant Henry Laurens wrote to Peter Furnell of Jamaica that "stout, healthy fellows sell to most advantage with us, the Country not material if they are not from Callabar [synonymous with Igbo, modern Nigeria] which slaves are quite out of repute from numbers in every Cargo . . . destroying themselves."[93] Even late in the eighteenth century, a witness in the slave trade investigation noted that slaves from the "Ebo [Igbo] country" were "remarkably high spirited," implying that they chose suicide because they did not "brook slavery so well as those from several other countries," while an early nineteenth-century tract described the Igbo as "turbulent, stubborn, and addicted to suicide."[94] As this quote suggests, and as Michael Gomez has shown, nowhere is the connection between ethnicity and suicide more apparent than in the case of the Igbo.[95] Other traders agreed that the Igbo were understood to be prone to suicide through obstinacy, despondency, and stubbornness.[96] If the Igbo were in fact more prone to suicide, this helps explain why the petitions for compensation in Virginia, where Igbo imports predominated, may have outpaced those of North and South Carolina.

Planters not only corresponded about the linkages between enslaved ethnicity and suicide, they also versified it in plantation poetry. For instance, in *The Sugar Cane: A Poem in Four Books* (1764), which was being reprinted in the United States as late as 1850, the West Indian planter and poet James Grainger counseled planters to avoid the "Coromontee," who "choose death before dishonorable bonds" and to "fly, with care from/The Moco-nation;

they themselves destroy."[97] Grainger directed others to avoid purchasing older slaves, who were "sullen and unteachable and frequently put an end to their own lives." As he explained,

> But, planter, from what coast soe'er they sail,
> Buy not the old: they ever sullen prove;
> With heart-felt anguish, they lament their home;
> They will not, cannot work; they never learn
> Thy native language; they are prone to ails;
> And oft by suicide their being end.[98]

Owners were warned to choose carefully and master competently. To the extent that they accepted these assessments, then, they believed that suicide could be controlled through careful scrutiny. *Caveat emptor* meant understanding African propensity toward suicide. If this failed, of course, owners and planters could attempt to warn slaves away from suicide through forced feedings, beatings, and postmortem desecration. Above all, however, owners and planters who acknowledged that enslaved people killed themselves during seasoning averred that the reasons they did so lay elsewhere than in the brutal and systemic features of the institution of slavery itself.

For enslaved people, like the unnamed woman discussed by William Byrd II in his diary in 1710, suicide remained a possible alternative to captivity and an acceptable escape from enslavement during seasoning in British American plantations. The initial years following Africans' arrival reproduced circumstances—the fracturing of social bonds, sexual abuse, physical brutality, labor regimes—that fostered self-destruction. As traders and owners sold and dispersed slaves across the American plantations during seasoning, the latter may have found, in fact, even more opportunity and reason to consider suicide over continued enslavement. Not the least among these reasons was their belief that self-destruction brought the possibility of spiritual rebirth.

Masters and owners appear to have rarely pondered deeply why enslaved men and women killed themselves, as illustrated by Littleton's chilling assessment that "no creature knows why" slaves in Barbados hanged themselves. Similarly, Virginian William Mayo wrote matter-of-factly that the "Negro Quaccoo Hang'd himself[,] the Women all in Health and [otherwise] all things goe on as well as can be expected."[99] Petitions to that colony's legislative house, in addition, did not typically discuss the reasons for slave suicide. Yet owners recognized the threat posed by slave self-destruction and punished such acts in order to attempt to forestall their incidence. Byrd punished his enslaved woman's runaway attempts in part because he suspected that she had tried to kill herself: in the end, she may have succeeded in doing so, and her death put her beyond his reach. Most surprisingly, perhaps, with all evidence to the contrary, some masters denied that slave self-destruction happened at all, although doing so did not diminish its visibility.

Enslaved people's deaths by suicides were a part of the Atlantic trade and remained evident during the early years of their seasoning on plantations across the British America. Newly arrived Africans struggled with the brutal processes of enslavement and, in response, some of them chose suicide over seasoning. Their self-inflicted deaths, whether achieved directly or indirectly, cast doubts on the reputations of their owners as well as on slavery as an institution. Yet that inquiries into the nature and circumstances of slaves' self-inflicted deaths surfaced in late eighteenth-century investigations into the slave trade reflects the way in which slave suicide exposed the paradoxes of slavery. Slaves' acts of self-destruction compromised the aims of owners and reflected badly on them; hence masters were reticent to discuss any deaths by suicide that occurred on their plantations. In this way, acts of suicide by slaves during seasoning laid bare the contradictions of slavery. As we shall see in the next chapter, those questions and paradoxes persisted and deepened alongside the development of slavery in colonial British America.

THREE

Slave Suicide in the Context of Colonial North America

WILLIAMSBURG, *July* 10

A few days ago, a fine Negroe Man Slave, imported in one of the late Ships from *Africa,* belonging to a Wheelwright, near this City, taking Notice of his Master's giving another Correction for a Misdemeanor, went to a Grindstone and making a Knife sharp cut his own Throat, and died on the Spot.

—*Virginia Gazette*, 1752[1]

In 1752, the *Virginia Gazette* published the story of an unnamed slave who slit his throat near Williamsburg, one of seventy-odd reports of suicide by whites and blacks that were featured in the weekly paper from its first publication in 1736 through the onset of the American Revolution. The story was preceded by an account of the execution of a felon in Annapolis and followed by a letter from the Reverend Samuel Davies who quoted Job: "Wherefore do I take my Flesh in my Teeth, and put my Life in my Hand?" Appearing to the right and slightly lower was a notice that the *Anne* had arrived from "Old Callabar" with a cargo of "choice, healthy slaves" destined for the auction block on 16 July. That item was followed by an advertisement for the sale of a "choice assortment of silks," fine fabrics, and other millinery (stays, gloves, fans, and the like), an array aimed at female consumers. Reports of execution, suicide, and despair appeared alongside advertisements for the sale of human beings and luxury goods. For the *Gazette*'s audience, death and commerce appear to have been the order of the day.

The confluence of these items is revealing. Most notably, their convergence mirrored the contradictions and contexts that shaped understandings of suicide in the emerging slave societies of pre-Revolutionary British America.[2] The masthead of the *Gazette* promised its readers the "freshest advices, foreign and domestic." Appearing in the latter section of the paper, sandwiched between news from Europe and notices of people and goods for sale, these brief pieces made the connections among suicide, moralizing, and commerce implicit rather than direct. Both the printed text of the felon's contrite confession as well as the Christian exhortation against Job's suicide stressed the traditional importance of obeying God rather than succumbing to sin and despondency. In the same breath, the advertisements for slaves and luxury goods emphasized the secular values of marketplace consumerism. By 1752, slave sale was central to Virginia's economy, while fine millinery functioned as a marker of gender and status, largely purchased by those individuals whose families could also afford to own slaves.[3]

While such juxtapositions were common in eighteenth-century newspapers, the 1752 issue offered the first account of slave suicide to be printed in the *Virginia Gazette*. The meaning of that suicide for the paper's audience was ambiguous. In the context of the stories that surrounded it, the account of suicide reflected tensions between secular and sacred understandings of self-destruction: while Davies's sermon strongly condemned suicide, the description of the unnamed enslaved man's self-destructive act contained hints of admiration. The paper also revealed competing understandings of slaves as both persons and commodities by positioning the account of the fully human act of self-destruction against the advertisement of slaves for sale. Moreover, the item itself was essentially a narrative transcript of suicide. The slave's actions were offered up by an unidentified onlooker whose point of view structured the account. From that perspective, this was no impulsive act of self-destruction. In this telling, the slave had telegraphed a calculated set of intentions: he had watched the beating of another slave, walked to the grindstone, whetted his knife, and wounded himself fatally. Did those actions constitute an improvised ritual? Did the slave say a prayer as he honed the blade that he would use to slit his throat? Or was the sharpening a practical matter, designed to ensure that the cut would be swift and sure and surpass any attempts to heal it?[4] Or, to put these questions differently, how did the enslaved man understand the meaning of his death and what did other observers make of this suicide?

Perhaps like no other act, suicide by enslaved people had the potential to expose the contradictions of slavery in colonial British North America. Those contradictions can best be comprehended first by analyzing the competing meanings of the unnamed Williamsburg man's act of self-destruction and second by situating slave suicide in the context of other accounts of self-inflicted death by early Americans. Some stories of slave suicide accentuated similarities between blacks and whites. In the case of the enslaved

Williamsburg man, for instance, the story appealed to masculinist ethics of choosing death before dishonor, a theme that resonated with the Anglo-American elite. Yet if some accounts of enslaved people's suicides reflected a set of reasons for choosing death that were shared across racial lines, others confirmed differences based on race and class. For instance, European missionaries' reports of suicide by indigenous Americans suggested that they, like enslaved people, viewed death as an acceptable as well as sometimes a good or honorable death. Similarly, like those of the laboring classes, the suicides of enslaved people were attributed to temperamental stubbornness. Such appraisals distanced the meanings of slave suicide from those of free Europeans, and sustained the disarticulation of suicide and slavery that had begun in the slave trade. Additionally, as we have seen, reports of slave suicide also contained critical estimations of masters, a theme that became more pronounced over the course of the eighteenth century. Enslaved people who killed themselves, some observers indirectly implied or directly averred, did so because their masters were unfit. In these ways as well, stories of enslaved people's suicides presented Anglo-American observers with a host of competing, contradictory, and charged messages that had the potential to unsettle the acceptance of slavery and assumptions about enslaved people.

The questions posed by the suicides of enslaved people were not resolved, of course, in the eighteenth century. However, whether or not slaves intended it, their self-inflicted deaths challenged ideas about slavery and about suicide in British North America. Their acts of self-destruction called into question prevailing Anglo-American assumptions about religion and commerce, personhood and commodification, and racial, class, and gender identity and difference. Well before the rise of organized antislavery movements, the attention that slave suicide focused on these contradictions both hinted at and openly exposed the moral quandaries of slavery.

In light of these evidentiary and narrative complexities, the contemporary historian may be tempted to discuss the suicides of slaves primarily in terms of agency and resistance, reading slaves' acts of self-destruction as defiant and destructive.[5] In killing himself, one might argue, the unnamed enslaved man in Williamsburg resisted his enslavement and ruined his master's valued property. Rather than read this suicide only as one slave resisting one master, however, it is more analytically productive to think of its broader political and cultural implications. Characterizing it as an isolated act of resistance by a single slave obscures the multiple and often unknowable forces that precipitated it and risks the implication that suicide was the result of a freely made decision. To the extent that it was a choice, it was one from an exceedingly narrow range of options and an alternative for which the enslaved man paid with his life. But considering this act of self-destruction in the context of colonization allows us to see how its meanings were culturally shared and circulated beyond one moment, one enslaved person, and one master. Accounts of enslaved people's suicides demonstrate not only their very real significance as individual acts but also the paradoxical and political implications of those suicides in the emerging slave societies of British North America.

The Williamsburg man's suicide conveyed varied meanings about honor and class, race and gender, and slavery and mastery to the mid-eighteenth-century readers who witnessed his suicide, however mediated, through print. Because early modern newspapers were shared widely and read out loud in a variety of situations—at home and work, in coffeehouses and taverns—the stories that they contained reached beyond immediate subscribers. Assessing the cultural implications of this report for the varied group of mid-eighteenth-century Americans who read or heard it requires close consideration of the details of the item and its printed context.[6]

For mid-eighteenth-century Anglo-Americans, the meanings of this suicide were informed, in part and perhaps surprisingly, by ideas of honor. Honor was a gendered concept, one associated most closely with early modern elite masculine identity. At least some of those who read or heard the story of this suicide would have conceded a grudging admiration for the courage with which the man approached death. Some may have been familiar with the idea, perhaps earliest voiced by Jean Barbot, that "in general" captive Africans were understood to regard death "stoically" and endured its pain with an indifference that was associated with bravery. Barbot attributed this quality to Africans' "Pythagorean" inclinations—that is, to their spiritual beliefs in reincarnation and their understanding that the soul lived on in new forms.[7]

Other observers might have admired the studied resolve and public staging of the slave's self-killing; as depicted, this was not the result of passionate impulse, but rather an act of cool reason and unflinching determination. For English elites, deliberate, rational suicide, typically using firearms, was a means of dying with honor. This belief appears to have been shared by at least some colonial southerners. William Byrd III, for instance, who shot himself on New Year's Day 1777, evidently believed that self-inflicted death was preferable to facing disgrace after he lost both his family's fortune and the political respect of his peers.[8] Similarly, in the antebellum period, at least one southern slave owner perceived himself to be an ineffectual master and believed that his slaves viewed him with contempt for his weaknesses. In imagining ways of gaining their respect and esteem, he contemplated suicide, believing that the act would make him appear to be firm rather than "permissive." This suggests the extent to which the beliefs of enslaved people regarding suicide might weigh heavily on their owners' self-images.[9] In addition, the ideas of the Stoics, along with neoclassical depictions of suicide as heroic and admirable, were frequent subjects in popular eighteenth-century Anglo-American plays, such as Thomas Southerne's 1695 adaptation of Aphra Behn's *Oroonoko* (1688) and Joseph Addison's *Cato* (1713). Some readers of the *Virginia Gazette* would have been familiar with the virtue sometimes attributed to self-destructive acts.[10] These suggestions of regard, then, attributed both integrity and honor to the unnamed enslaved man who killed himself in full view of the Williamsburg public in 1752.

The specific reasons for the man's suicide were made explicit to those who read the *Gazette*'s account. One set of explanations was, like honor and courage, related to class and rank. The slave, readers were told in the first line, was a "fine" man, meaning that he was "consummate in quality," "refined," in a word, "perfect." In the context of the slave market, "fine" carried a powerful commercial valence: this slave was a valuable commodity and a costly investment. The audience might have imagined "fine" to indicate a physically formidable and mentally adroit person, a man who possessed both the corporal strength and psychological resolve necessary to kill himself. These assessments could also have been related to complexion. Early modern Anglo-Americans assigned meanings and status to skin color, and they may have viewed the darkness or richness of the slave's hue as mark of physiological superiority—hence, a "fine" slave.[11]

The issue of class was also raised in the *Gazette* story by the occupation of the owner, a wheelwright likely training his slave for the trade. The suicide could be read as a rejection of menial, if skilled, labor and may have suggested to the audience that the enslaved man was high born in Africa. Anglo-Americans may have debased Africans on the basis of race, but rank was still a salient cultural category of respect. Other details might have furthered the associations with rank and class: the slave's expectation of imminent corporal punishment—"taking notice" of his master beating another slave—may have spurred his suicide. Certainly other slaves, as well as indentured servants, were understood to have killed themselves in response to labor regimes that they viewed as unsuitable or brutality that they experienced as shaming and painful. For instance, a physician described an enslaved man in Jamaica as a person "of consequence" in his own country who stubbornly refused to work for any "white man." Bound for transport, his hands tied behind him, the enslaved man leapt into a river and drowned.[12] Slaves were reportedly provoked to suicide when "they saw their fellow creatures punished," and believed that it would be the "same case with themselves in a short time."[13] Some of these slaves, including perhaps the unnamed man in Williamsburg, came from elite classes in Africa and therefore preferred death to these kinds of indignities, or so the reports of the enslavers suggest.

Thus, the story of the unnamed man's suicide pointed to a chief contradiction in the slave societies of mid-eighteenth-century British North America. This enslaved man, the object of debasement, possessed a code of honor that was recognizable to Anglo-American onlookers, particularly those who were owners and masters of slaves. The hint of admiration implied for this act of suicide differs sharply from the story of Caesar, the mid-eighteenth-century slave who ran away rather than decapitate a fellow slave who had committed suicide.[14] That account assigned no honorable motives to the suicide of Caesar's unnamed compatriot. Rather, his lifeless body was to be publicly dishonored by severing his head from corpse. We must therefore consider that, at best, the association of honor with slaves was emergent, circumstantial, or regional. Nonetheless, the possibility that readers would have understood the Williamsburg slave's suicide as an act that preserved his honor reveals a central contradiction in Anglo-American views of slaves as both persons and property as well as familiar and foreign. In effect, the account established social distance between the *Gazette*'s readers and the enslaved man who was the subject of the story while at the same time its details offered a means of breaching that divide.

The Williamsburg story also raised questions about where mid-eighteenth-century Anglo-Americans placed the blame for slave suicide. In particular, it allows for the interpretation that the owner was somehow at fault for his bondman's death. A couple of details suggest this line of reasoning. The first is that this owner was a wheelwright, a laborer himself, and therefore unfit to master slaves. The second detail is that he was correcting another slave for a "misdemeanor," a trifling offense, which further may have conveyed to readers that the wheelwright was unsuited for or unaccustomed to slave ownership and unable to demonstrate his authority legitimately. Implicitly, the item made a connection between the abilities of the owner and the enslaved man's choice of death by suicide. In doing so, it intimated that a "fine" man should not be enslaved to a plebeian and insinuated that the ownership and governance of slaves most safely rested in the hands of elites.

Yet if the story indicated that the enslaved man's motives for choosing death were honorable, the context contradicted that idea by offering outright condemnations of suicide. In the paper, the contrite felon and Job were figures that were expressly oppositional to that of the enslaved man. In contrast to his deliberate and intentional death, they endured the fate that God had meted out to them. The felon confessed his sin and faced execution, while Job suffered the loss of his property, his sons, and his health, but he never lost his faith in God. The stories of Job and the condemned man reflected the traditional view that suicide was anathema to the precepts of Christianity and an act that foreclosed the possibility of redemption. Setting these stories against the enslaved man's suicide, then, confirmed his status as a spiritual and cultural outsider and validated the superiority of the traditional European Christian emphasis on obedience, endurance, and suffering.

In the context of the *Virginia Gazette*, this report of slave suicide sent conflicting messages about honor, rank, and race and contained unresolvable meanings. Among these, the most critical contradiction was that a debased human commodity undertook a willful assertion of personhood for codes of masculine honor that Europeans understood, shared, and affirmed. At the same time, however, the story accented racial differences; in the end, Christian endurance triumphed over the stoicism exhibited by the pagan African. Still, the act was no longer viewed as simply the product of African ethnicity or purely as an incomprehensible response to slavery. The reasons for his suicide had become startlingly familiar but nonetheless aspects of the act itself remained, to use a word associated with newly imported slaves themselves, outlandish and distant.

Of course, enslaved people were not the only individuals who died by suicide in early modern British America, and so the cultural meanings of acts of self-destruction are better understood in comparative context. From the beginnings of European colonization of the Americas, for example, observers penned accounts of suicide by indigenous people in order to fuel imperial rivalries and to measure the human losses wrought by expansion. Girolamo Benzoni, for instance, and later Bartolomé de Las Casas averred that Native suicide in Latin America was a response to oppressive imperial labor regimes; by the seventeenth century, these and other observations were published and translated in multiple editions and languages across Europe. Being "intolerably oppressed and worked," Benzoni noted, the Natives "longed for death." His *History of the New World* (1565) illustrated this

3.1. Early Spanish accounts featured images of widespread native suicide in response to Spanish expansion in the New World. Benzoni wrote that "the Indians of La Espanola hang themselves in the woods, rather than serve Christians." Source: Girolamo Benzoni, *History of the New World, Shewing His Travels in America, From 1541 to 1556*, trans. and ed. W. H. Smyth (London: Hakluyt Society, 1857), 77. This item is reproduced by permission of The Huntington Library, San Marino, California.

point with an image showing Indians killing themselves by leaping off cliffs, hanging themselves from trees, and stabbing and poisoning themselves—the very methods often used by enslaved people. In *The Devastation of the Indies* (1552), Las Casas concurred, arguing that whole families and entire communities hanged themselves out of despair.[15] These assessments fueled imperial critiques, but at the same time they confirmed cultural differences. The illustration in Benzoni's text suggests an epidemical contagion of suicide, unlike anything in European accounts of themselves.

Similarly, across North America, missionaries—Jesuits in Canada, Quakers in Pennsylvania, and Anglicans in Virginia, the Carolinas, and Florida—remarked on Native American suicide as a source of cultural difference. Most of these observers agreed that among the Native people, principally

3.2. Native suicide in the Caribbean, 16th century. Girolamo Benzoni, *History of the New World, Shewing His Travels in America, From 1541 to 1556* (Venice, 1572), p. 52 verso. This item is reproduced by permission of The Huntington Library, San Marino, California.

Huron and Iroquois in the Northeast and Tutelo in the South, suicide was neither condemned nor condoned.[16] Missionaries cited multiple examples of individuals who poisoned themselves out of shame and asserted that suicide among the Indians was regarded as neither heroic nor cowardly; self-destruction was neither praised nor denigrated.[17] In addition, onlookers compared indigenous and enslaved propensities for suicide in the face of humiliation. Bernard Romans, for instance, told the story of a young Choctaw man who was chided by his mother: "he took so ill as in the fury of his shame to resolve his own death, which he effected with a gun." These sentiments, he continued, were "very similar" to the "sublimity of negroes sentiments in their own country."[18] Similar to enslaved people, some Native Americans viewed suicide as a means of spiritual reunion. In the late eighteenth century, for instance, one Seneca leader apparently concluded that he would "eat of the fatal root, and sleep with his fathers, in peace."[19] Anthropologist William N. Fenton reached similar conclusions in his study of suicide among the Huron and Iroquois but also noted that the greatest frequency of suicide occurred in these two groups in the period immediately following European contact. This finding indicates some congruity with the experience of captive Africans and suggests that suicide was a response to the violent, cataclysmic change and high mortality rates experienced by both enslaved and indigenous people during European colonization and settlement of the Americas.[20]

Acts of self-destruction by both captive Africans and indigenous Americans can also be viewed as responses to the dispossessions wrought by forced migration and imperial expansion. Self-destruction appears to have been an explicit and immediate reaction to the brutality, labor regimes, and the fracturing of social bonds that were central to enslavement. Dispossession was also related to the loss of territory. In 1715, for instance, Samuel Sewall reported that Isaac Nehemiah, a praying Natick, had killed himself. Nehemiah had participated in land and treaty negotiations with the English, and on September 15, the Naticks sold the last of their large-scale landholdings to the English; Nehemiah's suicide occurred on the very next day.[21] Daniel R. Mandell notes that Sewall did not comment on the parallel between Judas and Nehemiah, who may have viewed himself as a traitor to his community, but does note that suicide was "not uncommon" among those Indians who felt "emotionally abused or dishonored."[22] A coroner's jury declared Nehemiah a *felo de se*, but the nature of his burial is unspecified.[23] His self-inflicted death measured cultural dispossession and paralleled the experiences of enslaved Africans.

Death itself was a shorthand for measuring cultural differences. Suicide in particular had the potential to solidify notions of temperamental, ethnic, and racial characteristics that distinguished cultural outsiders, in this case indigenous and enslaved people, from Europeans.[24] Furthermore, African and Native beliefs, as we have seen, challenged European religious teachings, legal practices, and folklore surrounding what they referred to as self-murder. While Native and African concepts of honor and rank often accounted for their acts of self-destruction, their spiritual interpretations of suicide—especially the belief that suicide could foster rebirth or reconnections with ancestors—probably presented the largest challenge to European beliefs. These competing ideas about the meaning of death and suicide were of course not fixed, and the boundaries between them shifted alongside continuing forced migrations and European expansions. For indigenous and enslaved people, suicide had become imaginable and acceptable, an escape from enslavement and therefore perhaps even a good death. In the eyes of

European onlookers, however, those suicides confirmed ideas about racial and cultural differences that many of them viewed as irresolvable.

Discussions about indigenous Americans and enslaved people were used to measure their racial differences from Europeans, but in other cases, slave self-destruction carried class associations. While the suicides of Isaac Nehemiah in 1715 and the enslaved Williamsburg man in 1752 entailed concepts of honor and dishonor that were understood and shared by Anglo-Americans, they might just as readily attribute slave suicide to the dispositional features that enslaved people were said to share with laborers and criminals. Owners and overseers, justices and juries, and Atlantic and domestic traders alike all summoned ideas about temperament, and in particular assumptions about their natural temperamental stubbornness, in order to explain the suicides of their unfree laborers. An indentured servant drowned himself to escape an imminent beating; an unseasoned enslaved woman threw herself down a hill after an overseer gave her a few lashes; a Tutelo woman, the "last of her nation," poisoned herself for fear that she would not be treated according to her rank.[25] Explanations for these acts of self-destruction were linked to stubbornness and willfulness, passion and irrationality. Correspondingly, in colonial British America, servants, slaves, and Indian converts who killed themselves were also more likely to suffer postmortem punishments for their transgressions. Their corpses were subjected to desecration and profane burial more often than those of their free counterparts; this both punished their stubbornness and reflected their lack of social standing.

That slaves and servants were stubborn was a routine statement in the early modern world. Elite Europeans had long remarked on the inherent stubbornness of the laboring classes, and British American masters cast similar epithets on their laborers. In the seventeenth and eighteenth centuries, terms like obstinacy or stubbornness were frequently applied to servants as well as slaves.[26] For example, a newspaper printed the findings of a coroner's inquest on a seven-year-old servant who was beaten for being "stubborn and refusing to do what his master bid him." The servant died; the inquest attributed to the death to "stubbornness and manslaughter."[27] In addition, because suicide by slaves was viewed as a form of rebellion, masters judged it as they did organized slave revolts. According to a 1737 newspaper report of a slave uprising in Antigua, for instance, the enslaved remained steadfast in their "obduracy" when gibbeted, racked, or burned at the stake and "stubborn" in their refusal to name other conspirators.[28]

Laborers' stubbornness went by many adjectives: barbaric, distempered, obdurate, obstinate, refractory, sulky, sullen, troublesome, and willful. Even the typically terse coroners' reports filed in British American jurisdictions occasionally reflect stubbornness when describing servants' suicides. Usually inquest language attributed suicide and murder to the "instigation of the Devil" or "not having God before their eyes." Yet on occasion it explicitly linked self-destruction to the willfulness of servants and slaves. In Virginia, for instance, one inquest reported that a servant "willfully made himself away first by cutting of his throat with a drawing knife and afterward by drowning himself in a well where he finished his last breath."[29] Another "barbarously" tied a grindstone around his neck and drowned himself in a millpond. "Barbarously" is double-edged in this usage, referring both to the social condition of the worker and to the savagery of the act.[30] Barbarism could also extend to the method of self-slaughter: the grindstone was probably recovered, but given the taint of self-murder, it likely went unused.[31] Inquests on servants who destroyed themselves underscored that such acts were done "without provocation," "willfully," or "voluntarily." These documents not only reveal the very conscious connection between stubbornness and labor, they also definitively affirmed that these laborers who caused their own deaths were in no way *non compos mentis*.[32]

Stubbornness was also inflected with ideas of disobedience and criminality. *Felo de se* verdicts, of course, declared suicide to be a criminal act, but stubbornness was also associated with lawbreakers. In 1732, *The American Weekly Mercury*, for example, described one felon awaiting execution in London's Newgate prison as a "most obdurate and impenitent wretch" who eventually went to his death "stubborn and obstinate."[33] Other accounts questioned whether suicide could ever be honorable because it always reflected stubbornness. For instance, a 1733 newspaper article averred that the famous suicides from antiquity, Cato and Brutus, could not be considered to be truly great men. Their choice of suicide—"dying by their own hands" because Caesar had "destroyed the liberties of their country"—reflected a "rather sullen stubbornness." Truly great men, the writer asserted, had the fortitude to do their duty, regardless of onerous circumstances.[34]

Stubbornness implied temperamental challenges to cultural hierarchies and therefore was to be condemned. Empowered Europeans viewed acts of self-destruction by slaves and servants through a prism of prevailing hierarchies of class and race; acts of suicide were viewed as reproaches to temporal and spiritual authority. Servants and slaves were expected to obey their masters and mistresses as part of their God-given fate. Yet while their suicides were often described in formulaic language as offenses to God, the rhetoric also sometimes conveyed the idea that suicide by the unfree was more an act of defiance against earthly masters than it was an offense against divinely ordained hierarchies.

The association between suicide and temperamental stubbornness was not a solely southern phenomenon, and the meanings of self-destruction varied according to race and class across British North America. Among fourteen suicides recorded in his diary between 1688 and 1725, Massachusetts justice Samuel Sewall assessed the self-inflicted deaths of African Americans, servants, and Indians differently than he did those of the middling classes. In 1688, for instance, he noted that "Sam Marionn's wife hang[ed] herself in the Chamber, fastening a Cord to the Rafter-Joice. Two or three swore she was distracted and had been for some time, and so she was buried in the burying place."[35] Yet when "Mr. Pain's negro woman cast her self from the Top of the house above, 40 foot high," in 1712, Sewall recorded only that description, without any intervening commentary.[36] On another occasion, Sewall noted that the town was "saddened with the amazing news that a young gentleman of good parentage and good education had hanged himself in his Store-house," but seemed unsurprised to learn that "at night one who came over a souldier, and was diverted to a tanner, being himself of that trade, hang[ed] himself," implicitly linking suicide to his reversion to an undesirable status.[37] The lower orders perhaps merited less comment because their survivors (if any) were less likely to have the resources to avoid *felo de se* verdicts. Nonetheless, despite the widespread Christian assertion that suicide was a bad death and the work of the devil, Sewall's diary, very much like the attitudes of his counterparts in the Chesapeake, reveals that his interpretations of self-destruction were shaped by cultural understandings of race and class.

If temperamental stubbornness explained the suicides of slaves and servants, their methods of self-killing also resembled one another. Suicide by hanging or drowning had long been associated with the laboring and lower orders, and with women as well.[38] Lacking access to guns and even knives, members of these groups were more likely to avail themselves of millponds or rivers to drown themselves or use trees and vines to hang themselves. Indentured servants and slaves also threw themselves into sugar works or used grinding stones, flax, or other elements associated with their labor as instruments of self-destruction, making the connection between their work regimes and their deaths quite explicit.[39] In contrast, among the gentry, the use of certain weapons could lend a sense of honor to suicide.[40] These examples demonstrate the ways in which method of self-destruction carried class associations.

Race, however, remained a stubborn divide in regard to the means of self-destruction, and certain ways of dying by suicide were viewed as distinctive to enslaved and indigenous people. In such cases, observers often fixated on oral sustenance. Benzoni noted that the Indians in the Caribbean "starved themselves to death," while Las Casas reported that they swallowed stones and dirt.[41] Across British America, reports alleged that slaves killed themselves by refusing to eat, swallowing their tongues, or ingesting dirt or stones.[42] The last of these, referred to as geophagy, is often described as a "natural, if unconscious response" to thiamine and iron deficiencies. Yet in the early modern South and Caribbean, slaves reportedly made and ate clay cakes, and ingesting dirt in particular was associated with their attempts to destroy themselves.[43] While slaves who did this were reported to be attempting to kill themselves, it is unclear if that was truly their intent.

Still, the European preoccupation with what they viewed as oral pollution measured a racial divide between colonizers and enslavers, on one hand, and the colonized and enslaved on the other. While the former often embraced the popular belief that a little dirt was healthful, they decidedly viewed ingestion of dirt by slaves as distasteful and primitive. Medical authorities in the Caribbean designated geophagy as *Cachexia Africana*, giving it a scientific imprimatur and describing it as a sickness inherent to slaves. In 1798, Dr. George Davidson described it as a malady of West Indian slaves, most of whom were new to the country, but noted that it could also be found among those who had been in the Caribbean for "some time." Yet even this disease had its roots in temperament. Davidson described the first symptom of the disease as "a fondness for solitude" and "despondency," a typical late eighteenth-century term to describe the emotional state of enslaved people. When despondent, "the mind, partaking of the sufferings of the body, is affected with nostalgia"; slaves brooded over their "ill treatment, separated forever from their friends and relations, and doomed to suffer without daring to complain."[44]

If slave suicide shared elements with elite codes of honor, indigenous responses to dispossession, and assumptions about the stubbornness of servants, such acts were also set apart on the basis of race. Declaring geophagy to be an African disease, averring it as a method of self-killing that was distinct to slaves, and linking it to disposition had the effect of racializing this method of suicide. It was a means of measuring racial differences between the English, who in the eighteenth century were reported to be quite prone to suicide through drowning, hanging, and (for the upper class) shooting, and enslaved people in the colonies. Well into the nineteenth century, evolving understandings of suicide by enslaved people continued to disarticulate self-destruction from slavery and to reinforce ideas of differences in race, class, and disposition.

While masters and planters attributed the suicides of enslaved men and women to racial and temperamental differences, those who formed the ranks of the unfree on occasion challenged these associations. Concepts of honor may have been most closely associated with the gentry, but slaves and servants also had codes of honor. Some unfree laborers preferred death to corporal punishment. The unnamed Williamsburg slave whose story opens this chapter may have chosen suicide after viewing the punishment of another slave and assuming, probably quite correctly, that he was next in line for the lash. The deliberateness of his actions—he watched, walked, and whetted his knife—may have reflected his belief that such punishments were incompatible with his own sense of integrity and identity. That this choice may have been related to his understandings of honor may be gathered from the observation that he was a "fine" man.

Concepts of honor appear to have been related to gender. In 1712, an overseer reported in his account book that Roger, an enslaved man, had hanged himself in the "old 40 foot Tobacco House." The overseer first noted, seemingly perplexed, that Roger had done so "not [for] any Reason" except, he subsequently wrote, that the enslaved man had been "hind[e]red from keeping other negroe men's wifes." Roger might have been a newly imported slave who may have been entitled to polygyny, a marker of male status in some African societies. Polygyny was practiced across the Americas and Africa, and, according to twentieth-century anthropologists working among the Ashanti, a man who possessed only one wife was the object of derision.[45] The overseer's assessment was that Roger had transgressed his masculine entitlement by seeking to control (or "keep") more women than the overseer (who had "hindered" Roger in this regard) thought he had a right to do. He was angered at Roger's display of power: the power over women he sought and the power to kill himself.[46]

The responses of the unnamed Williamsburg man and Roger illustrate the ways in which understandings or honor and the entitlements of rank and masculinity were reported to have motivated the suicides of enslaved men. But if the importance of rank and honor were mostly attributed to men, occasionally the same themes also emerged in eighteenth-century accounts of women slaves as well. One woman reportedly could find "none of her equals" in Barbados, and refused to marry, eat, or talk with other slaves.[47] For others, the importance of rank led to self-destruction. For instance, a young enslaved woman whose country marks indicated nobility threw herself from a steep hill, suggesting that the lash and labor may have been a shameful fate to which she could not reconcile herself.[48]

On occasion, unfree laborers articulated their distinctive codes of honor by taking aim at their masters and assigning to them the responsibility for slave and servant suicide. The story of the enslaved man Tony in mid-seventeenth-century Maryland (chapter 2) came from Hannah Littleworth, an indentured servant in his household. She testified that Tony died because of his master's cruelty; in creating public knowledge of his brutality, she aimed to disgrace her master. Other indentured servants made similar choices. Several years after the inquest on Tony, indentured servant John Shorte was felling trees with his Maryland master, when the latter chastised Shorte about his work. Shorte stopped working altogether and fled to a nearby pond. His master gave chase with a tobacco stick; the wooden rod was typically hung with drying tobacco leaves, but masters also used it to punish servants and slaves. According to his master, Shorte ran into the pond and intentionally drowned himself.[49]

Fellow servants, however, laid the blame for Shorte's death squarely at the feet of their master. Like Hannah Littleworth, they provided some of the earliest legal linkages between the cruelty of masters and the indirect and direct suicides of servants and slaves in British North America.[50] One testified that he was called to the waterside, but his master subsequently bade him to "go about his business."[51] Two others servants swore that they went to "help to rescue . . . John Shorte from his Master," who only ordered them to "go into the water and fetch him out" just as he sank under for the last time.[52] Like Hannah Littleworth had done for Tony, Shorte's fellow laborers attributed his death to the negligence and cruelty of his master. Perhaps too they were Englishmen who despised suicide and were attempting to keep their fellow laborer from suffering the penalties of this most debased of deaths.

In response to indirect and direct suicide, servants—who had rights to testify in court that were lacked by slaves—put the fitness of their masters on trial and exhibited plebian standards of honor that sought to hold their masters accountable for the deaths of their laborers. That servants articulated their own sense of standards in both of these cases, however, had little impact on their legal outcome. Ultimately, courts sided with masters. Shorte was found to be a *felo de se* and was denied a Christian burial. That verdict did not just reflect the jury's inclination to accept as most convincing the master's testimony, but also perhaps the subtle way in which John Shorte's stubbornness—he had refused to work and then to come out from the water—pushed them to rule for suicide over accidental death. In both cases, the conflicts between masters and their bound laborers carried similar themes: heated exchanges, accusations of stubbornness, refusal to work, flight, silence, and, finally, resignation. More passive laborers might have merited different verdicts. In the end, the masters won the day, and courts and juries contained the contradictions exposed by these cases of suicide.

Like accounts of slave suicide along the Middle Passage and during seasoning, reports of slave self-destruction, such as the one printed in the 1752 *Virginia Gazette,* continued to disarticulate self-killing from the exigencies of enslavement. Instead, slaves' proclivities for self-destruction were associated with race, temperament, and class, rather than attributed to diabolical instigation. In the context of European expansion in North America, explanations for slave suicides in some respects paralleled those of servants and indigenous people. Yet while English servants were accused of drinking themselves to death, never in the evidence utilized in this study were they charged, as both slaves and Indians were, with obtaining death by ingesting dirt or stones. It was therefore not only the act of suicide itself, but also the method of suicide that became entangled with emerging cultural views of race, pollution, and temperament in eighteenth-century British North America.

These divergent representations of death by suicide created a social distance that was reinforced in burial practices. We have no clues about the manner of Tony's burial, but, given his master's inclinations, it was likely quick and unceremonious. Burial practices seem to have been erratic in early Virginia, as some masters used profane burials to punish laborers, although a 1661 law prohibited masters from privately burying their servants.[53] Shorte's jury was so certain of a suicide verdict—despite three depositions that he was not a suicide—that they specified that he "ought not to have a Christian burial by law."[54] Similarly, in 1661, a Westmoreland County, Virginia, jury ordered that a servant who had "willfully" killed himself should be buried at a crossroad with "a stake driven through the middle of him in his grave."[55] A New England jury ruled similarly when Thomas, "an Indian and very useful servant of Mr. Oliver" hanged himself in the brew house: Samuel Sewall noted that his body was to be buried "by the highway with a Stake through his Grave."[56] For slaves, such postmortem determinations were left to the discretion of their masters, who often ordered their corpses to be decapitated or left them to rot. Even slaves who died accidentally, rather than by suicide, were punished with ignominious burials or had their bodies sold for dissection.[57] These burial rites—or lack thereof—marked enslaved, indentured, and indigenous Americans apart from other Americans. Suicide had traditionally been deeply ingrained with ideas of pollution: the body, the method, and place of the suicide were unclean. In British North America, those cultural markers were reinforced by distinctly dishonoring postmortem rites accorded to suicides among the laboring, unfree, and indigenous communities.

Still, despite the reinforcement of these social distances through burial practices, like many of the accounts in this chapter, reports of slave suicide, like that of the unnamed enslaved man near Williamsburg in 1752, carried ambiguous, liminal, and conflicting meanings. Some contradictions emerged from the story itself, but its inconsistencies gained force from its placement amid traditional condemnations of suicide and the modern advertisements of consumer goods, including human chattel. The *Gazette*'s readership may have responded with revulsion or admiration, believed that the act should be lauded or punished, or attributed it to the devil, or to gender, temperament, class, or race. They also might have faulted the wheelwright. If masters laid the blame for suicide on stubbornness, servants and slaves pointed their fingers at the temperamental failings of masters who were cruel, unfit, and excessive. In the context of colonization, the interpretations and implications of this slave's suicide were competing and contrary.

Representations of suicidal slaves as stubborn and courageous, debased and noble, and stoic or barbaric persisted throughout the eighteenth and nineteenth centuries. Depictions of self-destruction that rested on stubbornness placed slaves (and others) beyond the sympathy of Anglo-American audiences; those that centered on honor conceivably lessened the social distance between the reader and the enslaved subject. These competing understandings of suicide shifted as slavery accelerated across eighteenth-century British America, and, in effect, exposed the paradoxes of slavery itself. The contradictions posed by slavery that were central issues raised by accounts of slave suicide in eighteenth-century Anglo-America were also manifested, as we shall see in the next chapter, in the law of slavery as well.

FOUR

The Power to Die or the Power of the State? The Legalities of Suicide in Slavery

> [His master tied Wiley] to a collar beam in the loft of said house and said [to him] that [he] no more belonged to his master but to the state and that after tomorrow [Wiley would be] tried for his life and hanged for his crime.
>
> [The next morning] when the family made from the bed the said [Wiley] had hanged himself with the rope that he was tied with. . . .
>
> —*Petition of James Anderson,* South Carolina, 1810[1]

While enslaved people's suicides were visible features of the Atlantic slave trade and seasoning and carried competing meanings across and beyond British North America, slave self-destruction also occupied a unique position in North American law. Although colonial statutes and justice of the peace manuals specified no particular legal penalties for suicide by slaves, accounts of their acts of self-destruction, such as that described in this chapter's epigraph, surfaced in southern courtrooms and legislatures throughout the eighteenth and nineteenth centuries. As we have seen, masters often privately punished slave suicide, but under certain circumstances they could also turn to the public for compensation for their loss of property. This was exactly what Wiley's master was doing in South Carolina in 1810. His telling phrase, that Wiley "no more belonged to his master but to the state" also reflects the two systems of power—one private, one public—that had been institutionalized by legislators across the slave societies of British America. Each system of law mattered to slave death, including death by suicide.

Beginning in the seventeenth century, officials from Barbados to Maryland enacted piecemeal laws and comprehensive slave codes that conferred extensive powers to owners of slaves.[2] Statutes authorized slaveholders to visit all manner of violence—commonly referred to as "plantation justice"—on their slaves. Alongside their private powers, owners of slaves could also rely on a public criminal justice system of state-sanctioned punishments specifically tailored for slaves. Hallmarks of this legal institution permitted summary court trials for slaves, authorized non-slaveowning whites to police slaves, and endorsed extraordinary corporal and capital punishments exclusively for slaves. Legislation also provided compensation for owners of slave felons who had been executed by the state or who had, like Wiley, killed themselves.[3]

Wiley's case reveals how the criminal justice system responded to enslaved men and women who stood accused of felonies and died by suicide before the state could carry out its punishment. In 1810, Wiley, an enslaved man about sixteen years of age, was accused of buggery, a capital offense in early national South Carolina.[4] His master, James Anderson, explained to Wiley that he would be remanded to the state for trial and executed for his offense. Having outlined this grim schedule—that Wiley would be "tried for his life and hanged for his crime"—his owner then used a rope to tie the slave to a crossbeam in the attic for the night. Sometime before morning, Wiley used the rope to fashion a noose and hanged himself. Because the law protected Anderson's investment in his slaves, he turned to the South Carolina legislature for reimbursement for his loss. The state would have presumably executed Wiley had he not hanged himself, and therefore, Anderson's claim was successful. The local court valued Wiley at four hundred dollars; his owner received the full amount as payment for his loss of human property.[5]

Wiley's suicide occurred at the turn of the nineteenth century, but the legalities of suicide in slavery reached back over a century, originating with lawmakers' efforts to establish control over and property rights in enslaved men and women. Colonial legislators revised English legal concepts of forfeiture, compensation, and outlawry, fusing together the legalities of suicide, slavery, and criminal justice in an original and, on occasion for slaveholders, remunerative way. These legal innovations helped to shape the cultural meanings and political understandings of enslaved people's suicides in British North America. For one thing, they bifurcated the legalities of suicide along the lines of race and freedom, and for another, they protected the property investments of owners by providing them, in certain instances, with state reimbursement for the deaths of their enslaved men and women. Equally important, a consideration of legalities also reveals both slaves' understandings of their relationship to the law and the circumstances under which they jumped into rivers, dashed their heads against rocks, took poison, and hanged themselves before the state or their owners had the opportunity to execute them. When, like Wiley, slaves stood accused of capital crimes—for instance, murder, insurrection, theft, running away—they sometimes chose the power to die in order to steer clear of, as Wiley's master put it, "belong[ing] to the state."

The significance of these legalities lay in the way that they made visible competing concepts of property and personhood that were fundamental to slavery. On one hand, compensation claims for slaves who killed themselves offered starkly secular and commercial assessments of slaves as property. From this viewpoint, suicide by slaves represented an economic loss for masters who sought through the legal system to recover the value of their investments. However slave owners might feel about this loss of their slaves, compensation schemes were designed to protect their proprietary interests.

On the other hand, however, suicide reflected the fundamental fact that the slave was a person under the law as well as in culture. Intentional suicide was the act of a person, a perpetrator, an agent of a felony. Criminally culpable, slaves who killed themselves were understood to have *mens rea* or the mental state required for the commission of a crime.[6] Moreover, even as owners sought to be reimbursed for their losses in property when slaves killed themselves, masters also wrestled with the ideas of slave personhood. Those who privately punished suicides through decapitation or dismemberment treated slaves as treasonous, fully human agents of rebellion who deserved, even after death, the worst spectacles of punishment.

As British American statute laws, local courts, and colonial and state legislatures forged the legalities of enslaved people's suicides, they revealed the tensions between legal concepts of slaves as chattel and as persons. Enslaved individuals' acts of self-destruction illustrate their struggles against not only private plantation justice, but also state-sanctioned punitive violence. Perhaps most importantly, they provide insight into the meanings of suicide for slaves like Wiley who appear to have rejected the disciplinary power of the state and instead died by their own hands.

Suicide, as Blackstone wrote, was a "peculiar species of felony." Like any felony under early modern English law, including that prevailing in early British North America, intentional self-destruction was punished in part through forfeiture, which gave the Crown or its representative the deceased's personal property. Forfeiture was a legal punishment for suicide that had existed across Europe at least since the Middle Ages.[7] The concept translated unevenly to the British colonies. In North America, Virginia, Maryland,

New Jersey, and the Carolinas practiced forfeiture; Massachusetts Bay and Rhode Island fashioned their own statutes, although their penalties mirrored English practice; Pennsylvania rejected the idea that suicide was a crime and forbade forfeiture.[8] In part, forfeiture was meant to deter as well as punish would-be suicides. Individuals contemplating self-destruction might be stymied if they considered the effects of the loss of property, if they were male heads of households, on their wives and children.[9]

Forfeiture did not apply to all suicides. Because the law recognized that not all acts of suicide were intentional, coroners' juries issued verdicts of either *felo de se*, a felon of the self, or *non compos mentis*, not of sound mind. The former was a felony; the latter was not, because the victim lacked the criminal culpability of intentional harm.[10] Juries thus held the power to palliate punishments for suicide.[11] This difference mattered a great deal to families as well as to the Crown, which pressured local officials, including those in the colonies, for its share of forfeiture income. In seventeenth- and early eighteenth-century Virginia, for example, the Board of Trade repeatedly asked the Governor's Council as to the whereabouts of forfeiture monies, a portion of which they certainly expected to come from *felo de se* rulings.[12] Local leaders responded to this pressure. In 1725, for instance, Robert "King" Carter (1663–1732) of Lancaster County, Virginia, sought to collect the personal estate of a man who had recently hanged himself. As the Crown's representative, Carter was entitled to the property because, as he wrote to the colony's attorney general, "a *felo de se* is the highest species of murder" and as a penalty for this offense, the property was due to him as the proprietor who held the grant.[13] By statute, coroners could be penalized—by having to pay the fines themselves—when they failed to report verdicts that would qualify for forfeitures.[14]

Forfeiture penalties also had a gendered dimension. When a husband and father killed himself, a *felo de se* verdict potentially consigned his widow and children to poverty. Early modern historians argue that more men than women killed themselves, often by a ratio of two to one.[15] Although suicide statistics are unreliable, it is clear that the state had a greater interest in prosecuting the suicides of men, since, under coverture, a free married woman's property belonged to her husband. Married women who killed themselves were unlikely to bring financial hardship to their families, as coverture vested their property in their husbands.

Suicide verdicts and forfeiture penalties were shaped by considerations of class as well. By the seventeenth-century, class deference played a significant role in separating the sound or intentional (*felo de se*) from unsound or unintentional (*non compos mentis*) suicides. In early modern England, for instance, the individual *least* likely to gain a verdict of *felo de se* was an elite male with a good reputation.[16] Forfeiture declined on both sides of the eighteenth-century Anglo-Atlantic, as juries were increasingly reluctant to enforce confiscation penalties in cases of suicide. They selectively presumed insanity (*non compos mentis*) and increasingly pardoned an ever-extending range of individuals.[17] Religious and community punishments eased as well for many, but not all, of those who died by suicide.[18] A number of currents combined to reshape the attitudes of local juries. Popular culture, particularly in the form of the cheap press, carried stories of suicide and debated its legitimacy.[19] Medical practitioners blamed suicide on mental illness over which individuals had little control. Philosophers, including statesman Thomas Jefferson, viewed suicide as a disease and defended it as an extension of natural rights; while tragic, he argued, self-destruction was an individual entitlement over which the state had no jurisdiction.[20] While none of these views went unchallenged, by the end of the eighteenth century, forfeiture was abandoned as suicide came to be seen more as a secular disease and a public dilemma to be managed and less as a religious sin and a crime to be punished.[21] Particularly in northern states, humanitarian attitudes toward and medical explanations for suicide had emerged by the last quarter of the eighteenth century. Even as self-destruction was increasingly understood as a disease rather than condemned as diabolical, however, this transformation in attitudes occurred unevenly.[22] In slave societies, elite whites in particular continued to view suicide as the worst of crimes. Free southerners continued to view suicide as an act that had no justification although they no longer, as they had in the seventeenth century, punished self-destroying free persons through profane burials.[23]

Glaring exceptions to these changes, however, can be seen in the response to the suicides of the least advantaged people—indentured, unfree, and Native Americans—who were more likely to be judged felony suicides.[24] For instance, the suicides of felons and slaves continued to spark particularly virulent responses in local communities in both Europe and British America; through the very end of the eighteenth century, their bodies were defiled, dismembered, desecrated, and displayed.[25] Criminals who were deemed to be, as one was described, especially "hardened" in their "wickedness" and who killed themselves before they were executed were the focus of noteworthy community wrath. Robbing the public of its spectacle of punishment was so egregious a violation that, in one English instance reported by the *Gentleman's Magazine* in 1735, a Bristol mob exhumed the body of a suicide from its crossroads burial site. They subsequently "dragged his guts about the highway, poked his eyes out, and broke almost all his bones."[26] Similarly, in Amsterdam between 1732 and 1795, nine of fourteen accused felons who killed themselves were singled out for postmortem punishments. Although these men had not confessed to the crimes for which they stood accused, their suicides were understood to be *ex conscientia sceleris*, a moral awareness of guilt. The last public display of such a suicide's corpse in the city occurred in 1792.[27] During the same period, New Englanders responded violently to white murderers who killed themselves before the state could execute them. In one case the corpse of such a suicide was put on display and left to rot, but impatient and enraged townspeople kidnapped it, dragged it to a river, and threw it into a hole for summary burial.[28] In effect, the mutilations and public displays of corpses took the place of the (expected) execution rites, since self-destruction was taken to be an implicit admission of guilt, especially if it happened before a trial had taken place. The community insisted on its ritual of punishment, and the felonious suicides necessitated impromptu displays of postmortem desecration.

Spectacles of postmortem punishment continued across British North America for alleged felons, including enslaved ones, who killed themselves before the state could punish them. In slave societies, the responses to the suicides of enslaved people were often distinctly virulent and violent. Owners continued to view enslaved people's acts of self-destruction as forms of rebellion, and the public continued to demand spectacles of retributive justice. Well into the nineteenth century, the state used spectacular punishments on the bodies of enslaved people, penalties that were also designed to discourage other enslaved people from criminal, rebellious, and suicidal behavior. While across the eighteenth-century Anglo-Atlantic, the extension of mercy to suicides and secular explanations for self-destruction spread, the commercial imperatives of slavery forestalled the extension of such clemency or compassion to slave suicides. Planters may have extolled their paternalism, but when it came to slaves who died by suicide, the limits of slaveholders' charitableness were all too clear. The treatment of suicidal slaves remained another way of reinforcing their racial and social differences from whites, a grisly means of marking their debasement into perpetuity.

Forfeiture would seem to have no relevance for enslaved people because they had no civil standing under the law; as property, they had nothing left to forfeit except their corpses.[29] Sometimes even those were forfeit. Charles Ball described the treatment of Paul, a serial runaway who endured increasingly cruel punishments, including the attachment of an iron collar—with bells—around his neck to discourage further escape. Nonetheless, he hanged himself in the wood. Although his master was apprised of his suicide, Paul's dead body was never taken down; turkey buzzards had destroyed him beyond recognition, but the iron collar—its bells ringing, echoing his self-inflicted death—still remained.[30] When five slaves from Butler Island boarded a dugout against their overseer's command and drowned in rough seas, he ordered that they should be buried like "*dogs*, for not one of them should have a coffin." He further warned that if any other slaves drowned in violation of his orders, he would "sell the bodies to be cut to pieces by the doctors.'"[31] Like these slaves, others who died through disobedience, including suicide, were denied the privilege of regular burials.

Ironically, however, when slaves killed themselves, their status under the law altered dramatically. Above all else, suicide was the crime of a person; slaves who killed themselves were felons, persons under the law who were simultaneously defined as the property of slave owners. Across British North America, compensation provided a solution to this legal conundrum and reinforced the property side of the equation. Given particular conditions, slave suicide was a loss for which masters could and did collect compensation. Thus, when alleged slave felons killed themselves, the state paid out by reimbursing masters for their losses in slave property. Yet the act of suicide itself, as well spectacles of postmortem punishment, viscerally acknowledged that the self-destructive slave was a person. Treating slave self-destruction both in legal terms of property and personhood, in effect, placed their suicides in a distinct legal category and distinguished them from the suicides of free persons.

When Wiley hanged himself in South Carolina in 1810, his master immediately petitioned the General Assembly of South Carolina for compensation. Like forfeiture, the idea that offenders should compensate victims of certain, usually violent, crimes had a long history in English law. In British North America, however, legal compensation was modified to encompass slavery. It placed a monetary value on executed slaves, including those who had died by suicide, and identified their owners as injured parties who could collect monetary damages.[32]

By the early nineteenth century, seeking reimbursement was a fairly routine act for southern masters, but compensation for suicide was neither assured nor automatic. Slave suicides had to meet specific criteria in order for their owners to qualify for compensation. In 1800, for instance, William Wilson petitioned the General Assembly of Virginia for the value of his slave, Jacob, an alleged participant in Gabriel Prosser's Rebellion. The petition noted that Jacob, Wilson's "only slave," was a "valuable waterman and always supposed to be (until the late insurrection of the slaves) an honest inoffensive negro." After Jacob was implicated in the conspiracy, apprehended by patrollers, and confined to the hold of a vessel, he fatally stabbed himself. "Thus," Wilson pleaded, he was "deprived of his chief support in maintaining a large family." Because proof of Jacob's conspiratorial activities "would have been addressed against him had he been brought to trial" and his master had "little doubt" that Jacob would have "suffered as a conspirator," Wilson asked the court for compensation.[33]

Compensation for slave deaths, especially those by suicide, depended on the status of the slave as an outlaw. Masters had to demonstrate to often parsimonious and budget-conscious legislators that the slaves for whom they sought reimbursement were legally outlawed. For instance, Virginia's legislators denied Jacob's master's petition for compensation, perhaps because the slave had not been formally charged, but nonetheless Jacob's captor received just over twenty-nine pounds for his efforts in retrieving the alleged rebel. Wiley and Jacob revealed their familiarity with the criminal justice system as well: both knew they faced certain execution by the state. Wiley's owner assured him of this case. Jacob also probably knew that his fate was sealed: twenty-six enslaved men were convicted of conspiring in Gabriel Prosser's Rebellion; all had been hanged in September and October of 1800, well before Jacob was apprehended by patrollers.[34] Facing imminent death, both men denied the state its prerogative when they died by suicide.

Traditionally, to be an outlaw was to exist outside of the law's protection and meant that one had no enforceable legal rights. As a common law category with a history that stretched back well into antiquity, the concept of the outlaw originally was an accepted and often used legal mechanism in England and its colonies.[35] The Latin *civiliter mortuus,* civil death, captures the essential meaning of outlawry. English jurist Sir William Blackstone wrote that in ancient times, an outlawed felon existed in a state of *caput lupinum,* that is, as one who might be "knocked on the head like a wolf by any one that should meet him," because, "having renounced all law, he was to be dealt with as in a state of nature, when every one that should find him might slay him."[36] The eminent legal scholar, writing in the eighteenth century, noted that this ancient "inhumanity" no longer applied because outlaws faced justice rather than summary execution.[37] In his assessment, however, Blackstone failed to consider how the status of outlaw operated for enslaved people who routinely faced the "ancient inhumanity" in British America.

Across the Anglo-American colonies, lawmakers altered the legal category of the outlaw in order to fit the goals of a growing slave society. Their actions reflect the ways in which the legalities of slavery and criminal justice were powerfully intertwined, particularly but not exclusively in the southern colonies.[38] In English criminal law, the category of the outlaw referred to serial absconding or flight after the alleged commission of a felony. In contrast, North American legislators modified the concept in an attempt to control a large and unfree labor force. To be an outlawed or outlying slave was to lose the public protection of the state and the private protection of masters, both of which were already slim and dubious. And these legal codes were modified, making it possible for any free person to kill an outlawed slave, and, what is more, often compensating the agent of the slave's death.

By the very beginning of the eighteenth century, colonial statutes defined the terms under which slaves could be declared legal outlaws. North American colonies modeled their laws on the slave code of Barbados: Virginia enacted outlaw statutes for slaves in 1691 and 1705, South Carolina did so in 1712, and North Carolina followed suit in 1715.[39] The terms of Virginia's statute declared slaves to be outlaws for a variety of offenses, but particularly for "unlawfully absent[ing] themselves from their masters and mistresses service" and by lying, hiding, and lurking in "obscure places, killing hogs and committing other injuries to the inhabitants of this dominion."[40]

The traditional penalties for outlaws—for instance, stripping them of property or legal rights—had no bearing on enslaved persons, of course; slaves were instead punished through their bodies.[41] For slaves, maiming, dismembering, whipping, and confinement took the place of the deprivation of rights that free outlaws endured. In effect, for enslaved people, colonial British American law revived the "ancient inhumanity" referenced by Blackstone: any enslaved outlaw in fact might be "knocked on the head like a wolf" by any free individual. Initially, legislation in Virginia stipulated that if outlawed slaves resisted recapture, the law empowered the "person or persons" capturing the outlaws to kill them. By 1705, however, slave law in the Old Dominion went even further, authorizing "any person or person whatsoever" to "kill or destroy" outlawed slaves "by such ways and means as he, she, or they shall think fit."[42] The gender specificity of this statement ("he, she, or they") is truly remarkable for an era in which legal personhood and the terms of statutes were typically described in masculine pronouns.[43] These statutes conferred on all whites—men and women, rich and poor, slave owners and wage laborers—the power to use violent means to compel outlawed (or presumed to be outlawed) slaves to submission. All whites could, at their own discretion and by whatever means they chose, apprehend and kill outlawed slaves. What is more, the legislature paid them for so doing. Those who fatally wounded outlawed slaves at the point of recapture or while in custody—where they could be subjected to any punishment the patrollers or local justices deemed fitting—faced no penalty.[44]

To assist in recapture efforts, the names of outlying (outlaw) slaves and the penalties they faced were publicly announced. The intent was to empower all whites in specific recovery efforts, although the system also alerted enslaved people of their status as outlaws. In Virginia, sheriffs proclaimed the details of the 1705 statute and posted the names of outlying slaves on the door of every church and chapel in every county immediately after Sabbath services. After these public proclamations, slaves who did not return to their masters were officially outlawed and legally defined as felons.[45] To be an outlawed slave brought a heightened and ubiquitous vulnerability. For the state, outlawry was a valuable legal mechanism for disciplining, terrorizing, and apprehending escaped slaves and for giving all free white persons the power of life and death over their enslaved counterparts.

These statutes provided the identical mechanism for compensating owners whose outlawed slaves died by suicide as it did for masters whose slaves were executed for capital felonies. In Virginia, the same statute that defined the slave outlaw simultaneously authorized compensation.[46] The earliest legislation gave masters four thousand pounds of tobacco for each lost slave; by 1705, each slave had to be valued by the court of public claims.[47] North Carolina lawmakers made similar provisions.[48] Compensation applied regardless of how enslaved felons or outlaws died. If the state hanged or burned a slave felon, if patrollers killed an enslaved outlaw, or, more to the point here, if alleged slave felons or outlaws killed themselves, masters were compensated for the value of their lost slaves.[49] The system aimed for nothing less than to control the movement of enslaved individuals, provide incentives for every free white to apprehend slave outlaws, and secure the financial interests of masters in their slave property.

Compensation also helped to consolidate the supremacy of the wealthiest slave owners, often at the expense of all subjects. In North Carolina, for instance, the funds for policing outlying slaves and the cost of reimbursing their masters were provided by provincial taxes. That meant that all taxpayers—those who owned many slaves, those who owned few or no slaves, former slaves, and free black men and women—paid the costs of apprehending outlawed slaves and compensating their owners.[50] Unsurprisingly, the wealthiest slave owners appear to have held all the cards. In some parts of North Carolina, for example, the wealthiest slave owners collected 100 percent of all compensation monies awarded, but whether this was typical of other jurisdictions is uncertain.[51] Smaller planters seem to have been less likely to have the resources to legally prove their slaves to be outlaws. When he sat as legislator in 1755, Virginian Landon Carter noted in his diary that William Southall sought compensation for a slave who reportedly had "hanged himself after he burnt his master's tobacco house." Some of the assembly had supported the claim, but it was ultimately rejected when Burgess George Wythe persuaded the committee that it was not "within the letter nor the meaning of the law relating thereunto," which meant that the slave had not been formally outlawed.[52] The petitioner complained that his slave "set fire to his barn and with it consumed all his tobacco, corn, wheat, and oats, and other goods, and then hanged himself" and pleaded that he had a large family of small children and was "utterly ruined" by the loss of the slave and the rest of his property. Still, the petition was declined because Southall had no opportunity to outlaw his slave between the alleged commission of the crime and his suicide.[53] Legislators rejected similar petitions from other planters as well. Other masters who sought compensation for the deaths of their non-outlawed slaves were typically unsuccessful. When Peter Richeson's seven slaves ran away together, for instance, and were "shortly thereafter found dead" in the Mattapony River, his claim was disallowed.[54]

Without overseers, planters who owned few slaves had little opportunity to formally declare them outlaws. In contrast, Wiley's master, James Anderson publically established awareness of Wiley's crime a full day before he was found dead. In fact, although Anderson had been counseled by some neighbors to take Wiley "out of the way of the law," he refused, claiming that he did not want to conceal the slave's crime. Conceivably, his interests were also financial: running Wiley "out of the way of the law" would not garner any compensation, while submitting him to the criminal justice system would almost certainly do so.[55] Outlawry and compensation were mechanisms, then, not only for controlling slaves, but also for subsidizing the losses and consolidating the power of the elite planter class.

Compensation schemes challenged long-standing European understandings of suicide and reinforced modern notions of property rights. Traditionally, forfeiture punished the families of suicides by seizing the personal estate of the victim. Yet successful petitions for compensation for slave suicide meant that the colonial government remunerated slave owners, rather than demanded property from the families of suicides. What the Crown made of this legislative innovation is unclear, since it stood to lose revenue. Yet because slaves were defined as property, southern lawmakers and slave owners anchored themselves to compensation that made slave suicide, like slave felonies, an act to be punished as well as a proposition of financial value.

When slaves killed themselves before the justice system executed them, then, intentionally or not, they avowed their personhood before their owners and the state. Although suicide was an awful alternative, such enslaved individuals were understood to have rejected the power of the law to make living spectacles of their bodies and their deaths. Instead, in the act of taking their own lives, they shaped the meaning of death on their own terms. The circumstances that surrounded their acts of self-destruction allow us to more closely consider their motivations. While the petitions to the eighteenth-century Virginia House of Burgesses and other legislative bodies reflect the specific goals of slave owners seeking compensation, those brief documents also offer clues to the conditions that fostered suicide by enslaved people and illustrate the circumstances that precipitated their acts of self-destruction.

An account of a runaway named Dick in 1754, for instance, illustrates how the prospect of recapture and execution may have influenced slaves' decisions to kill themselves. Dick was accused of various unspecified crimes: he ran away, was captured, stood trial, and was sentenced in a summary slave court; the justices ordered that one of his ears be severed. About ten days later, Dick absconded again and was duly outlawed. Faced again with recapture, he vigorously resisted, but a patroller eventually wrestled Dick to the ground, stunned him with a blow, tied him to a horse's tail, and dragged him to a nearby farm.[56] The symbolism of dragging projected criminality: being dragged behind a horse was the typical means of getting felons to the gallows in early North America as well as in much of Europe.[57]

By the time patroller and slave arrived at the farmstead, however, Dick was dead. A coroner's jury was soon assembled and examined the corpse, a routine matter in any suspicious death, although less routine for the suspicious deaths of slaves. Puzzled when they found no bruises or marks that would account for Dick's demise, they asked the patroller for an explanation. He swore under oath that he "saw [Dick] take something out of his pocket and swallow it, and that he was soon after taken with a vomiting." While the coroner's jury did not initially "take much notice" of the patroller's testimony, one of them later recited the evidence to support the owner's petition. Given the circumstances and the fact that Dick "was in due form of law outlawed" by his master, he received £40 as a compensation for his loss. It is likely that the patroller was paid as well.[58]

The patroller's testimony, however imperfect, offers a possible glimpse into Dick's state of mind. The patroller claimed that Dick, like Wiley, killed himself before the state had a chance to carry out its own execution. The patroller swore, for instance, that Dick refused recapture, "saying he was outlawed, and if he was carried to prison he should certainly be hanged."[59] Other enslaved men and women echoed these sentiments. In 1755 the enslaved Jasper "dashed his brains out against a rock" to "avoid hanging, which he often said he expected if he was brought back into [Virginia]."[60] "Fear of the gallows" was a common Anglo-American explanation for the suicides of felons, and the *Virginia Gazette* as well as other colonial newspapers carried reports of English, Native Americans, and enslaved people who killed themselves before facing trial or execution.[61] Perhaps the patroller simply voiced an explanation for suicide that was familiar in his cultural repertoire.

Owners' petitions for compensation in eighteenth-century Virginia account only for the suicides of those slaves, like Dick, who were outlawed or charged with felonies. Many more suicides of enslaved men and women existed outside of these specific categories; some slaves were not formally charged with felonies or explicitly outlawed, and most slaves did not commit capital crimes. Still, according to the petitions, fully 40 percent of slave outlaws and felons died by suicide before the state could execute them. If we add petitions that indicate but do not explicitly mention suicide—those that describe slaves as having been "found dead shortly" after absconding—the figure rises to 53 percent.[62] While no evidence of self-murder was apparent in these cases, slaves may have ended their lives through means not comprehended by patrollers. Still other slaves did not directly take their own lives but engaged in behavior that was life-threatening or likely to result in their deaths; in the context of slavery, these actions might be termed suicidal, and these deaths suicide-like.[63] One enslaved man aimed a gun at his pursuers and another broke jail; both were fatally shot. Another man was killed when his pursuer was "obliged to give him several blows."[64] Other enslaved people burned to death; seven of these were described as deliberately setting fire to their jails and were possibly deliberate suicides. Although self-immolation was rare, in 1773 the *Virginia Gazette* reported that an enslaved man killed himself by setting fire to a building and walking inside to burn with it.[65] The majority of petitions named enslaved men as suicides; men accounted for 72 percent of certain suicides, women accounted for 14 percent, a probable reflection of sex ratios in Virginia.[66]

Causes of slave death in eighteenth-century Virginia, House of Burgesses Petitions

Cause of death	Males	Females	Unknown	Total
Suicide	31	6	6	43
Found dead	10	2	2	14
Died in jail*	23	2	4	29
By fire	11	1	0	12
By frostbite	8	0	1	9
Unknown	4	1	3	8
Killed	10	1	7	18
Accident	1	1	0	2
Totals	75	12	19	106

*The category "died in jail" is subdivided by specific cause of death, and because the numbers in those subdivisions are already captured in the "died in jail" category, they are not used in calculating column totals.

Source: H. R. McIllwaine, *Journals of the House of Burgesses, 1712–26, 1727–40, 1742–49, 1752–58, 1758–61, 1761–65, 1766–69, 1773–76* (Richmond, VA: Colonial Press, E. Waddley Co., 1905–1915)

The prospect of execution by the state, and perhaps torture in jails, likely influenced the suicides of enslaved people. For about a third of slaves described in the petitions, suicide occurred after the alleged commission of interpersonal and homicidal violence.[67] Typical cases included an enslaved man who had allegedly murdered his owner and then "destroyed himself," and the enslaved Sacco, who stood accused of murdering his overseer and, in response, ran away and hanged himself.[68] Other suicides appear to be the culminating acts of violent outbursts in which self-destruction followed on the heels of homicide, robbery, and arson—actions that may have been preludes to concerted rebellion. In 1736, for instance, a slave woman broke into her master's house, wounded his son, burnt his tobacco house, killed three other slaves, her own children, and then drowned herself. Similarly, in 1774, a slave named Juda murdered her son, set fire to the dwelling house, and rushed inside.[69]

When slaves destroyed themselves after allegedly injuring or killing other slaves, the accused may have acted in accord with African legal codes. Igbo legal concepts, for instance, called on murderers to hang themselves. Sally E. Hadden has recently argued that scholars ought to consider the ethnic African origins of slaves' legal perceptions and respect the "underlying principles that guided legal relations, conceptions about guilt and innocence, and presumptions about human nature."[70] Following this line of thinking, if Igbo imports predominated in early Virginia, what approaches might they have brought to the law, and how might these have shaped their responses to suicide? The Igbo understood law to be both divine and man-made, and the greatest penalties were reserved for severe breaches of the former, such as murder. According to Hadden, Igbo murderers were not even put on trial, since earthly courts had no jurisdiction over such crimes. Rather, for violating divine law, the community expected the accused to hang themselves.[71] This may help explain why slaves in Virginia destroyed themselves after allegedly killing other people. At the same time, compensation claims indicate that, upon death, the ethnicity of slaves had ceased to matter to slave owners. Runaway ads might distinguish among Igbo, Angolan, and French-born slaves, but masters' claims of compensation made no notice of the African origins of their slaves.[72]

Those enslaved women and men accused of violence against others may have faced reprisals not only from masters but also from the slave community. African rivalries may have followed some slaves to the New World, and, despite the bonds forged between diverse groups of newly arrived slaves, conditions on plantations may have exacerbated interpersonal tensions among them. Domestic discord among the slaves on Thomas Thistlewood's Jamaican plantation, for instance, accounted for violent disputes among slaves. In at least one instance, Moll drowned herself after violently beating another enslaved woman.[73] When it came to violence against whites, slaves expected swift and certain punishment. In cases of homicide and interpersonal violence, the prospect of death and probable dismemberment at the hands of the local justice system may have spurred slaves to kill themselves. According to Philip Schwarz, between 1706 and 1739, slaves convicted of killing, wounding, or attacking other slaves were likely, but not certain, to hang for their crimes; but when their alleged victims were whites, they faced certain hanging, as well as burning or dismemberment.[74] For instance, in 1727, the *Virginia Gazette* reported that an enslaved woman who confessed to killing her mistress received "the sentence of death, and is since burnt."[75]

Surprisingly, perhaps, the petitions suggest that the greater percentage of enslaved men and women who died by suicide did not stand accused of crimes against persons. Yet serial absconding and property crimes were capital felonies in this era, and slaves who committed these crimes killed themselves to avoid being captured and likely executed. Two slaves accused of arson were burned at the stake in Virginia. One enslaved man who was noted only to be a "notorious villain" was sentenced to death.[76] Other slaves had escaped their plantations and killed themselves before being recaptured. One petition noted that an unnamed runaway slave "to prevent being taken, leaped from on board a ship in the river and drowned himself."[77] Another woman ran away; patrollers found and tied her, but she somehow escaped and similarly drowned herself.[78] Sometimes slaves killed themselves on a first escape attempt or without being formally outlawed, as in the case of a woman who "was endeavoring to make her escape by water, in a canoe; and being closely pursued, threw herself into the water, to avoid being taken and was drowned."[79]

Even if enslaved people did not face certain execution, there was much to fear. Penalties could include whipping, beating, confinement, and dismemberment—nose slitting and ear cutting, the loss of toes or feet, or castration. One enslaved Virginia man was jailed for hog stealing and cut his throat, but a surgeon repaired the injury. It is not clear whether he was subsequently executed; perhaps the state paid to revive him, only to later hang him.[80] A consciousness of such reprisals might have spurred slaves to take their own lives.

In the context of the legal system, such suicides sent a political message to all southerners, slave and free, rich and poor, male and female. These suicides deliberately or unintentionally denied the state its ritual of retribution and robbed it of an opportunity to exemplify its authority through spectacles of execution.[81] Executions and punishments in eighteenth-century America were public; whites sought to "impress upon the blacks in attendance the folly of violence against whites" and made sure their bondpeople attended these spectacles.[82] In the quarter century preceding the Revolution, slaves faced extraordinary punishments, even by eighteenth-century standards. Some slaves were burnt alive, others drawn and quartered, gibbeted, and dismembered (losing hands or testicles) before hanging. After death, the state further mutilated alleged slave felons, often displaying their decapitated heads.[83] In eighteenth-century Georgia, for instance, many capital sentences decreed that after a slave had been hanged until "Dead, Dead, Dead," her or his head was to be cut off and set upon a pole "erected at, or close to, the scene of the crime."[84] As Kirsten Fischer has observed, "one gets the impression that in the 1760s, especially, the public display of mutilated and rotting corpses had become a rather common sight" in much of the upper South and the Caribbean.[85] Of course there was a racialized dimension to postmortem punishments. In the last two decades of the eighteenth century, Virginia courts ordered the display of the decapitated heads or bodies of enslaved blacks on at least twenty-six occasions. No evidence exists that white corpses were ever mutilated in these ways.[86]

If the prospect of execution made suicide seem like an acceptable alternative for enslaved men and women, even the punishments faced by those accused of noncapital crimes were chillingly grisly. As awful as it was, suicide was an alternative to the prospect of ear slitting, castration, or the loss of a foot, punishments that were not meant to produce immediate death.[87]

4.1. The gibbeting and display of the bodies of rebellious slaves. Slaves who killed themselves were similarly gibbeted and their corpses displayed to warn others away from acts of self-destruction. Source: "Sketch of Street Scene Depicting Two Negroes Killed by Soldiers and Exposed out on the gallows," undated. Du Simitiere Papers Relating to the West Indies 1748–1773," Box 4, 968.F.19H. This item is reproduced by permission of The Library Company of Philadelphia.

Confinement to jail carried similar risks; as a consequence of frostbite, slaves lost limbs and died from exposure to the cold.[88] Even slaves like Dick, who were already familiar with the pain and disfiguration of mutilation or suffered from ongoing infection, might have contemplated the possibility of suicide out of desperation even when they were not condemned to die.

Slaves also had much to fear in the form of physical violence from patrollers who apprehended them and jailors who kept them confined; although a dreadful alternative, suicide conceivably provided an escape from potential reprisals. Slaves knew that they could be shot, raped, beaten, whipped, or tortured by the patrollers; incarceration was equally dangerous and made slaves vulnerable to extralegal violence. In some cases, the language of petitions indicates that incarcerated men and women consciously took life-threatening risks by starting fires to facilitate escape attempts. For instance, in 1738, a slave imprisoned on suspicion of felony reportedly "set fire to the prison and was burnt to death," and in 1775, the enslaved Lemon "set fire to the gaol of [Prince George] County, to which he was committed, with two others, in order to make his escape and perished in the flames."[89] Some fires were clearly accidental, others were the work of vigilantes, and still other petitions simply note that the prison was "set" on fire.[90] Some of these were acts of murder, some were probably accidents, and others were attempts at suicide. The story of the enslaved Hampshire, recounted on the first page of the 23 December 1773 *Virginia Gazette*, for instance, reported that he killed himself the first night of his confinement by setting fire to the jail and walking into the flaming structure.[91]

In the end, however, while suicide by enslaved people deprived the public of its spectacle of execution, nothing prevented owners of slaves from exercising their private powers of plantation justice. Across the slave societies of British America and the United States, owners punished enslaved suicides with postmortem indignities. In mid-eighteenth-century South Carolina, Caesar's master ordered him to decapitate a slave who killed himself; in antebellum Georgia, an owner ordered the body of a slave suicide to be left in the slack tide to rot.[92] In 1837, Charles Ball declared that suicide among slaves was "regarded as a matter of dangerous example, and one which it is the business and the interest of all proprietors to discountenance and prevent." Slave suicides were "always branded in reputation after death, as the worst of criminals; and their bodies are not allowed the small portion of Christian rites which are awarded to the corpses of other slaves." And yet, he continued, "if any thing can justify a man in taking his life into his own hands, and terminating his existence, no one can attach blame to the slaves on many of the cotton plantations of the south, when they cut short their breath, and the agonies of the present being, by a single stroke."[93] Still, regardless of what occurred to their bodies after death, slaves who killed themselves—regardless of what they intended—were often understood to have willfully exhibited their own politics of death, a politics that contradicted the aims of slave owners as well as those of the state. In the narrow range of choices available to the enslaved, the alternative of suicide when faced with state-sanctioned violence, for better or worse, perhaps most fully measured the meaning of the power to die.

As Wiley's story illustrates, lawmakers in the eighteenth-century and early nineteenth-century upper South reconfigured traditional legal categories and created a unique hybridized system of criminal justice to fit the needs of slave societies. This legal system served the financial interests of slave owners and bolstered the commercial institution of slavery. Along with compensation, the category of the slave outlaw created a legal regime of private and public violence that attempted to control the rising numbers of Africans imported to the upper South in the early to mid-eighteenth century. Yet by choosing the awful alternative of suicide, enslaved men and women, like Wiley, rejected the private supremacy of their masters and the public authority of the state.

The power of the criminal justice system, however, was not absolute or unchanging. In theory, in some southern jurisdictions, enslaved people, even when they were felons or outlaws, fell within the compass of the King's Peace. Colonial British American legislators enacted both specific and general provisions to restrain violence against slaves. Some laws even limited masters' abilities to obtain compensation, and stipulated that owners' claims would be disallowed if they had poorly provisioned, clothed, or housed slaves or subjected them to undue cruelty.[94] In 1740, South Carolina legislators agreed to fine owners for failing to provide sufficient food and clothing to their slaves. In 1753, North Carolina went further, stipulating that masters seeking compensation had to provide evidence that their slaves had been "sufficiently clothed" and fed for the preceding year. The colony threatened masters with damages if they failed to sufficiently provision their slaves and, as a consequence, they were forced to steal corn, cattle, hogs, or other goods in order to survive.[95] Despite the limited will and capacity to enforce these statutes, these laws forged a connection between owners' cruelty and alleged slave crimes, including the crime of suicide.[96]

The legalities of slave suicide also reflected tensions in existing concepts of slaves as persons and property under the law. When they stood accused of criminal acts, including suicide, slaves were assumed to possess *mens rea*, intentionality or the mental state required to have committed a crime. When they killed themselves before the state could punish or execute them, their acts were construed as conscious rejections of the state's power, dangerous examples for other slaves. The mixed character of enslaved people under the law, as Jeannine DeLombard argues, "located their personhood in their punishable acts."[97] In legal terms, slave suicide was not just willful or intentional, it was, ironically, a powerful claim to personhood. At the same time, the system of compensating masters for their suicidal slaves underscored the idea that slaves existed as property. As enslaved people's acts of self-destruction came under the purview of the criminal justice system, they exposed the legal contradictions of slavery. Over the course of the eighteenth century, the intertwined systems of plantation and criminal justice, the legal tensions in slaves as persons and property, and the choices of self-destruction by slaves may have laid the groundwork for the emerging criticisms of the institution of slavery itself. By the 1770s, the contradictions of slave suicide in law and, as we shall see next, in print were becoming all too visible to be ignored.

FIVE

The Paradoxes of Suicide and Slavery in Print

> This Gentleman among his Negroes had a young Woman, who was look'd upon as a most extraordinary Beauty by those of her own Complexion. He had at the same time two young Fellows who were likewise Negroes and Slaves, remarkable for the Comeliness of their Persons, and for the Friendship which they bore to one another. It unfortunately happened that both of them fell in Love with the Female Negro abovementioned, who would have been very glad to have taken either of them for her Husband, provided they could agree between themselves which should be the Man. . . .
>
> After a long Struggle between Love and Friendship, Truth and Jealousy, they one Day took a Walk together into a Wood, carrying their Mistress along with them: Where, after abundance of Lamentations, they stabbed her to the Heart, of which she immediately died. A slave who was at his Work . . . discovered the Woman lying dead upon the Ground, with the two Negroes on each side of her, kissing the dead Corps, weeping over it, and beating their Breasts in the utmost Agonies of Grief and Despair. He immediately ran to the *English* family . . . who upon coming to the Place saw the Woman dead, and the two Negroes expiring by her with Wounds they had given themselves.
>
> —Joseph Addison, *The Spectator*, 1711[1]

As the contradictions exposed by slave self-destruction surfaced in British North America, themes of suicide also emerged in the novels, periodicals, and plays that circulated across the eighteenth-century Anglo-Atlantic.[2] Joseph Addison's *Cato: A Tragedy* (1713), for instance, enjoyed wide appeal among British and American audiences, particularly among those men, like gentry slaveholder William Byrd II, who viewed honor as a cardinal virtue of elite manhood. As a theater enthusiast, Byrd would have seen *Cato* staged, perhaps during a trip to London or at a Williamsburg production in 1736.[3] The play culminates with the suicide of the main character and applauds the stoic virtue of choosing death rather than accepting the dishonor of tyranny.[4] Such themes of liberty or death would later lend themselves to the rhetoric of revolution as well as that of antislavery activism.

Suicide was also a subject of less imaginative writing in the eighteenth century.[5] Among other notable works, *The English Malady* (1733), by George Cheyne, was especially popular across the Anglo-Atlantic; American planters purchased and perused these studies and sometimes knew their authors. Byrd, for instance, owned titles by Cheyne, and they shared membership in the Royal Society; the two men frequented the same London coffeehouses.[6] In the kind of reading materials that appealed to British American slaveholders like Byrd, suicide was "debated, anatomized, castigated, celebrated and even satirized in writings from every press across Britain and its colonies."[7] Byrd himself collected bits of suicide humor in his commonplace book, most of which lampooned husbands driven to suicide by unhappy marriages or brabbling wives.[8] As self-styled cosmopolitans, avid readers, and book collectors eager to keep up with London currents, planters across British America would have come across suicide as a kind of leitmotif in a range of early print materials as well as on the stage.

Accounts of self-destructive slaves were part of the flourishing theme of suicide in early eighteenth-century Anglo-American print and theater. These depictions, often set in British American colonies and based on allegedly true events, conveyed a distinct politics of suicide in slavery and explored its paradoxes. Stories of slave suicide appeared in the venues aimed at middle- to upper-class readers and theatergoers, a group that included merchants, investors, and absentee owners with interests in slavery. Moreover, these were literary fusions: not exactly fact or fiction, but fiction putatively based on fact. They did not debate suicide, provide fodder for humorous anecdotes, or outwardly condemn slavery, but instead, these stories explored the implications of colonial slavery. In particular, they considered the characteristics of slaves—rank, passion, beauty, and temperament were prominent themes—and assessed the nature of colonial slavery. Tales of slave suicide were a means for scrutinizing the imperial politics of slavery from the safe distance of print.[9] Variously focused on the slave trade, the temperament of Africans, and the nature of English authority, accounts of slave suicide probed the ramifications of slavery in British American plantations.

Stories of slave self-destruction in pre-Revolutionary Anglo-America appeared in periodicals, in novels, on the stage, and in the earliest memoirs of enslaved Africans, conveying a range of competing cultural and political meanings. For instance, suicide in print and plays underscored and confirmed assessments of the loyalty, honor, and virtue of slaves on one hand, and their passionate and savage nature on the other. One of the more striking features of these materials is the way in which suicide by enslaved men and women differed along the lines of gender. Pre-Revolutionary pre-abolitionist eighteenth-century Anglo-Atlantic literature and drama also featured stories of suicide as a way of probing the meaning of slave resistance and exploring the ramifications of the trade in slaves. Yet if stories of slave suicide momentarily tested structures of white dominance and planter authority or offered mild condemnations of dishonest traders or unjust governors, in the end they typically justified slavery. Print and dramatic accounts of slave self-destruction did not explicitly debate the morality of suicide. Instead, these stories of suicide surveyed the nature of slave character, the ramifications of imperial expansion, and the violence endemic to England's colonization of America.

The story of slave suicide quoted above, titled "A Kind of Wild Tragedy," exemplifies these themes. The tale is reportedly based on events in the Leeward Islands in the 1690s.[10] In its full version, the account depicts the enslaved male friends as possessing both admirable virtues and inexplicable passions and offers a reflection upon the character of all slaves. The report portrays the men as noble and loyal, while the woman is epitomized as obedient and compliant. Owners and slaves are nameless in this anecdote, a detail that is meant to emphasize the anonymity and universality of the players' natures. That the male subjects are so exceedingly loyal to one another but turn suddenly violent exposes the fineness of their character and the depth of their savagery. Their inability to regulate their passions is evidence of their barbarism and an implicit justification for their enslavement. Moreover, the violence in the scene has nothing to do with the institution or commerce of slavery; it is linked only to the fervent and fierce temperament of the enslaved. Here, as in accounts of suicide in the Atlantic trade, during seasoning, on American plantations, and in law, slave suicide is disarticulated from the processes of enslavement or the institution of slavery. Instead, unrestrained passion measures the differences between the cultural categories of civilization and barbarism.[11]

While "A Kind of Wild Tragedy" explored the nature of slave character, other stories of slave suicide examined slaves' resistance to authority. Some of the most celebrated and enduring works of the late seventeenth and early eighteenth centuries, like Aphra Behn's *Oroonoko* (1688) and Thomas Southerne's stage adaptation of the novel, take on this theme in earnest. Both presented readers and theatergoers across the Anglo-Atlantic with depictions of suicide as the virtuous and admirable choice of enslaved people who suffered injustices engineered by tyrannical colonial governors and duplicitous traders. Ballads, novels, essays, and plays explored the idea of the enslaved people's momentary resistance to authority; in the end, however, the resisting slave dies at his own hands—and it is almost always a "he"—confirming ideas about white dominance, the rightness of slavery, and the superiority of the Anglo-American audience.[12] That the protagonists in these stories are largely male reflects the importance of a patriarchal structure in slavery; only men are figured strong enough to take their own lives. Imaginative literature could momentarily give expression to slave mistreatment and discontent, but at the same time it also quickly foreclosed challenges to the institution through the suicide of the protagonist. Print assured readers that, even when slaves contemplated suicide or killed themselves, such acts had little to do with slavery as an institution, although certainly some of its representatives were blamed. Still, by exploring injustices done to enslaved people, cultural products in print and on the stage exposed the contradictions of slavery before Anglo-American audiences. These representations fostered the idea that self-destruction was a regrettable act driven by uncontrolled passions, a "wild tragedy," for which thinking persons might feel empathy.

In pre-Revolutionary Anglo-America, stories of suicide encompassed slave resistance to authority, extolled the loyalty and virtues of slave manliness, and explored the exoticism and passionate violence that was linked to blackness. Yet even as the politics of these depictions assured Anglo-Americans of the rightness of slavery and justified their commercial interests, they also raised doubts about the institution: in the context of slavery, accounts of suicide had begun to carry an increasingly moral valence. The cultural products analyzed here unmasked the deepening contradictions of slavery and exposed the paradoxes of suicide by enslaved people. By the late eighteenth century, the power to die would become a weapon that would be turned against the institution of slavery itself.

When depictions of slave suicide began to appear in print and theater in the late seventeenth and early eighteenth centuries, they centered on themes of plebeian resistance that had long been a tradition in English popular culture. One example can be seen in the early modern ballad, *A Lamentable Ballad of the tragical End*, first published in 1658. Set in Rome, the ballad featured a blackamoor servant who, having been unfairly punished for some unnamed affront, sought revenge on his master. The blackamoor complained, "My Master he did me correct,/My Fault not being great," and, in retaliation, the servant rapes his master's wife and afterward kills her as well as the couple's children. The full title captures the plot: *A Lamentable Ballad of the tragical End of a gallant Lord and a virtuous Lady, and the untimely End of their two Children, wickedly perform'd by a heathenish black-a-moor, their Servant, the like never heard of before.*[13]

The ballad turns on an unwarranted physical punishment. Early modern ballads often chronicled the ways in which dependents resisted the excesses of their superiors; such themes were not only popular fare in traditional seventeenth- and eighteenth-century English songs, they were particularly prevalent in those that featured suicide.[14] For instance, some ballads focused on the self-inflicted deaths of the young who resisted parental authority and social convention. Their self-destructive acts were blamed on forced marriages, inconstant lovers, or out-of-wedlock pregnancies. These themes in suicide ballads also suggest a longstanding popular recognition that not all suicide was inspired by the devil. On the contrary, these ballads suggest that a not-so-subtle acknowledgment of the secular, as opposed to diabolical, causes of suicide predates the modern period.[15] In the popular mind, at any rate, suicide was linked to injustices caused by cruel or autocratic authorities.

Suicide ballads invited audiences to identify with the victims of various wrongs, as in *A Lamentable Ballad*.[16] In this regard, the ballad is both typical and unusual. In traditional songs, suicide was the outgrowth of injustice—doomed romance brought about by intransigent parents, for instance—and, similarly, *A Lamentable Ballad* asks listeners to identify with the blackamoor as a victim of excessive authority. According to Catherine Molineux, some members of the audience must have "enjoyed its particular working through of the implications of resistance."[17] Likewise, later depictions of slave suicide set in the Americas presented readers with similar images of blacks as victims of unjust authority.[18]

The blackamoor's desire for revenge was also a vehicle for exploring racialized depictions of violence. This theme, too, was translated to literary explorations of suicide in the Americas. In *A Lamentable Ballad*, the blackamoor raped his master's wife, dashed one child's brains against the wall and "pluck'd" the other child from its mother's breast, cut its throat, and threw its body into the moat. While the audience might sympathize with the blackamoor's feelings of affront, they would hesitate to endorse the violence that evidenced his "heathenish" and "savage" nature. Having destroyed the family, the blackamoor jumps into the moat to drown in order to escape punishment from angered villagers. Having begun the ballad as victim of unfair violence, he has now been transformed into a principal agent of brutal aggression that far outweighed his own treatment by his master. The revenge of the blackamoor could be viewed as honorable response to wrongful corporal authority, but his violence conveyed his innate savagery.

The suicide of the blackamoor ultimately resolved the tension between insults to plebeian honor that were aimed at criticizing elites' unreasonable use of power and his own violence against those elites. By the ballad's end, the master and his innocent family have paid for his moment of tyranny with their lives. In all of this the wife exists simply as an object upon which violence is enacted; although she did no wrong, she and her children suffer in her husband's stead. All of these themes—resistance of the unfree, honor and loyalty, violence and patriarchal privilege—would be picked up in stories of slave suicide written in English that were set in the Americas.

One of the most enduring and popular literary and dramatic vehicles for exploring both injustices done to enslaved people as well as their resistance to slavery, was Aphra Behn's novel *Oroonoko* (1688), adapted to the stage by Thomas Southerne. Set in Africa and English Surinam, few other plays were more popular or successful on the eighteenth-century British stage; beginning in 1695, it was performed every year through 1829.[19] The main character, Oroonoko, appears to have been modeled on Cato the Younger, the Roman stoic most closely associated with choosing suicide over tyranny. In Addison's version, Cato is defeated in war and kills himself rather than sacrifice his ideals and honor by submitting to Caesar's oppressive rule. As Cato reflects in the play, "It is not now a time to talk of aught/But chains or conquest, liberty or death."[20]

In addition to relying on classical models that enjoyed popularity on the British stage, *Oroonoko* surveyed the nature of slavery and suicide in England's New World colonies. Much of *Oroonoko's* content is focused on the injustice of and resistance to slavery. It does not so much attack slavery, however, as question the enslavement of the royal prince Oroonoko, who came from a slave-owning family in Africa.[21] The theme of the wrongly enslaved royal African, as we shall see, also surfaces in some of the earliest slave memoirs published in England; *Oroonoko* is a fictional forerunner of these. In the novel and play, slaves' resistance to unjust and wrongful authority is coupled with suicide: aboard ship Oroonoko refuses to eat, but relents when he is assured he will be freed. On land he attempts to establish his freedom through legal means; when this fails, he organizes an unsuccessful revolt. In its aftermath, he attempts suicide. His courage and defiance are points of contrast to his captors and enslavers; he is depicted as virtuous and brave, while they are cruel and unjust. Ultimately the novel portrays his death as violent and stoic: he cuts a piece of flesh from his throat and throws it at the English, declaring that he will kill himself before he falls "a victim to the shameful whip." Then, as did Cato, Oroonoko rips up "his own belly; and took his bowels and pull'd 'em out."[22] He survives (as did Cato) and is revived so that he could be executed for treason.[23] In the final scene of the novel, he sits calmly and smokes a pipe while his ears, nose, and arms are cut off. At his death, his corpse is quartered, his divided body sent to various elites; one refuses to display his portion, arguing that "he could govern his negroes without terrifying and grieving them with frightful spectacles of a mangled king," a plea for paternalism alongside an orgy of absolutist gore. In stark contrast, the stage version features a milder version of torture, and more importantly, Oroonoko dies at his own hands, a conclusion that underscores his heroism in choosing death over slavery.

To much a greater extent than in *A Lamentable Ballad,* readers and audiences were encouraged to admire Oroonoko's resistance to slavery, and his display of manly courage. For these reasons, the play was banned in Charleston in 1795 and never performed at all in Kingston. In addition, Oroonoko's refusal to "live as a slave or be separated from his wife"—who in the stage version was a white woman—were not sentiments that the slave-owing, theater-going public in those ports wished to see emulated.[24] Indeed, although he enacts much violence in the course of the story, at its conclusion, the enslaved man remains a stoic hero. Rather, *Oroonoko* faults ineffectual leadership—from the jealous African king who sold Oroonoko and his beloved into slavery to the British governor whose overzealous punishments and injustices thwarted Oroonoko's quest for liberty—rather than the commerce of slavery itself. The play suggests that suicide was an honorable choice when confronted with tyranny, even, or perhaps especially, when it was the choice of a male slave.

Enslaved women, in contrast, were held to standards that measured their virtue through their obedience to patriarchal authority. Men can resist, but women must obey. For instance, the novel depicts Oroonoko's wife, Imoinda, as "heroic," but her heroism is predicated on loyalty to her husband. In the wake of Oroonoko's failed revolt, he plans to murder her and kill himself; not wishing to be separated, they hope that after death, they will "be sent [to their] own country" and reunited. Once Imoinda understands his purpose, her resolve to die is described as "noble": she smiles that she should die "by her husband's hand." The reader is told that in their homeland, "wives have a respect for their husbands equal to what other people pay a deity; and when a man finds any occasion to quit his wife, if he loves her, she dies by his hand; if not, he sells her, or suffers some other to kill her." As Charlotte Sussman points out, Imoinda is a possession before she is a slave, so her move from Africa to Surinam is "not so much a transition from freedom to slavery as a transition from one code of property relations to another."[25] When Oroonoko kills Imoinda to safeguard her virtue, he does so by severing her head from her body.[26] To an English audience, beheading signaled treason, but of course, Imoinda is innocent of such a charge. Perhaps Oroonoko's thought was to prevent the postmortem desecration of her body and protect her, even after death.

In the mid-eighteenth century, the *Gentleman's Magazine* reported on two Africans, a prince, William Unsah Sessarakoo, and his companion, who attended a performance of *Oroonoko* in Covent Garden in February 1749. Like Oroonoko, the pair were noble and had been tricked into slavery by duplicitous traders; unlike Oroonoko, however, they were rescued by Englishmen and returned to London. Their appearance at the play caused a sensation, and others in the audience greeted the two Africans with a round of applause and monitored their reactions to the play. The *Gentleman's Magazine* informed its readers that the two Africans were strongly moved by viewing "persons of their own colour on the stage, apparently in the same distress from which they had been so lately delivered," that is, enslavement, betrayal, injustice. Giving in to a "generous grief which pure nature always feels and which art had not yet taught" the two youths to suppress, the prince in particular was "so far overcome" that he left the play at the end of the penultimate act, missing the final death scene, the suicides of Oroonoko and Imoinda. In Southerne's stage version, Imoinda was transformed into a white woman who assists Oroonoko in plunging the dagger into her breast; he then kills the governor and finally himself. According to the *Gentleman's Magazine*, the remaining African in attendance reportedly wept for the rest of the performance, evidencing the sensibility admired by metropolitan Londoners.[27] The accounts blended life and art and, in the process, infused acts of self-destruction by slaves with increasingly politicized meanings.

The popularity of *Oroonoko* may have inspired the onset of stories and accounts of suicide by slaves in Anglo-American print; slave suicide was a theme that resonated with readers and audiences. Most of these accounts similarly revolved around themes of slave resistance, honor, loyalty, and violence. In addition, *The Spectator* and the *Gentleman's Magazine*, periodicals that could be found in the households of gentry slaveholders across British America, also featured accounts of slave suicide.[28] Although these accounts were never as numerous as articles on self-destruction by free persons, slave self-murder was distinctively newsworthy. Like *Oroonoko*, these publications extended the neoclassical trope of heroic or "honor suicide" and sometimes modeled enslaved men on the figure of Cato.[29] For those who championed the choice between "liberty or death," as Addison's Cato put the matter, suicide was honorable, even when it was the choice of a slave.

The focus on the virtue and honor of enslaved people was sustained in other accounts of British American slavery. In 1711, for instance, *The Spectator* published the account of slave suicide in St. Christopher, "A Kind of Wild Tragedy," that opened this chapter. In a later version (1775), an almanac kept the essential details of the story, but changed its setting to Virginia.[30] The unrestrained passions of the men in the story conveyed assumptions about the barbarism of slaves, a trait that existed in opposition to English civilization. Addison's purpose in this story was to illustrate that this "instance of barbarity" and other "strange disorders" occur in slaves because their "passions are not regulated by virtue and disciplined by reason."[31] Yet the story also hinted that slaves—male slaves at least—possessed virtue: their friendship was so great, their love for the woman so intense, that they were hopelessly deadlocked. Their passions in fact defined their limitations; they stabbed her together because they could not reason their way out of the situation. At the same time, the account projected sentimentalism, as they lay "beating their breasts in the utmost agonies of grief and despair."[32] Unlike *A Lamentable Ballad* or *Oroonoko*, the "Wild Tragedy" did not explore suicide as an outcome of confrontations with unjust authorities. Rather, the piece played upon the virtues of male companionship: two men who refused to betray their friendship for the love of a woman. The story revolves around men unwilling to live without one another, men whose love for one another was so profound that neither could not deprive the other of the object of their romantic affection. She was truly an object, a vehicle upon which men enacted manliness and honor. While the account may have reassured readers that suicide could be admirable, it nonetheless confirmed prevailing ideas about the passion and inferiority of slaves.

Accounts of slaves who killed themselves to demonstrate their loyalty—rather than to resist slavery—surfaced repeatedly in the early eighteenth century and widened the gulf between conceptions of African versus English identities. Sometimes the accounts illustrated slaves' loyalty to their masters. For instance, in addition to the "Wild Tragedy," *The Spectator's* 1711 issue also included this item:

> When one hears of Negroes, who upon the death of their masters, or upon changing their service, hang themselves upon the next tree, as it frequently happens in our *American* plantations, who can forbear admiring their fidelity,

> though it expresses it self in so dreadful a manner? What might not that savage greatness of soul, which appears in these poor wretches on many occasions, be raised to, were it rightly cultivated?[33]

Similarly, in 1756, Jamaican planter Thomas Thistlewood recorded an event in his diary in which a slave "so soon as he heard his old Master was dead went to the negro house privately and shot himself, to accompany him into the other world and there wait upon him."[34] What is striking in both accounts is the depiction of the slaves' identities as so dependent upon those of their masters that the former will destroy themselves rather than exist without ownership. These representations were early versions of the myth of the contented slave, a trope that may have assuaged rising doubts about slavery. From an owner's point of view, loyalty was a valuable trait in enslaved people. That they would kill themselves because their identities were so bound up with those who governed them may have appealed to the audience of investors, masters, and traders who read *The Spectator*. The story reflects a need to depict slaves as faithful and domesticated, not wholly unlike their frequent presentations in eighteenth-century portraits.[35]

At the same time, these same depictions of slave loyalty could prove to be unsettling to Anglo-American audiences. In part, they illustrate what Orlando Patterson calls the "human parasitism" of slavery and capture not only the asymmetrical relationship of domination but also the complexities of masters' dependency upon their slaves.[36] These stories illustrate not simply an individual but a cultural dependency on the myth of slave loyalty: in these stories, masters are already dead and other Englishmen tell the tale. What is more, these representations also contain a glimmer of a theme that will be revived in the early antislavery writing: suicide in slavery is presented as both admirable and troubling. Like other accounts in print, the depiction of the loyal slave hints at the importance of culture over nature and civilization over barbarism but suggests that slaves could overcome their innate selves and aspire to "greatness" over "savagery." These rhetorical questions actually open up other possible meanings of the slave's act of suicide for the audience. What might slaves achieve if they were subjected to the cultivation of sensibility, if they enjoyed liberty, if they were given education? The deep feelings that led to suicide could be channeled toward more progressive ends. Addison concludes by asking the following.

> What colour of excuse can there be for the contempt with which we treat this part of our species that we should not put them upon the common foot of humanity, that we should only set an insignificant fine upon the man who

> murders them; nay that we should, as much as in us lies, cut them off from the prospects of happiness in another world as well as in this, and deny them that which we look upon as the proper means for attaining it?[37]

Here, the challenge to slaveholders, merchants, and the general audience grows even bolder. Addison recounts a story that reflects the mythical loyalty of enslaved people, an account that presents them—rather than owners or investors—as models of virtue. In doing so, he implicitly offers a critical misgiving for his readers to consider: how is enslavement of human beings justified?

Later in the eighteenth century, in 1784, James Ramsey, an antislavery activist, would directly pose this question to an Anglo-American readership. He drew on some of the same themes of honor, loyalty, and suicides among slaves but used them for expressly antislavery purposes. He related an incident from the 1750s, the "famous" legend of Quashi, a story that celebrates the slave's fierce sense of loyalty as it is expressed in an act of suicide that is described as "worthy of a Spartan."[38] Quashi had never been brutalized: the "smoothness of his skin," Ramsey reports, had been left "unrazed by the whip." Accused of a crime he did not commit and sentenced to the lash, Quashi ran. He encountered his master in a field, gave chase, and the two men wrestled together. When Quashi had the upper hand, he "firmly seated on his master's breast, now panting and out of breath, and with his weight, his thighs, and one hand, secured him motionless." The ensuing dialogue between the two men, which Ramsey invented to "give words to the sentiment that inspired it," is as follows.

> [Quashi] then drew out a sharp knife, and while the other lay in dreadful expectation, helpless, and shrinking into himself, he thus addressed him. 'Master, I was bred up with you from a child; I was your play-mate when a boy; I have loved you as myself; your interest has been my study; I am innocent of the cause of your suspicion; had I been guilty, my attachment to you might have pleaded for me. Yet you have condemned me to a punishment of which I must ever have borne the disgraceful marks; thus only can I avoid them.' With these words, he drew the knife with all his strength across his own throat, and fell down dead without a groan, on his master, bathing him in his blood.[39]

This powerful image has the effect of fusing master and slave. Ramsey suggests that Quashi's sensibility was laudable, and that had he enjoyed, in the parlance of 1776, the "inalienable rights" to which all people are entitled, he might have furthered the progress of humanity in the arts, sciences, or philosophy. At the same time, the slave's protectiveness of his integrity (the virtue reflected by the smoothness of his skin) and his highly developed sense of honor may have struck a sympathetic chord with the readership even as it set Quashi apart from them. In Ramsey's hands, however, at the particular historical moment of the rise of antislavery organizations, the self-inflicted death of this loyal slave carried a host of political meanings.

What did it mean, in the pre-Revolutionary era, to admire the virtue, nobility, and honor of enslaved men who chose suicide? Did it reflect antislavery or proslavery sentiment? In fact, these depictions presented readers, both then and now, with a paradox; they suggested both support for slavery even as they sowed the seeds of antislavery themes. One could argue that the institution of slavery was reinforced by these representations. Endorsing ideas of rank and nobility and embracing virtues of friendship and courage, the suicides of slaves in print and on the stage ultimately underscored their loyalty and fitness for slavery. In print, some slaves were so exotically, passionately loyal to their masters—rather than to freedom—that they were willing to kill themselves. Some slaves hung themselves after their masters died; and, in the case of Quashi, killed themselves rather than suffer punishment. Yet on the other side of the coin, some undeniably antislavery themes were emerging: admiration for slaves' virtues, sympathy for their resistance to injustice, esteem for those who chose death over tyranny, and regard for their patriarchal manliness. Oroonoko is a good example here: in the novel he beheads Imoinda; in the stage version he assists in her suicide; in both cases, he prevents her from being subjected to sexual violence after his death. Similarly, in the novel he plans to kill himself and in the stage version he succeeds in doing so. He chooses heroic death rather than suffer tyranny, punishment, and the dishonor of enslavement for a man of his rank. Framed within a patriarchal structure, the image of rebellious, honorable, and loyal black slaves may have "caught popular imagination" despite the fact that their deaths foreclosed future possibilities of insurgency.[40]

Despite their diverse interpretations of resistance to authority, all of these printed accounts of slave suicide featured a veritable pornography of violence, treating audiences to a spectacle of unrestrained passion that included murder, necrophilia, and lamentation, scenes meant to underscore the dangerously passionate nature of the enslaved self. In "A Kind of Wild Tragedy," for instance, the unnamed female was stabbed in "the heart"; a nearby slave heard her "shrieks," ran to see what was the matter, and found her "dead upon the ground, with the two negroes on each side of her, kissing the dead corpse, weeping over it, and beating their breasts in the utmost agony."[41] The emphasis on the strength of Quashi's thighs as he sits astride his master and bathes him in his blood—a visual expression of the dependency of the master on the slave—is similarly not only graphic in its depiction of violence, but sexually suggestive. In print and on the stage, slave suicide might be used to probe the injustice of and resistance to slavery, but the centrality of themes surrounding rank, loyalty, and honor also reinforced the values of slave owners and the institution of slavery. Such accounts emphasized the resistance, courage, and loyalty of enslaved men; women, when they appeared at all, were vehicles for the display of the central attention to male virtue. In particular, Quashi's master, pinned beneath his slave and bathed in his blood, appears as a culpable cultural agent of the injustices of slavery.

The earliest slave memoirs printed in English in the first half of the eighteenth century echoed many of the literary and dramatic themes in depictions of self-destruction by enslaved people. Suicide plays a small and indirect role in early autobiographies, particularly in contrast to nineteenth-century North American slave narratives in which suicidal ideation or accounts of slave self-killing are abundant. The depictions of self-destruction in the earliest memoirs of Africans focused on issues of rank, virtue, and race, and like the periodical and literary treatments of slave suicide considered above, their primary objective was to affirm rather than to protest slavery. In fact, like the fictional Oroonoko, the captive Africans whose memoirs were published in English before the American Revolution themselves owned slaves or belonged to families that were actively involved in the slave trade. Two accounts of Africans' enslavement were published in English before 1750: one by Ayuba Suleiman Diallo (1730), more commonly known as Job ben Solomon, and a second, published anonymously as *The Royal African* (1749), which relates the story of Prince William Ansah Sessarakoo, although he is never named in the text.[42] The former was taken into captivity when he went to an English ship to sell slaves and buy paper.[43] The latter's father, a principal trader in gold and slaves, instructed a ship's captain to take his son to England via Barbados to be educated in order to strengthen trading ties, but when the ship reached the West Indies, the captain sold Sessarakoo into slavery.[44] Diallo's story was taken down by Maryland lawyer Thomas Bluett, who helped free him; it was reprinted "many times in French and English."[45] The author of *The African Prince* is unknown, but the biography enjoyed a second and perhaps a third printing. Pictures of both men appeared in *The Gentleman's Magazine*.[46]

5.1. The Priest Job ben Soloman (Ayuba Suleiman Diallo) and the Prince William Ansah Sessarakoo. This illustration and brief accounts of both men appeared in the *Gentleman's Magazine* and emphasized their upper-class status. Job was noted to be a "person of great distinction in his own country" where he was wrongfully seized and sold as a slave in Maryland in 1731. Sessarakoo was noted to be the son of "John Banishee Corrantee Chinnee of Anamaboe, and of Eukobah, daughter of Ansah Sessarakoo, King of Aquamboo, and niece to Quishadoe king of Akroan." Source: *Gentleman's* Magazine, vol. 20 (London, 1750). This item is reproduced by permission of The Virginia Historical Society, Richmond.

Neither *The Memoirs of Job* nor *The Royal African* opposed slavery as an institution. Rather, among other things, these accounts explore the wrongful enslavement of the African upper classes; Diallo was a priest, while Sessarakoo was a prince. In this sense, their accounts are like that of *Oroonoko*. Moreover, the themes that appear in later eighteenth-century and nineteenth-century North American slave narratives—the Middle Passage, family separation, the brutality of corporal punishment, suffering, the tyranny of mariners, traders, and owners—are absent in these pre-Revolutionary memoirs.

Rather than questioning slavery, the stories of Diallo and Sessarakoo accept slavery as part of natural social hierarchies and express admiration for the enlightened English who rescue these protagonists from enslavement. For instance, Diallo was kidnapped by warring Mandingoes and eventually sold into slavery in Maryland; he was able to distinguish himself through his "affable carriage and the easy composure of his countenance" as no "common" slave. In Bluett's transcription, Diallo notes that many in his nation were suited to a "hard and low life," but that he was, in contrast, a civilized African, unsuitable for enslavement because he was part of the "better sort" of people who "apply themselves to study and reading."[47]

The Royal African similarly sets apart its author from other captive Africans. Sessarakoo is a prince, "the greatest favorite" of his father; his mother, the chief wife of his father, was the daughter of "one of the principal persons" of the country. As Sessarakoo traveled to Barbados, unaware that he is to be sold into slavery, he views "numbers" of Africans who had been enslaved "from a variety of accidents." In retrospect, he remarks that none of them had experienced anything in any degree "comparable to that which had brought this heavy lot upon him," a reference to his wrongful enslavement as a prince. English slavers with whom he traveled admired Sessarakoo as well and called him "Cupid" for his "sweet and amiable temper." His eventual wrongful enslavement, then, is made all the more egregious because of his rank, which could not protect him when he was sold by the ship's captain to cover a debt and enslaved in Bridgetown.[48]

Both memoirs anticipate the ways in which suicide will serve in later slave narratives to measure the inhumanity of enslavement, but they do so from a distinctly eighteenth-century viewpoint. For instance, both protagonists consider suicide because they feel dishonored and disgraced: men of their rank should not be enslaved, and they suffer because of their distance from those royal kin who might intercede and protect them. While Sessarakoo protests his "rough usage" at the hands of two other slaves, unlike the brutality expressed in later nineteenth-century ex-slave narratives, neither he nor Diallo reports being beaten, chained, shackled, or confined to the hold of ships. Sessarakoo makes the crossing as a free man, so the Middle Passage is irrelevant to his story, but Diallo does not mention it either.[49]

In both accounts, the protagonists suffer psychologically rather than physically, and self-destruction is intimated rather than openly contemplated. Diallo's owner, for instance, ordered the captured African to work in the tobacco field, where he felt "more and more uneasiness" in his labor and eventually grew too sick to work, a reflection of his despondency. He was "in no way able to bear" his labor. Rather than administer a flogging, his master gave him a simpler task of watching cattle. Diallo periodically withdrew into the woods to pray, but when a "white boy" taunted and threw dirt on the enslaved former priest, he could bear no more indignities. Diallo grew "desperate" and simply ran away, hoping to "meet with some lucky accident, to divert or abate his grief."[50] This allusion to achieving death indirectly is as close as the narrative comes to suggesting suicide. Since the religious beliefs of Diallo proscribed suicide, a more direct reference to the act was probably implausible, given that he was described a "high priest" of his nation.[51] Diallo wandered through the countryside and was eventually imprisoned. His confinement continued until Bluett heard of Diallo and engineered his freedom.

Sessarakoo more openly contemplated self-destruction, perhaps because he was a prince rather than a priest. His "distress" and "horror" left him with "scarce a glimmer of hope" that evolved into "bitterness" when he reflected on his "sudden and undeserved reverse of fortune." The "rough usage" given to him in Barbados, along with his distance from "father, family or friends" pushed him toward thoughts of suicide. "He had before him a prospect so gloomy, that he stood in need of superior greatness of Mind to bear the shock without sinking under it, or taking some desperate Method to remove the Load." Unlike other slaves, however, the Prince's rank rescues him from thoughts of self-destruction: as a member of the ruling class, he did indeed possess "greatness of mind," which he feared losing.[52] The phrase echoes Addison's assertion that slaves possessed a "greatness of soul" that, although expressed in a "dreadful" manner through suicide, might be channeled in more useful directions.[53]

Rather than "sinking under" the shock of enslavement and giving into a suicidal impulse, Sessarakoo persevered. Still, his sense of injustice remained and nothing could remove the "melancholy" of his countenance, although the author was quick to add that Sessarakoo's melancholy "was not attended with any tincture of sullenness or obstinacy" that would associate him with the lower orders.[54] As we have seen, sullenness, stubbornness, and obstinacy were descriptive terms often connected to the suicides of enslaved people. In contrast, Diallo's lack of obstinacy reinforced the importance of his class affiliation for his audience.

Like other accounts of slave suicide in literature and periodicals from the pre-Revolutionary period, the stories of Diallo and Sessarakoo reinforced the humanity of English enslavers and, therefore, suppressed distressing questions about the slave trade itself. To be sure, both accounts point out that the commerce in slaves was corrupted—by warring Mandingoes and dishonest ship captains in these narratives—but these troubling aspects of the trade could be overcome, as both narratives suggest, by an exclusive reliance on English traders.[55] Anglo-Americans, in fact, prevent both men from committing suicide and rescue them from slavery. Their rescue, in turn, benefitted English-African trade relations: Diallo, for instance, gave "repeated assurances" that he would promote the English trade "before any other."[56] Similarly, although much "odium" had been cast upon the English for Sessarakoo's kidnapping, an associate of his father's devises a plan to "restore" his country's "good opinion" of them. He arranges for his own son to accompany traders, a move that he believes will rehabilitate regard in particular for English traders.[57] These accounts do not impeach the transatlantic commerce in slaves.

At the same time, these early memoirs prefigure themes found in later slave narratives and antislavery literature. While accounts of suicidal ideation are brief in the stories of Diallo and Sessarakoo, their stories echoed themes of suicidal despondency, melancholy, alienation, and isolation that emerge in later eighteenth and antebellum writing by and about slaves. In that sense, these early memoirs lay the groundwork for later explicitly antislavery work in print that will assign blame for suicide to actions of mariners, owners, overseers, and traders and use suicide to indict the commerce of slavery. Moreover, these accounts also offer partial critiques of slavery by questioning Anglo-American assumptions about the inferiority of Africans. Sessarakoo in particular objects to racism even as he esteems the British Empire above all others.[58] Such protests are, however, more credible coming from these men of high rank who, at other turns, offer no complaints about the continuing enslavement of their countrymen and women.

Into the era of the Imperial Crisis, other writers of the Black Atlantic modeled their life stories on the literature of Christian confession and suicide to illustrate crises of conscience. The enslaved James Albert Ukawsaw Gronniosaw, for instance, contemplated suicide out of an awareness of his sinful and corrupt nature. Although he was kidnapped in Africa and transported to North America, neither the Middle Passage and natal alienation, nor punishment and labor regimes fostered thoughts of self-destruction. Rather, his suicide attempt occurred during a crisis of conscience that precipitated his conversion to Christianity.[59] Gronniosaw also linked himself to the tradition of the African prince in his title: *A Narrative of the Most Remarkable Particulars in the Life of James Albert Ukawsaw Gronniosaw, an African Prince, as Related by Himself* (1772). However, his story is not about being rescued from slavery. It is about being rescued from sin. Rather than momentarily highlighting slave resistance or assuaging the anxieties over England's commercial investment in slavery, Gronniosaw's memoir instead sought to ignite the sacred worldview of his audience. His story was worthy of the notice of "every Christian reader."[60]

According to his memoir, Gronniosaw's inclinations toward suicide, in fact, began in Africa, where he was a "melancholy" and "unhappy" child. Words like "grave," "reserved," "dejected," and "dissatisfied" pepper the opening pages of his recollections; he also notes that he especially labored under "anxieties and fears" when celebrating the "Sabbath" of his nation.[61] A traveling merchant offers to take Gronniosaw with him, in the hope of curing his despondency. In the course of this trip, Gronniosaw is sold into slavery. Initially disembarking in Barbados, he accompanies his first master to New York and continues his Christian education.[62]

Doubt and paranoia, however, continued to plague Gronniosaw and led him to consider suicide. Resolving to "put an end" to his life, he took a large knife and went into the stable "with an intent to destroy" himself. As he "endeavoured" with all of his strength to force the knife into his side, it doubled and bent. Suddenly aware of what he is doing—and of the Christian prohibition against suicide—Gronniosaw is horrified. He realizes that had he succeeded in killing himself, he "probably [would] have gone to hell."[63] His full conversion to Christianity follows quickly. In many respects, his narrative does not offer any criticism of slavery or decry his enslavement. Rather, slavery brings him closer to God. His suicidal thoughts preceded his spiritual awakening, and his retreat to the barn with a knife represents a crisis of faith from which he emerged as a full believer. Yet despite this orientation, Gronniosaw's account helped initiate a tradition of black autobiographical writing that later transformed into the genre of the slave narrative.[64] Gronniosaw's crisis of conscience, attempt at suicide, and subsequent spiritual conversion fused elements of enslavement, suicide, and Christian morality in ways that, in later iterations, would be one means of attacking slavery.

In the first half of the eighteenth century, accounts of suicide by slaves appeared in a variety of printed genres. Like "A Kind of Wild Tragedy," novels and news items, plays and essays, memoirs and narratives alike featured enslaved men who contemplated self-destruction or killed themselves outright. Drawing on classical models, accounts of British American plantations, and descriptions of Africa, this literature generated competing meanings of suicide by enslaved people. Relying on the trope of the African prince, these representations presented suicide by enslaved men as variously indicative of their resistance to tyrannical authority and their possession of honor and virtue. At the same time, stories of slave suicide in pre-Revolutionary print did not uniformly or consistently attribute suicide to slavery. Enslaved men in particular chose suicide in response to physical insults or disgrace, or the denial of liberties, but also out of loyalty to one another or even to slave owners. From the vantage point of literature, theater, and periodicals, suicide by enslaved men reflected themes of justice, honor, rank, and patriarchal privilege. In this context, acts of self-destruction were to be admired, the result of sentiments that were virtuous and worthy of emulation. In this genre, in this period, paradoxically, literary, periodical, and dramatic representations offered much to appreciate in the character of captive royal Africans and very little to deplore in the commerce of slavery.

At the same time, these representations presented contradictions between virtue and barbarism that were central to understandings of suicide in slavery. The enslaved killed themselves because of their irrational and passionate natures, as "A Kind of Wild Tragedy" suggests; even their virtues, like those of loyalty and honor, were depicted as so extreme as to lead them to self-destruction. In this sense, the extremities of slave passion and emotional differences from their enslavers as well as from investors, merchants, and the ordinary English, were, from a very early point, a theme in print and illustrated the divide between Anglo-American cultural categories of civilization and barbarism.[65] The emotional extremes of slaves were accompanied by depictions of their capacity for violence. Particularly in scenes emerging from the West Indies, slaves' propensities for violence toward others accompanied depictions of violence that they turned against themselves. Of course, the subjects of most of these accounts were enslaved men; women were simply vehicles through which, if not upon which, violence was enacted.

These paradoxical depictions went a far distance to justify slavery, the commercial expansion of the English trade, and the growth of the institution in British American colonies. Assurances about racial and temperamental differences allowed the English to justify enslavement as well as to disarticulate suicide from the circumstances of enslavement. Moreover, stories of African royals featured the English as liberators, that is, those who rescued wrongfully enslaved elite Africans from a life of forced labor. In doing so, the rescuers, ironically, secured their networks for the commerce in slaves and tightened their hold on the international slave trade. In the accounts that circulated in the Anglo-Atlantic prior to the onset of the Imperial Crisis, suicide by slaves manifested all of these justifications for slavery and the slave trade.

The proslavery leanings of print and dramatic representations, however, tell only part of the story. As we shall see, accounts of suicide by slaves in British American plantations cast some doubts on the morality of slavery. The admiration for suicide in the face of tyranny remained a popular theme in print and on the stage. The figure of the wrongly enslaved prince was initially a successful vehicle for conveying objections to slavery, conceivably gaining the attention and sympathy of royalist audiences. Yet such representations would lose ground after the American Revolution, as slavery itself—rather than enslavement of a royal—was an increasingly politicized question. Most importantly, these early depictions of enslaved resistance to tyrannical authority—and especially a resistance that culminated in suicide—prefigured the importance of slave self-destruction to the earliest antislavery literature. Moreover, commentary on some of these representations pitted nature against nurture and put forward the idea that, were captive Africans and African Americans not enslaved, they might further human progress. As the Imperial Crisis deepened, the competing meanings of slave suicide took on an increasingly politically radical implication and a decidedly antislavery tone. In the coming decades, suicide in slavery, the power to die, would become a force for revolutionary political change.

CHAPTER SIX

The Meaning of Suicide in Antislavery Politics

Tuesday a Black, Servant to Captain Ordington, who a few days before ran away from his Master and got himself christened, with the Intent to marry his Fellow Servant, a white Woman, being taken and sent on board the Captain's Ship in the Thames, took an Opportunity of shooting himself through the Head.

—*Virginia Gazette*, 1773[1]

Arm'd with thy sad last gift—the pow'r to die,
Thy shafts, stern fortune, now I can defy;
The dreadful mercy points at length the shore
Where all is peace, and men are slaves no more.

—*The Dying Negro, A Poem*, 1775[2]

In 1773, as the British North American colonies and England moved toward armed conflict and activists leveled challenges to the transatlantic trade and the legalities of slavery, a radically new era in antislavery politics commenced. It began with a newspaper account, given above, of the suicide of an unnamed enslaved man in London. Two lawyers, Thomas Day and John Bicknell, were outraged by the report, and used the story to fire the opening salvo in the fight against slavery. Their efforts took the form of a poem, *The Dying Negro*, through which they sought to expose the injustices of slavery and the cruelties endured by enslaved people. The poem was widely popular: after its initial printing and subsequent revisions, it circulated in multiple editions in England, Revolutionary America, and the early United States.[3]

The Dying Negro was not purely the product of its authors' imaginations, and the newspaper report on which it was based, while brief, conveyed specific political messages to an eighteenth-century Anglo-American readership. For one thing, it noted that the West Indian owner of the unnamed enslaved man had brought him to London, where he subsequently ran away. The legal status of slavery was uncertain in England in the 1760s and 1770s, and other enslaved African Americans who had traveled with their masters to England had similarly sought their freedom.[4] Their aims intersected with the goals of activists who sought to challenge slavery's legalities in England. Second, the news story stated that the unnamed, formerly enslaved man ran away to be baptized so that he could marry his fellow servant, a white woman. Both baptism and wedlock were viewed as possible avenues for slaves to secure their freedom under English law.[5] In addition, while the suggestion of miscegenation and interracial marriage would have shocked North American audiences—where both were proscribed by law—mixed-race marriages, particularly among the working classes, were tolerated in England.[6] Before the wedding could take place, however, the enslaved man was seized by his master and confined to a ship in the Thames, where he awaited transport to certain slavery. "Preferring death to another voyage to America"—stoically choosing suicide over tyranny—he killed himself. The report specified that he used a firearm, but the authors of *The Dying Negro*, indulging in poetic license, armed their protagonist with a dagger, a classical and theatrical allusion to honorable suicide.[7] In print, the attack on slavery had begun.

Memorialized in Day and Bicknell's poem, the African's suicide ignited antislavery debate across the Anglo-Atlantic.[8] The authors recognized the political potential of their poem and quickly revised it accordingly; in 1775 they altered the first word of the opening line, substituting the comparatively mild opening word "Blest" with the more seriously militant term, "Arm'd with thy last sad gift—the pow'r to die"[9] Moreover, the newspaper report was used as the epigraph to the poem and endowed it with the force of authenticity. The poem positioned the enslaved man as a protagonist whose life history and inner thoughts were conveyed in epistolary form. Despite its structure, the poem was, in effect, a suicide note from the protagonist to his beloved. Inventive in its focus on the political implications of an actual suicide by an enslaved person, the poem fused antislavery politics, personal history, and emotional pathos to indict slavery.

In part, the power of *The Dying Negro* derived from the ways in which the protagonist's suicide revealed the paradoxes of slavery; the popular, legal, and cultural foundations for its influence had long been established across the eighteenth-century Anglo-Atlantic. As we have seen, acts of suicide by enslaved people highlighted the many contradictions of slavery. Slave suicide, both implicitly and directly, exposed not just the brutality of slavery but also the legal, social, and cultural inconsistencies of human bondage. *The Dying Negro* was successful in part because it capitalized on occasions of, themes in, and assumptions about suicide by enslaved people that were broadly familiar to Anglo-Americans.

The Dying Negro also foreshadowed themes of suicide in antislavery literature in the early national and antebellum United States. Read and circulated widely, accounts of slave suicide—whether penned by antislavery activists or written or related by formerly enslaved men and women themselves—were to become powerful testimonies to the injustices of slavery. Beginning with Olaudah Equiano, who quoted *The Dying Negro* in *The Interesting Narrative of the Life of Olaudah Equiano, the African* (1789), suicide remained a potent theme in the slave narratives published through the eve of the Civil War.[10] Accounts such as Charles Ball's *Slavery in the United States* (1837), Harriet Ann Jacobs's *Incidents in the Life of a Slave* Girl (1861), and Matty J. Jackson's autobiography, *The Story of Matty J. Jackson* (1866), used suicide to compellingly measure the human response to the multiple injustices of slavery. Even after slavery was abolished, some ex-slaves and their descendants interviewed in the 1930s related incidents of suicide in slavery. In each of these genres—poetry, memoirs, slave narratives, and WPA interviews—acts of suicide by enslaved people were powerful, visible reminders of the moral, political, and, with the formation of the United States, national wounds caused by slavery.

The implications of slave suicide in Revolutionary British North America and the early United States took on explicitly political meanings as antislavery activists, including former slaves, used accounts of self-destruction in order to attack slavery. Representations of slave suicide made evident the contradictions of property and personhood that had long lingered in Anglo-American settlements, legalities, literature, and culture. The task of former slaves and antislavery activists was to make the suicides of enslaved people meaningful on the national stage, both as a testimony to the wrongs of slavery and to illustrate the unfinished legacy of the American Revolution. Not all antislavery activists, however, shared the same aims. The earliest efforts, illustrated by *The Dying Negro,* used suicide to attack very specific aspects of slavery: the legal ambiguities of slave status in England, the ways in which slave owners existed above the law, or the brutality of the international slave trade.[11] These materials also asserted that slave suicide was a response to specific harms: imminent transport, the Middle Passage, and familial separation led enslaved men and women to commit despairing acts of self-destruction. In focusing on these and other precipitating moments, early antislavery activists challenged the long-standing disarticulation of slavery and suicide that had emerged in the Atlantic trade, was sustained by traders, masters, and lawmakers throughout the slave societies of British America, and persisted in prose and periodicals that circulated across the Anglo-Atlantic. Suicide, then, came to represent a host of specific injuries caused by slavery.

The earliest antislavery accounts of slave suicide were also politically powerful because they exposed the inconsistency between the ideology and rhetoric of democratic revolution and the institution of slavery. For some, slave suicide measured the denial of natural rights central to Revolutionary era claims for liberty or death. In their introduction to the 1775 edition of *The Dying Negro*, for example, the authors describe slavery as antithetical to the "rights of nature." Similarly, the 1776 edition pointed to the contradiction between American cries for liberty and their reliance on slavery and averred that there was no more ridiculous object than the "American patriot, signing resolutions of independency with one hand, and with the other brandishing a whip over his affrighted slaves."[12] If the rightful legacy of the Revolution was to resist arbitrary power, slaves, too, could choose "liberty or death." As other historians have demonstrated, this phrase, along with the idea that suicide was a tragic if principled alternative to the tyranny of slavery, resonated in antislavery writing up through the Civil War.[13]

Furthermore, these natural rights—both to enjoy liberty and, correspondingly, resist arbitrary authority—were understood differently in relationship to enslaved men and women. Just as notions of citizenship in the new United States were bifurcated along the lines of sex, the political meanings of suicide in antislavery literature were explicitly gendered.[14] The suicides of enslaved men, for instance, measured not only the denial of natural rights, but also the lack patriarchal privilege accorded to them. Indeed, this is seen in the newspaper account of the protagonist of *The Dying Negro*: slavery not only deprived him of his natural right to freedom, it also robbed him of the patriarchal privilege to marry. In contrast, the suicides of enslaved women gauged their lack of domestic stability and patriarchal protection. Much as in literary and dramatic treatments of slave suicide, men might heroically choose self-destruction in response to the tyranny of slavery, but women more often passively or unintentionally sought death. Early antislavery writing confirmed that the injustices of slavery differed for men and women, who, in turn, responded to them in distinctly gendered ways in the early Republic.

In contrast to the earliest antislavery activism, later antebellum abolitionism staked its claim on more radically expansive visions of racial equality as well as demands for slavery's ends. Yet even as the aims of antislavery activists diverged after 1820, suicide by enslaved people remained a persistent theme in abolitionist literature, and specifically in the narratives of former slaves. Despite the evolution in the scope and purposes of antislavery organizations, accounts of slave suicide remained linked, as they were in Revolutionary America, to themes of natural rights and differed along lines of gender.[15] They also continued to focus on pathos and suffering in which episodes of sale and separation, as well as incidents of physical and sexual brutality were precipitating events for suicidal ideation in ex-slave narratives. Because the accounts so prominent in antebellum abolitionism were written or related by former slaves—rather than by abolitionist onlookers, however well-intentioned—they carried the force of lived experience. Narrators revealed their own suicidal ideation, providing uniquely personal insight into the experience of slavery and self-destruction. They also commented on suicides by other slaves; in doing so, they revealed that self-destruction was deeply—and perhaps shockingly, for some readers—imbedded in slavery. The narratives of former slaves had an avowedly political purpose, in which suicide illustrated the multiple emotional, psychological, and physical tragedies of slavery.

The significance of suicide in antislavery politics, then, has a history that begins with the publication of *The Dying Negro* in 1773 and extends through the narratives of former slaves published in the antebellum period. In these works, self-destruction by enslaved people was used to represent weaknesses of the law and the cruelties of the slave trade, to illuminate contradictions in Americans' beliefs about natural rights and Christian morality, to expose a host of specific injuries experienced by enslaved people, and to demand human rights for them. Whatever their precise political intentions, accounts of slave self-destruction in antislavery literature also carried meanings related to gender, race, and nation. In order to fully capture the diverse political implications of slave self-destruction in antislavery efforts, I first examine why slave suicide became explicitly politically meaningful in the era of the American Revolution, and then analyze the implications of slave suicide in antislavery writing ranging from *The Dying Negro* in 1773 to the story of Anna's Leap, discussed in the preface, in 1815. I conclude by exploring the significances of slave suicide in antebellum slave narratives and interviews with ex-slaves from the 1930s. Despite differences in focus and changes over time, accounts, images, and representations of enslaved women and men who killed themselves as an alternative to enslavement were powerful and enduring forces for political change in the early United States.

In order to understand why the image of the suicidal slave was so compelling and persistent in antislavery writing, it is useful to consider the ways in which slave self-destruction animated philosophy, religion, law, and politics, both local and national, at the moment of the American founding. Most prominently and enduringly, suicide illustrated the slave's lack of natural rights. Key passages of political philosophy used suicide and slavery to illustrate the meaning of natural rights and liberty most relevant to the democratic revolution and originating documents of the United States. In *The Persian Letters* (1721), for instance, French philosophe Baron de Montesquieu accepted suicide as a legitimate expression of individual liberty. He concluded the volume with the suicide of a slave—Roxanna, a woman of the seraglio—who sought in death liberation from further sexual and patriarchal submission.[16] Similarly, English political theorist John Locke explicitly used the suicide of a slave to illustrate the meaning of natural rights and liberty. Although in one instance he wrote that individuals did not possess the liberty to destroy themselves, in another he averred that slavery was an exception to this rule.[17] As he argued, whenever a slave "finds [that] the hardship of his slavery out-weigh[s] the value of his life," he has the power "by resisting the will of his master, to draw on himself the death he desires." Enslaved people may of their own volition seek death to end the condition of slavery, a state that, in Locke's theoretical formulation, they endured as a penalty for some criminal act or fault of their own.[18] Suicide, then, constituted the slave's escape from arbitrary power.

In eighteenth-century colonial North America, the natural right to resist arbitrary power was given explicit political force in the language of democratic revolution. The rhetorical choice between liberty or death was a galvanizing idea during and after the Imperial Crisis, one invoked in the preface to *The Dying Negro*, which refers to slavery as the "rights of nature invaded."[19] Equiano, for instance, "called on death" to free him from slavery and take him to a place, quoting from *The Dying Negro*, "where slaves are free, and men oppress no more."[20] Into the antebellum years, black activists like David Walker, Frederick Douglass, and Henry Highland Garnet would use the phrase to illustrate the national crime of slavery, defending the legitimacy of slave death by suicide as a political and moral choice.[21] Those who advocated liberty or death, in effect, overlooked some of the subtleties of Locke's formulation in favor of his main point: suicide was a legitimate choice in response to the tyranny of arbitrary power for slaves; since they could not choose liberty, they are permitted to choose death.[22] The Revolutionary generation's use of Locke, especially his formulation of a right to be free from arbitrary power, might have been an abstraction.[23] Nonetheless, the idea that liberty meant resisting tyranny—even unto death—articulated in the political philosophy and rhetoric that influenced the American founding would be particularly salient for abolitionists and slaves in the early United States.

If the image of slave suicide was effective for antislavery activists because of its resonance with natural rights philosophy, it also gained force from religious and moral objections to slavery. As early as 1740, George Whitefield protested the sinfulness and injuriousness of slavery. In a letter to the "Inhabitants of Maryland, Virginia, North and South Carolina" published in the *Pennsylvania Gazette,* Whitefield refused to comment on whether or not slavery was "lawful," but he was certain that it was "sinful." What is more, the clergyman continued, "considering what usage" enslaved people commonly met with, he wondered "that there were not more instances of self-murder among the negroes, or that they have not more frequently rose up in arms against their owners." In his letter, Whitefield suggests that suicide by slaves was part of a holy war, one in which suicide and revolt by enslaved people were justifiable responses to their unchristian treatment, to the sin of slavery.[24] Traditional Christian treatises on suicide argued that self-destructive acts by soldiers in battle and religious martyrs were exempted from definitions of suicide.[25] Later, abolitionists and the African American press would indeed frame the sectional crisis as precisely a kind of holy war, one in which enslaved people's suffering and deaths, including those that were self-inflicted, exemplified martyrdom.[26]

If representations of slave suicide contradicted ideas about natural rights and religiosity in the new United States, they also clashed with the emerging cultural ethos of Anglo-American sensibility. Accounts of slave suicide stressed emotion and sensation: self-destruction was fostered by the cruelties of the slave trade, the violence of slave owners, and the brutalities of labor regimes; all of these revealed the acute human suffering produced by the institution of slavery.[27] By the era of the Imperial Crisis, some of these kinds of representations were front-page news that commented on local politics, even in southern papers. For instance, in 1773, the story of the suicide of "poor Hampshire" appeared in the *Virginia Gazette* as a means of revealing the ruthless, if completely legal, harm that he had endured at the hands of his owner, named only by the initials, R.M. According to the story, R.M.

had heaped a series of increasingly violent punishments on Hampshire; the slave endured ear cutting, castration, whipping, and dismemberment of his legs. Although it seems inconceivable, Hampshire managed to run away. Upon recapture, the article noted, he "chose to die" rather than "perish by his master's hand," a choice of suicide over tyrannical authority. Confined to a not-too-secure jail, he lit the structure and faced a fiery death.

The newspaper's explicit description of the suicide of the martyr-like Hampshire took aim at the cruelty of his master, but it also indicted the failure of the law, a key theme hammered on by early antislavery activists. The piece averred that even a slave like Hampshire, who suffered at the hands of his "tyrant" owner, ought to have enjoyed the protection of the legal system. R.M had "imbrue[ed] his hands with the blood of his miserable slaves" and ought to have been "brought to punishment" for his crimes. Despite this failure of the law, one way or another, the article warned, the owner would be ultimately punished by God, who would rest his judgment on R.M, despite the fact that he had eluded the "force of law."[28] To be a slave meant to exist outside of legal protection; because he was denied the law's protection, Hampshire's act of self-destruction was a reasonable response to slavery. His story captured the multiple political meanings of slave suicide in early America. His suicide highlighted the natural right to resist arbitrary authority, the sinfulness of slavery, the cruelty of slave owners, and the feebleness of the law and local authorities to either protect the slave or punish the master.

Slave suicide took on a prominent role in national politics in the immediate post-Revolutionary period as well, as can be seen in negotiations following the Treaty of Paris in 1783, which ended the American Revolution. When General George Washington argued that Britain was bound by the terms of the treaty to return those slaves who had escaped or were seized by the British to their American masters, Governor General Sir Guy Carleton refused. When Washington repeated his demand, Carleton replied that the treaty terms did not apply to slaves because they were, in fact, no longer "property": they were free men and women and to return them to their masters would be as good as killing them. As Carleton explained,

> a great number of those negroes would have conveyed themselves away and been secretly assisted in so doing, on the common principles of humanity in spite of his utmost diligence and authority. A further number, possibly very great, would have laid violent hands on themselves and, in all likelihood, have destroyed their wives and children rather than have been thrown upon a fate probably not less severe.[29]

Those who threatened suicide, according to Carleton, were all men from British North America who were prepared to kill themselves rather than return to slavery. What is more, the men also asserted that they would slay their wives and children, implying that as heads of households—subjects bearing natural rights—they controlled the fate of their dependents. While we do not know whether these men used the language of "liberty or death," Carleton implies as much when he notes that they would choose to annihilate themselves and their families rather than face a fate "probably not less severe." In short, reenslavement meant death; suicide, in a tragic irony, was liberty.

The threats of the enslaved men, as recounted in this exchange, echoed connections among slavery, natural rights, and patriarchal privilege that had been popularized, as we have seen, by the play *Oroonoko*. Carleton's exchange also relied on the image of the heroic slave drawn from that play as well as from other, equally well-known, antislavery writings like *The Dying Negro*. The exchange also echoed experience: throughout eighteenth-century British America, slaves threatened suicide, and they made good on those threats, as Washington, a Virginia slave owner, quite likely knew. Carleton's warning was probably partly true. It was also partly rhetorical, built on the natural rights talk of the American founding as well as on popular images of the suicides of noble slaves.

One could simply write off these exchanges as the political positioning of powerful men, neither of whom had the interests of the former slaves at heart, but the evidence suggests that the black loyalists had urged Carleton to lead an army and reopen hostilities. At least according to one reading, they declared that following him, even into death, was preferable to returning to the United States and living as slaves. In effect, they used the language of the American founding to question its legitimacy, since slavery remained intact in much of the new nation.[30] What is clear, however, is that the figure of the slave who chose self-destruction over slavery was culturally familiar and politically potent; slave suicide powerfully exposed contradictions embodied in the American founding. In that sense, the implications of suicide in slavery had become revolutionary.[31]

Beginning with *The Dying Negro,* antislavery poetics drew on all of these themes in order to attack slavery. Regardless of the specific timing or changing aims and constituencies of antislavery activism, suicide remained an especially potent symbol of the gendered injustices of slavery. The self-destructive acts of enslaved people illustrated the contradictions between natural rights, arbitrary power, and slavery and exposed the paradoxes of slaveholding in a Christian republic. Slaves' acts of suicide revealed the fundamental cruelty at the heart of slavery, a horror that was incompatible with an enlightened, rational sensibility, and reflected the failure of the rule of law that undergirded democratic republics, including the United States.

While philosophy, religion, cultural, and national politics fueled the moral meanings and political efficacy of slave suicide in ways that abolitionists would find useful, they, of course, coexisted alongside negative assessments of race and self-destruction. In 1785, the *Pennsylvania Evening Herald* published a series of anecdotes that reflected a confluence of ideas about slavery and suicide. The first item captured the fact that the Revolution and the rise of antislavery crusades had not as yet slowed the commerce in slaves, observing the notable prices for "new negroes" in Charleston, 45 to 50 pounds sterling cash. The second item announced the formation of a society to promote the manumission of slaves. The third and most developed item lamented the African influence on the suicide of free, presumably white Americans. It was remarkable in its assessment that Christianity was not civilizing slaves as much as the implied barbarism of slave religion had, in fact, not only infected free white Americans, but was an alarming agent in their degeneration. As the paper stated it,

> Our last paper contained some reflections on the enormity and actual prevalence of suicide—sorry we are to find that some more infatuated wretches have in different parts put a period to their existence, among whom was a Mr. Parker, a merchant of Charleston, who shot himself with a pistol on the 7th instant. It appears, that in the New England states, where this fatal delusion rages with the most fatal violence, many persons have lapsed into such a horrible system as to be firmly persuaded that when taken away from their country, they shall return thereto by killing themselves. This creed, after having abandoned Christianity, they have adopted from the *refined* negroes.[32]

The economics of slave sale, the politics of abolitionism, and racialized beliefs about the meaning of suicide were compressed together in this short series of items. In context, these anecdotes signaled the collision course between the slave trade and antislavery projects; more importantly, they underscored a common knowledge of—and articulated a disdain for—African and African American beliefs that transmigration followed death, even when it was self-inflicted.[33]

The exchanges between Carleton and Washington and the pieces in the *Pennsylvania Evening Herald* reflect the competing political implications of slave suicide in the early United States. On the one hand slave self-destruction was a justifiable act of liberty or death; on the other, it exerted a degenerating influence on the religiosity of European Americans. The work of the earliest antislavery activists and enactment of gradual emancipation statutes in the post-Revolutionary North had transformed the political and social landscape there and intensified the perception that slavery contradicted the espoused ideals of the United States.[34] Yet slavery as a legal, political, and social institution in the South remained unchanged. Regardless of region, moreover, European-American beliefs that slavery was an immoral system coexisted with their assumptions about the innate inferiority of blacks.[35] For instance, a petition made to the Virginia legislature in the wake of the Revolution acknowledged that blacks had been debased by slavery but that gradual manumission might be a means of improving them.[36] In an odd dovetailing of the aims of pro- and antislavery advocates, these denunciations based on race, as David Brion Davis has argued, became the "central excuse for slavery" for proslavery advocates.[37] The *Pennsylvania Evening Herald*'s caustic reference to "*refined* negroes" reflects how natural rights arguments against slavery competed with negative assessments of Africans and African Americans as a race and fears over cultural contamination.[38] These rival viewpoints coexisted up through the eve of the Civil War, in part through the figure of the self-destructive slave. Nowhere are these oppositions better seen than in the history and reception of *The Dying Negro*, which fused these multiple implications of suicide into one of the earliest and most influential statements against slavery.

The immediate inspiration for *The Dying Negro* was a story printed in several London newspapers in May 1773. As recounted at the beginning of this chapter, the news item focused on an American slave who had failed in his attempt to seek freedom (and marriage) in London and killed himself as he awaited transport back to the colonies. Three months later, the story crossed the Atlantic to America, where it was reprinted verbatim in a variety of papers, including the *Virginia Gazette*.[39] Printed editions of the poem, which appeared later that same year, featured a version of the original news item as an epigraph or advertisement. The poem was resoundingly popular on both sides of the Atlantic. It was reviewed favorably in the *Gentleman's Magazine* and *Monthly Review* and continued to be published into the nineteenth century.[40] The poem was also the apparent inspiration for several antislavery songs (see figure 6.1).[41] While these songs capitalized on the popularity of the poem by borrowing its title, the lyrics did not actually reference direct suicide but did present the slave protagonist as welcoming death. In one version, the chorus refrains that "the strong arm of Death is the arm of a Friend."[42]

6.1. Songs were written using *The Dying Negro* as their title. The lyrics elided references to suicide or self-destruction and described death as a welcome friend. Source: Music Collections, The British Library Board, London. *The Dying Negro: A Much Admired New Song, By Mr. Hook.* Published by Him at his Musical Circulating Library (Dublin, 1800).

The Dying Negro used the guise of an autobiographical epistle, but its protagonist did not, of course, compose the poem. Yet like later eighteenth-century slave narratives, most notably the account of Olaudah Equiano, *The Dying Negro* recounts the protagonist's African origins and his capture by Europeans before describing the cruelty of separation from his homeland and the brutality of labor regimes in the Americas.[43] After suffering these hardships, however, he sees a chance for liberty when he travels with his owner to London, where, once on British soil, as he believes is his right, he runs away to claim his freedom. According a contemporaneous issue of the *Virginia Gazette*, the belief that there was no slavery in England was "prevalent" among American slaves.[44] In order to allow readers to understand the protagonist's choice of death over slavery, the first chord *The Dying Negro* strikes is the denial of natural rights: the unnamed slave has the right to chose death over the tyranny of slavery. As he explains, slavery is an erasure of personhood: slavery is like "becoming a thing without a name" in a traffic directed by those who lust for gold. He has a natural right to refuse the tyranny constituted by that erasure.[45] According to Brycchan Carey, this was "probably the first time many people had come across" a natural rights argument against slavery.[46]

In addition to the political currency of natural rights philosophy, *The Dying Negro* struck a note with a religious readership as well. The poem treats the protagonist's suicide as a moral response to the sinfulness of slavery.[47] Civilized readers were to fear God's "dreadful mercy"; and yet the unnamed slave's power to die was depicted as divinely sanctioned. "Flashing lightning" is a "dreadful sign" that God approves of the suicide. In the last stanza, the slave notes that it was at God's "great call" that he has "spilt" his being.[48] The idea that God approved of suicide was a radical one in terms of Anglo-American law and religion. In this sense, the writers framed the slave as a religious martyr who died in the service of a greater good. How this played with an Anglo-American audience, however, is less than clear. In England, where the poem was first published, the traditional penalties for suicide—forfeiture, profane burial, postmortem desecration—persisted longer than elsewhere in Europe, well into the nineteenth century, despite escalating arguments for decriminalization.[49] Criminal suicide remained on the books in some North American jurisdictions until after the American Revolution.[50]

At the same time, some phrases in the poem echoed the traditional religious condemnation of suicide. Portions of the poem, for instance, have double meanings that reveal tensions between longstanding beliefs that suicide was the worst of deaths and God's apparent sanction for this particular slave's act of self-destruction. The slave imagines a "wretch's grave" upon which "serpents hiss and night-shade blacken," suggesting revulsion and punishment for suicide. He also protests being "dragg'd" across the ocean, which may have alluded to the customary dragging of the bodies of suicides.[51] In the end, however, and as is made clear in the illustration that accompanied the poem, *The Dying Negro* presents the slave's self-destruction as an act that has God's full approval.

In addition to singling out slavery's denial of natural rights and its sinfulness, *The Dying Negro* also indicted the failure of the law to protect the unnamed protagonist. The immediate legal context for this idea was the famous *Somerset v. Stewart* (1772) case, in which abolitionists used the ambiguity of slave status in England to raise larger issues about slavery.[52] It is worth noting that nearly seventy years before *Somerset* was litigated, Virginia lawmakers had given this jurisdictional issue some thought. In 1705 they decreed that a slave's "being in England, shall not be sufficient to discharge" her or him from slavery, but it was unclear what force, if any, this law had in Great Britain.[53] At any rate, the lawsuit centered on the status of James Somerset, a man born in Africa and forcibly imported to Virginia in 1749, where Charles Stewart purchased him. In 1769, Somerset attended his owner on a trip to London; after arrival, he ran away but was recaptured by Stewart, who intended to ship him to Jamaica. Abolitionists interceded with a writ of habeas corpus on behalf of Somerset, and his case was remanded to the King's Bench, which allowed that slavery was not supported by English common law and, therefore, enslaved people could not be treated as property in or removed from England against their will.[54] The decision was followed closely in British North America; within months accounts of the case were reprinted in newspapers ranging from Massachusetts to Virginia, with widely varying accuracy.[55] *Somerset* stirred debate in the colonies as well as in the metropolitan center of government, and British American planters were anxious to clarify the status of slavery in England.[56]

By including the news item as its epigraph, *The Dying Negro* directly pointed to the *Somerset* decision—which should have protected the protagonist—and thereby exposed the glaring failure of the law as a precipitating factor in his suicide. Despite *Somerset*, the slave protagonist existed without legal protection and was subjected to the arbitrary authority of his owner; in response, he chose death over the tyranny of slavery. Slave owners who read the news item on which *The Dying Negro* was based may have felt reassured by the knowledge that the terms of *Somerset* were basically unenforced. If the law in England had any potency with regard to slavery, this unnamed enslaved man would not have been carried on board ship to be sent back to British North American slavery. This was precisely the political point that the poem's writers hoped to raise.

The cruelty of slavery was also measured through the protagonist's loss of companionship. Like natural rights, sentiments and feelings were understood as an essential part of the self in society; and the loss of companionship was expected to be an empathetic point of connection with an enlightened, sensible readership.[57] Having suffered through capture and enslavement, the protagonist experienced a brief moment of freedom in the form of romantic love, only to find himself barred from marriage and facing a return to slavery in America. If slavery robbed him of liberty—of self-ownership—it also denied to him the companionship of marriage—a further spur to suicidal despair. For a readership of largely free individuals, this personal loss may have induced a large share of sympathy. As the protagonist states:

> Ere yet this hand a life of torment close,
> And end by one determin'd stroke my woes,
> Is there a fond regret, which moves my mind
> To pause, and cast a ling'ring look behind?
> —O my lov'd bride!—for I have call'd thee mine,
> Dearer than life, whom I with life resign,
> For thee ev'n here this faithful heart shall glow,
> A pang shall rend me, and a tear shall flow.—

For all of its protests against slavery, however, the poem stops short of demanding racial equality because the death of the protagonist forecloses the possibility of a racially mixed marriage. The newspaper accounts identify the protagonist's betrothed as a white woman, and the poem describes her as a "gentle virgin" with "glowing features," "winning softness," and "languid eyes." Their relationship was depicted as companionate: she did not despise the enslaved man by whose side she performed domestic labor but, rather, was his "mistress and a friend."[58] Antislavery accounts often linked the denial of natural rights and patriarchal privilege with the loss of romantic and marital love. Few of them, however, suggested that those affections should cross the color line.

Perhaps this in part accounts for the circulation, reprinting, and popularity of *The Dying Negro*: the death of the protagonist does not ask readers to imagine a sexually consummated, racially mixed marriage. *The Dying Negro* may have linked slave suicide to Christian objections to slavery, natural rights philosophy, and enlightenment sentiment, but it also reflected prevailing legal and cultural prohibitions against love and marriage across the color line. As Philip Gould writes, having achieved the "moral high ground," the convention of African suicide "manages cultural fears of degeneration" through the death of the protagonist.[59] On one hand, suicide in early antislavery activism is used as an index of injustice but, on the other, it does not imagine a society characterized by racial coexistence.

In all of these ways, *The Dying Negro* makes the act of suicide by an enslaved man into a politically principled, spiritually sanctioned, morally laudable, and emphatically sentimental act. It drew on classical models of heroism and ideals of masculine virtue and affirmed a natural rights understanding of human freedom with which slavery was incompatible. The protagonist's self-inflicted death was a metaphor of liberation, as first Locke and then the American Revolutionaries had affirmed.[60] The poem also appealed to spiritual values with God's approbation of the protagonist's act of self-destruction and shocked readers' sensibilities through its depictions of suffering and the cruelty of lost dreams of domestic stability. The protagonist's heroism and endurance of distress are meant to elicit the readers' empathy for his act of self-destruction and, at the same time, his suicide contains fears about racial mixing.

The illustrations that accompanied *The Dying Negro* and other antislavery literature encapsulate these tensions between honorable resistance to tyranny and assumptions about slave inferiority. The various images feature a man who, whether he is depicted on the African savannah or in the hold of a ship, wears a clout or loincloth. The depictions emphasize the classical physical perfection of the male form; his musculature reflects his strength and telegraphs his virtue. The artist also changed the instrument of suicide for dramatic effect, depicting the use of a dagger, which was likely an allusion to Cato.[61] In the first example (figure 6.2), the figure is set against a landscape that features other images of the cruelties of slavery—separation of mother and child, labor regimes, corporal punishment—that appeal to the sentiments of the onlookers. The second version (figure 6.3) was more direct and radical in its indictment. Against the figure of the heroic male, in contrast, allusions to commerce in the background connect the slave trade and suicide. The deck of the ship is visible along with ordnance, store, and crew; the Union Jack flies in the background, while next to the slave, there is evidence of the poetic epistle, his suicide note. These elements both contextualize suicide as part of the slave trade and allude to the rationality of the slave who provides a written account of his reasons for destroying himself. In contrast, the image that accompanied John Gorton's poem, *Tuba to*

THE

DYING NEGRO,

A

P O E M.

The THIRD EDITION, Corrected and Enlarged.

LONDON:

Printed for W. FLEXNEY, opposite Gray's-Inn-Gate, Holborn; J. WILKIE, in St. Paul's Church-Yard; and J. ROBSON, in New Bond-Street.

M.DCC.LXXV.

[PRICE ONE SHILLING AND SIX-PENCE.]

6.2. Thomas Day's poem sentimentalized the theme of slave suicide and enjoyed wide publication across the Anglo-Atlantic beginning in 1773. Source: Thomas Day, *The Dying Negro, a Poetical Epistle supposed to be written by a Black (Who lately shot himself on board a vessel in the river Thames;) to his intended Wife* (London, 1775). This item is reproduced by permission of The Huntington Library, San Marino, California.

Sebal: The Negro Suicide (figure 6.4), published in 1797, reverts to a more pastoral setting.

The images that capture the enslaved male figure in the moment of choosing death over slavery are distinctive compared to other representations of male suicides from the period. For instance, Peyron's portrayal of the death of Seneca (1773) is much less a study in physicality, although he too is depicted with a flowing wrap around his groin. Seneca's suicide takes place in an interior setting, accompanied by supporters and mourners (figure 6.5). In contrast, *The Dying Negro* stands outside, in a landscape, alone, a tableau

6.3. *The Dying Negro*, frontispiece, 1793. Source: Thomas Day, *The Dying Negro, a Poetical Epistle supposed to be written by a Black (Who lately shot himself on board a vessel in the river Thames;) to his intended Wife* (London, 1773). This item is reproduced by permission of The Library Company of Philadelphia.

that persisted into the nineteenth century, as we see in the 1838 illustration of the suicide of the slave Paul, who hung himself with twisted hickory bark (figure 6.6). The physical beauty and emotional expressiveness of *The Dying Negro* figures is meant to reflect the courage, virtue, and morality of slave self-destruction. In contrast, Paul's mangled body, a testimony to his suffering, hangs inertly. He is depicted as beyond resistance, and his corpse is left hanging—a punishment for suicide—until the "flesh fell from the bones or was torn off by birds."[62] Antislavery illustrations like *The Dying Negro, Tubal to Seba,* and *The Suicide of Paul* variously align the enslaved male subjects with nature, savagery, and violence, even as they convey admiration for their classical form and principled aims and sympathize with their suffering.

Well into the early nineteenth century, the figure of the virtuous slave who chose an honorable death in resistance to tyranny was gendered male in antislavery writing. For instance in 1803, an anonymously published pamphlet, *Reflections on Slavery, With Recent Evidence of its Inhumanity,* tells the story of the enslaved Romain and his unnamed wife who had escaped from Saint Domingue to North America. Their owner intended to ship them back

6.4. *Tubal to Seba: The Negro Suicide*. The suicide of enslaved men was a persistent theme in antislavery poetics. Source: General Reference Collection, The British Library Board, London. John Gorton, *Tubal to Seba: The Negro Suicide* (London, 1797).

6.5. Depictions of the suicides of classical male figures share some features with those of slaves but typically frame their subjects within doors amidst a commiserating community. Here Seneca catches his blood over a tub, while others weep, while, in contrast, suicidal slaves spill their blood on the earth in isolation. Source: *Seneca Committing Suicide in a Bath*, J. F. P. Peyron, 1773. This item is reproduced by permission of Wellcome Library, London.

to the Caribbean, and with harsh memories of slavery, the couple plan to save their child from such a fate; his wife escapes with the infant and Romain faces shipment to the Caribbean alone. As he contemplated this situation, Romain became "maddened," "rendered desperate," and "complicated by misery." With his "faculties benumbed by oppression," he seized a pruning knife and slashed his throat three times, the repetition fostered by his "dread" that a spark of life should remain and he be revived.[63]

The illustration that accompanied the pamphlet offers a contrast to *The Dying Negro* because the landscape in *Reflections on Slavery* is urban. That visual fact indicted the domestic slave trade and illustrated its troubling implications for its readership in the United States.[64] Moreover, the centrality of commerce to Romain's story can also be seen in the image that accompanied the pamphlet. The ordinary street scene, with its orderly geometric panes of urban architecture—bricks, panes, shutters—frames the separation of the family (figure 6.7a). In contrast to *The Dying Negro,* here the enslaved individuals are rendered in middle-class clothing in order to emphasize their respectability. The violent self-destruction of Romain was brought on as a result of the slave commerce, itself symbolized by the largest element in the image, the carriage awaiting its human cargo.

However, if suicide symbolized the fact that enslaved men unjustly existed outside of the newly minted social contract, enslaved women often existed only on the margins of the earliest antislavery literature. The illustration for *Reflections on Slavery* visually gestures to this gendered difference: Romain's wife and child literally depart from the narrative; the wife is at the edge of the frame, her fate secondary to its message (figure 6.7b). Similarly, in the 1770s, Abbé Raynal recast the Caribbean-based "A Kind of Wild Tragedy," discussed in the last chapter, for antislavery purposes. The unnamed enslaved woman who appears in the story is not the subject of explicit remark, save for her beauty and obedience to men.[65]

In these early examples of antislavery writing, enslaved women are either absent from the narrative (*Dying Negro*), dead ("Wild Tragedy"), or disappearing (*Reflections*). When antislavery poetics focused on women, they often centered on themes of dependency and possession: that is, to whom, other than the slaveholder, does the enslaved woman belong? In *Scene in*

6.6. The *American Anti-Slavery Almanac for 1838* illustrated the suicide of the slave Paul, who, according to fellow slave Charles Ball, had "suffered so much in slavery that he chose to encounter the hardships and perils of a runaway. He exposed himself, in gloomy forests, to cold and starvation, and finally hung himself, that he might not again fall into the hands of his tormentor." Source: Nathaniel Southard, ed., *American Anti-Slavery Almanac for 1838* (Boston, 1838). This item is reproduced by permission of The Huntington Library, San Marino, California.

6.7.a–b Humanitas, *Reflections on Slavery; with Recent Evidence of its Inhumanity*. Philadelphia, 1803. Source: This item is reproduced by permission of The Library Company of Philadelphia.

the West Indies (1783), for instance, an enslaved couple seeks to leave the bitterness of slavery. As Francis calls Myrtilla to join him, she hesitates, "I am that cruel white-man's slave by right,/And dare I wander in your arms away?" Convinced that she belongs to her beloved, she joins him and together they "headlong plung'd" off a cliff.[66] Another early example, *Avenia* (1805), relates the story of an enslaved African princess who plunged from a cliff after having been raped by her master. Her suicide became the occasion for a revolt of other slaves who seek revenge for the violations, both rape and enslavement, that she suffered. The subtitle of the poem refers to the "Infringement" on the "Rights of Man"; those rights will have been attained only when women like Avenia are protected from the slave trade.[67]

In early republican antislavery print, representations of enslaved men's and women's suicides paralleled the gender bifurcation found in theories of natural rights and the privileges and practices associated with male citizenship in the wake of the American, French, and Haitian revolutions. In the era of democratic revolutions, rights accrued to free male subjects; in antislavery literature, the argument is that at least some if not all of these rights ought to accrue to all men, privileges that depend in part upon the subordination of women subjects. The gender dynamics in early antislavery literature correspond to larger political developments under way in eighteenth-century America, especially the exclusion of women from the public sphere. As Mary Beth Norton has argued, the proper place for eighteenth-century Anglo-American women was "positioned apart from the public realm."[68] By coding enslaved women's suicides to conform to this cultural model, antislavery poetics aimed to reach a wider audience.

The emphasis on female dependency, domesticity, and passivity, however, did not prevent accounts of enslaved women's suicides from emerging as powerful forces for political change in the early United States. A turning point in this regard was the story of Anna's leap in 1815, recounted in the preface (figure 6.8). Here too there is a pattern: in contrast to men, accounts of women's suicides were depicted as less intentional—they leap out of windows rather than draw knives across their throats. The account of Anna's attempted suicide was used in an effort to redirect the national conversation on slavery and became a local and national controversy after abolitionist Jesse Torrey interviewed her in 1816. Her story was published as part of Torrey's exposé on slavery in Washington, D.C.; it ignited a "national debate" and created a "national consciousness" about the human damage done by slave trafficking in the nation's capital.[69] Specifically, that damage was to motherhood, as Anna's story made clear. She explained that she jumped out the window to avoid being sold to Georgia and separated from her husband and children: "They brought me away with two of my children, and would'nt let me see my husband—they did'nt sell my husband, and I didn't want to go."[70] She did not say that she was trying to kill herself; perhaps such a conscious act of self-destruction would have appeared less feminine. Rather, her account emphasizes the unintentionality of her act. She was not attempting a *felo de se* or deliberately trying to kill herself, but, rather, she leapt out of the window because she was confused

6.8. This illustration, which appeared in the antislavery tract *A Portraiture of Domestic Slavery in the United States*, focuses on the separation of mother and child that led the former to suicide. Source: Jesse Torrey, *A Portraiture of Domestic Slavery in the United States* (Philadelphia, 1817). This item is reproduced by permission of The Huntington Library, San Marino, California.

and distracted. These words illustrated a *non compos mentis* state, an "alienation of mind" that rendered her "frantic or destitute of the use of reason."[71] Yet if depictions of enslaved women's suicides proved to be political powerful, this would be the model that they would follow.

Anna's attempt at suicide stirred Virginia representative John Randolph, a supporter of slavery, to argue for the formation of a committee to investigate the "inhuman and illegal" slave trade in Washington, D.C. Earlier legislation from 1794 and 1812 had prohibited the sale of slaves in the nation's capital, but traders regularly sold slaves in Alexandria and housed them in Washington taverns or hotels. The large numbers of slaves marching through the city indicated a thriving slave market.[72] Randolph was in a delicate position because he supported slavery, and his speech made it clear that any prospective legislation would not compromise the slave owners' rights to their human property. However, since most slaves brought through the capital were either purchased from "cruel masters" or kidnapped, or were free blacks who had been illegally sold into slavery, the city had become a "depot" for "nefarious traffic." Much of his argument—his speech did not mention Anna by name, but the committee also heard Torrey recount her story in his deposition—focused on slaves who were separated from spouses and children.[73]

Although Randolph's committee achieved no concrete results, Anna's story and others like it put forth by the first generations of American antislavery activists in the wake of the American Revolution raised troubling doubts about the moral economy of slavery and, more particularly, the consequences of the domestic traffic in human beings throughout the United States.[74] In the future, slave narratives would not be limited to the "struggle of men throwing off their chains," but they also addressed slavery's impact on domestic relations, and, specifically, on women.[75] Thenceforth, for both enslaved men and women, suicide came to illustrate the injustices of slavery along distinctly gendered lines. For men, self-destruction illustrated the denial of natural rights and the weaknesses of the law; for women, suicide exemplified a lack of patriarchal protection. Yet in the hands of antislavery activists, these gendered representations of self-inflicted death would powerfully illustrate the suffering caused by slavery to increasingly larger audiences, particularly as women assumed a central place in antislavery efforts in the second decade of the nineteenth century.[76] By the 1830s, abolitionist reformers like William Lloyd Garrison consciously worked to recruit women to the antislavery movement.[77]

The story of Anna can be seen as a transitional moment in the politics of slave suicides in abolitionist print. As antislavery constituencies, aims, and tactics evolved in the early United States, so did the movement's use of suicide by enslaved people. The earliest phase of Anglo-American abolitionism, from roughly 1773 through the 1820s, used suicide to expose the injustices of the Atlantic and domestic slave trades. Initially, the antislavery movement comprised an elite, mostly male group of activists. Their tactics were directed largely at raising legal questions over the free status of individuals, as in the case of protagonist of *The Dying Negro*; attacking the transatlantic slave trade in depictions like those offered by Equiano; depicting the cruelty of masters or the sinfulness of slavery as in Hampshire's story; or invoking the suffering wrought by domestic sale, as in Torrey's account of Anna's leap. This tradition of antislavery reform did not always attack slavery as an institution; it was gradualist and conservative.[78] Beginning in the 1820s, in contrast, formerly enslaved and other free black women and men, as well as white women, entered the ranks of the abolitionists in increasing numbers and changed the nature of antislavery print culture, including its treatment of suicide.[79] In addition, after Nat Turner's rebellion in 1831 and particular in the 1840s, a radical wing of antislavery activists emerged, demanding an immediate end to slavery. They declared a "virtual war" in which slavery, rather than suicide, was a "sin against God and a Crime against man."[80] Suicide by enslaved people continued to measure the multiple injustices of slavery, but the shift from the imperial to the national stage and the evolution of abolitionism altered the political and gendered implications of suicide by enslaved people.[81]

Of profound importance to post-1820s abolitionism were narratives written by formerly enslaved men and women that focused on the lived experience of slavery—and suicide—as a principal means of igniting the antislavery cause. Slave narratives had their genesis in the eighteenth century. Over sixty-five autobiographies were published in separate book or pamphlet form between 1740 and 1865, but the genre grew in numbers, scale, and scope after 1840.[82] The focus on the experiences of enslaved men and women is evident from their titles: words like *History*, *Narrative*, and *Incidents* conveyed the emphasis on the life stories of slaves. Promoted and published by antislavery organizations, slave narratives were widely read across and outside of the United States. For instance, Olaudah Equiano's *Interesting Narrative* (1789) went through thirty-six editions by 1850; Mary Prince's *History of Mary Prince* went into three printings when it was issued in 1831; similarly, the *Narrative of the Life of Frederick Douglass, an American Slave, Written By Himself* sold 30,000 copies between 1845, when it was first published, and 1850.[83] The authenticity of life history appealed to nineteenth-century readers who understood that the narratives divulged the consciousness of formerly enslaved American men and women and revealed the "truth" about slavery. In particular, the "epic character of individuals who first *willed* their own freedom, then *wrote* the story proved irresistible" to readers across the United States and Great Britain.[84] Collectively, pre–Civil War slave narratives form a history of slavery from the viewpoint of enslaved people themselves. Despite often being formulaic parables of good and evil that served as "effective abolitionist propaganda," these life stories were intended to expose the injustices of slavery, including slaves' reasons for suicide.[85]

While antebellum slave narratives shared experiential and ideological continuities with their Revolutionary-era forebears, they also fundamentally changed the basis for understanding suicide in slavery. First, slave narratives treated suicide as only one in a range of possible events in the lives of enslaved people. As in earlier antislavery poetics, self-destruction measured the deprivation of natural rights endured by slaves, emphasized their suffering, and exposed the incompatibility of slavery with an enlightened Christian democratic republic, often through distinctly gendered lenses. However, because the narratives embedded suicide in the extraordinary and everyday experiences of former southern slaves, discussions of self-destruction were given more authenticity and power than found in earlier accounts and pointed to the quotidian experience of suicide as a fundamental part of slavery. Earlier antislavery literature like *The Dying Negro* asked readers to contemplate a single, seemingly isolated and limited act of self-destruction. Second, antebellum slave narratives provided a crucial shift in perspective because they presented accounts of suicide from the enslaved individual's viewpoint. In the earliest examples of abolitionist literature, white authors imagined or transcribed the subjectivities of enslaved protagonists. Framing through the viewpoints of often anonymous sympathetic onlookers, rather than through enslaved subjects themselves, obscured the distinction between the enslaved person as human subjects and objects of pity. In contrast to the earliest depictions of suicide in antislavery materials, those of the later period gave representations of self-destruction the political force of lived experience.

Third, and perhaps most important, slave narratives reframed the meaning of self-destruction in slavery through the triumph of the narrator. In the earliest examples of abolitionist poetics, the suicides of enslaved men and women brought an end to the story, foreclosing the possibility of black freedom, not to mention equality or citizenship. Even Anna, who was disabled by her fall, exists more as an object of curiosity than as a free subject, although her story is certainly given moral weight through her survival. In contrast, in the antebellum narratives of former slaves, protagonists prevailed by escaping slavery and telling their stories. Slave narratives include admissions of suicidal thoughts and descriptions of self-destructive actions, but precisely because the narrator survived, suicide does not forestall—as it did in Revolutionary-era abolitionist poetics—the possibility of freedom, the prospect of citizenship and racial equality, or the hope of domestic stability.

The framework of survival allowed narrators not only to bear witness to their own thoughts of self-destruction, but also to expose and memorialize the suicides of other enslaved people. Narrators made suicide a point of reference for conveying the brutal realities, emotional vicissitudes, and political injustices of slavery. This can be seen in their use of specific circumstances or themes in relationship to suicide. Along with the African American press, Mark S. Schantz argues, slave narratives used suicide in order to "identify specific features of the slave system that critics found reprehensible." Similarly, Richard Bell maintains that beatings, sale, and escape were three of the "most generic scenes" in abolitionist print that were linked to suicide. While these and other themes suited the avowedly political agenda of abolitionism, it is also the case, as David Silkenat observes, that these accounts reflect former slaves' attitudes toward suicide.[86]

Despite their formulaic qualities, however, the narratives of former slaves drew on the long history of suicide in slavery, embedded it in the framework of lived experience, and infused it with renewed political power. The narratives heightened the tragedy of slave suicide by measuring the triumph of protagonists, both men and women, who escaped slavery with their lives against others who died by suicide—or contemplated destroying themselves. In doing so, these narratives used suicide to illustrate all that it meant to survive slavery: the suffering that led some slaves to self-inflict death was tantamount to that which had been endured by the protagonists. Narratives maintained the earlier antislavery emphasis on natural rights and patriarchal privilege by focusing on slavery's impact on domestic relations, offering personal accounts of suicide that often differed, as they had in the earlier periods, along the lines of gender. Yet to a greater extent than before, the rise of female-authored narratives moved enslaved women to the center of the antislavery debate and brought attention to their unique struggles under slavery.

These gendered dimensions of suicide are reflected in the distinct ways that men and women wrote about self-destruction. While men like Charles Ball (*Slavery in the United States*, 1837) openly contemplated suicide, women more typically courted death indirectly. This was a longstanding theme in abolitionist print culture: Romain deliberately drew a knife across his throat, but Anna jumped out of a window, afterwards saying that she did not mean to do so; these methods were inflected by understandings of masculinity, femininity, and gender. Similarly, in antebellum narratives, formerly enslaved women wrote that they wanted to die, but they did not discuss directly inflicting death on themselves. Similar associations between women and a more passive, indirect form of suicide can be found in autobiographies written by enslaved men. In addition, while suicide as a response to sale can be found repeatedly in slave narratives, women's choices to die by suicide also were fostered by sexual exploitation—concubinage, rape, and sexual assault—that men typically did not discuss in relation to themselves.[87] These stories revealed the experiences of women in slavery and were effective in eliciting the sympathies of northern white women as well.[88]

Solomon Northup in *Twelve Years a Slave* (1853), for instance, related the story of Patsey, the "slave of a licentious master and a jealous mistress." Patsey did not directly attempt suicide; rather, she requested that Northup assist her in putting an end to her life. As he relates, she gave him "bribes to put her secretly to her death, and bury her body in some lonely place in the margin of the swamp." Northup refused to assist Patsey in obtaining death, although later, after she was whipped relentlessly, he concluded that it would have been "blessed" if she had died. From that beating forward, he tells us, the "burden of a deep melancholy weighed heavily on her spirits."[89] Patsey wanted to die, but she did not want to kill herself. Similarly, in *Incidents in the Life of a Slave Girl* (1861), North Carolinian Harriet Jacobs, who was pursued by her owner and punished by his wife unremittingly, also sought death passively. In response to sexual coercion, she wrote that she often "prayed for death"; after one beating she needed a physician's assistance, but she "begged" her friends to let her die rather than "call a doctor."[90] These themes intersected with cultural models of gender differences.

Nineteenth-century medical experts agreed (as they do today) that men, across racial groups, are more likely to seek death by violent means and to achieve death by suicide.[91] Charles Ball relates the story of Paul, a newly imported African and serial runaway who hanged himself rather than suffer another beating; as Ball remarked, Paul was now "beyond the reach of his master's tyranny."[92] Similarly, in his 1857 narrative, Austin Steward recounted the story of an unnamed escaped man who, when faced with the possibility of return, "rightly thought death was far preferable" to reenslavement. Aboard a steamer from Albany to New York, the man fatally cut his throat.[93] Women were (and continue to be) understood to be less capable of killing themselves. Compare, for instance, the following accounts. In 1831, Caribbean-born Mary Prince related an incident in which her owner tied her to a ladder and gave her one hundred lashes for breaking a jar. She contemplated suicide indirectly, noting only that she "wished more than ever to die."[94] Harriet Jacobs does provide an example that contradicts female passivity in seeking suicide; she related the story of an unnamed wet nurse whose mistress had ordered her stripped and whipped; the enslaved women took flight to "escape the degradation and the torture" and "rushed to the river, jumped in, and ended her wrongs in death."[95] Yet Jacobs does not confess that she ever considered such a direct act of self-destruction, and thereby she maintains moral authority in her story by conforming to prevailing medical models and cultural assumptions about the gender of suicide. The accounts that emphasize the passivity of Patsey, Harriet Jacobs, and Mary Prince in particular, would have made their experiences more meaningful to a female readership.

In antislavery literature that addresses rape in unequivocal terms, however, enslaved women were depicted as actively choosing the power to die. Lewis Hayden was an escaped slave from Kentucky who moved to Boston, where he became an abolitionist leader and later a state representative.[96] In 1857, he related the story of his mother, who was subjected to the attentions of a man "who made proposals of a base nature to her." She refused him, but he declared that "she need not be so independent." As he threatened to do, he purchased and raped her. According to Hayden, his mother refused to live with her owner, but he raped, flogged, and punished her until at last she began to have "crazy turns." The beating and rape broke her mind periodically, and she "tried to kill herself many times," at least once with a knife and once by hanging. At moments of lucidity, temporarily recovering from the trauma of sexual violence, however, she related her story to her son.[97] In effect, he witnessed her abuse and passed her story along as part of his own history of slavery. Other accounts suggest that death by suicide was viewed as preferable to sexual dishonor for enslaved women, reflecting a longstanding literary theme of suicide in response to sexual violation. William Craft's 1860 narrative of his escape with his wife recounts the story of the enslaved Antoinette who avoided rape by breaking loose from her attacker and "pitch[ing] herself head foremost through the window" to her "bruised but unpolluted" death. The moralizing detail suggested that suicide was preferable to rape.[98] Unlike enslaved people who killed themselves upon occasions of sale, suicide in response to rape or sexual harms did not often appear in litigation, probably because it was not a crime to rape an enslaved woman. One legal case alleged that "improper and cruel treatment" drove an unnamed enslaved woman to drown herself; this may have been an indirect reference to sexual abuse.[99]

Still other narratives emphasized women's roles as moral guardians and therefore, more likely to obey Christian prohibitions against suicide.

For instance, Harriet Jacobs's uncle Benjamin ran away; upon recapture he "broke away" from his pursuers and considered "casting himself in the river." He was stopped, however, by thoughts of his mother, a statement that reflects an appeal to the prevalent cultural understanding of women—even enslaved women—as spiritual leaders of the family. When he confessed his thoughts of suicide to her, she advised him to endure slavery and trust God; in reply, he said that he could not because he lacked her goodness.[100] After he escaped to New York, he reflected back on his thoughts of suicide and remembered it differently. He considered that "in the old jail he had not valued" his life. "Once he was tempted to destroy it; but something, he did not know what, had prevented him; perhaps it was fear. He had heard those who profess to be religious declare there was no heaven for self-murderers." This knowledge of Christian beliefs may have been conveyed through the "goodness" of his mother. Yet safely on free ground, he also satirized the idea that suicide would lead to hell. He noted that "as [his] life had been pretty hot [on earth], he did not desire a continuation of the same in another world."[101]

Sale and separation of spouses and children, however, continued to foster suicidal ideation in slaves, regardless of their sex. Charles Ball, for instance, considered suicide when he was sold away from his wife and children in Virginia. Although he admitted that he "longed to die" when the sale was made, because he was chained for transport, "even the wretched privilege of destroying myself was denied to me."[102] His suffering was tempered with resolve, however, and he concluded that somehow his situation would improve. After all, having been sold and separated from his children and wife, how could his circumstances possibly worsen? Doubts began to gnaw at him, however. Passing though Virginia and North Carolina, he described a wasteland of deserted farms, an abandoned landscape where tobacco crops had depleted the soil, and landowners had departed for better prospects. The wasteland was spiritual as well; even the church stood empty. Slavery was literally and figuratively destroying the land and dispersing the families it sustained. When Ball arrived in South Carolina, he was filled with dread; he understood the state to be a "bottomless pit" and a "horrid" place where slavery was a "hundred fold worse" than it had been in Maryland.[103] Here again, he was plagued with suicidal thoughts. He wrote that he "seriously meditated on self-destruction," and had he been "at liberty to get a rope," he would have "hanged [himself]."[104]

Ball not only revealed his own suicidal thoughts; he also reflected on the psychologies that fostered self-destruction in other enslaved men and women. Slaves considered suicide, he poignantly argued, "from the dreadful apprehension of future evil." He experienced this dread firsthand upon his arrival in South Carolina; he described the onset of a kind of intolerable anxiety that "harassed and harrowed" him.[105] Ball suggests, not unlike Anna's description of her confusion and distraction in 1815, that profound uncertainty over the future fostered thoughts of self-harm. The horrors of being sold south or "down the river," as it was often phrased, loomed large in antebellum slave narrators' discussions of suicide, regardless of gender. Emotional separation from family and kin, the psychological terror of uncertainty, and the physical deprivation and corporal punishment associated with sale and transport were circumstances in which some enslaved men and women were haunted with thoughts of self-destruction.[106]

Owners and speculators also understood that slaves chose death by suicide as an alternative to sale and transportation. The issue was not only abolitionist propaganda; or, to put it another way, the propaganda was based on authentic experience. In 1836, for instance, Samuel Williams of Paris, Kentucky, purchased an enslaved man to sell "down the river" and confined him to the jail for safekeeping. When Williams returned the next day, the slave had hanged himself.[107] Although Williams wrote that the hanging was a "sad incident," he meant that it was unfortunate for him; he compared his losses in property to the suffering of Job. He also suggested that the man's suicide was no isolated event. This was "about the tenth [slave] we have lost and like to [lose]." "About the tenth" was a curiously vague phrase for a speculator concerned with numbers and values, but Williams may have been suggesting that some if not all of the slaves died by suicide.[108] The incident may have made him cautious as well and perhaps even fearful that other slaves might follow suit. Two weeks after the unnamed man's death, Williams wrote to his son that he had proposed shipping south two of his slaves, Adam and Sandy, but they declined, he reported, objecting too much "to going down the river." Williams could have forced the issue, surely, but as they were "so old" doing so "hardly seem[ed] worth while."[109]

The connection between slave suicide and domestic sale was also raised as a matter of law in antebellum courtrooms. Owners sued to recover their losses when recently purchased enslaved men and women killed themselves.[110] These suicides raised legal questions: who was responsible for slave death by suicide? Did self-destruction void the financial contract between buyer and seller? For example, in 1857 in Alabama, the enslaved Ellick hanged himself after being sold away from his wife. He and his wife were aware of the transaction and asked their owner to rescind it, which he had done previously and attempted to do again in this case. When the buyer refused, Ellick killed himself.[111] The trauma of separation from family and the dire prospect of heading south were sources of terror for slaves, regardless of whether the trip was to be made with a new owner, like Ellick, or by coffle, as with Charles Ball, or by boat, as was intended for Samuel Williams' enslaved man. Separation from family and community and sale to the South fostered self-destructive thoughts and outright suicide. Ball thought about hanging himself not only because he feared the deprivation and rigors of cotton planting, but also because he believed at that point that he had "no hope of ever again seeing my wife and children, or revisiting the scenes of my youth."[112] In slave narratives, abolitionist fiction like *Uncle Tom's Cabin*, and the African American press, as well as in planters' accounts and courtrooms, sale and suicide were inextricably linked together.[113]

It is also the case that many slaves who authored narratives in the antebellum era did not fault those who chose the power to die by suicide. Although Charles Ball, Harriet Jacobs, and Frederick Douglass agreed that slave suicide was a "frequent occurrence" in the South, only Douglass cautioned slaves not to "abandon yourselves, as have many thousands of American slaves, to the crime of suicide."[114] Yet even he would eventually endorse suicide as a principled alternative to slavery, a stance associated with radical antislavery activism in the 1840s and 1850s.[115] Similarly, Charles Ball argued that self-destruction was "much more frequent among the slaves in the cotton region than is generally supposed," adding that, based on his own experience of anguish over separation from his family and despair occasioned by domestic sale, he did not "marvel" that the slaves who were "driven to the south" often destroyed themselves. He also flatly stated that suicide by slaves did not violate the "precepts of religion, nor of the laws of God."[116] Likewise, Elizabeth Keckley was matter-of-fact about the death of her uncle, but it was a story that had been "strongly impressed" upon her by her mother. He had hanged himself, choosing suicide over imminent punishment for losing a second set of plow lines. When her mother went to the spring one the morning for a pail of water, "looking up into the willow tree which shaded the bubbling crystal stream, she discovered the lifeless form of her brother suspended beneath one of the strong branches." Keckley ended her reflection with the ambiguous statement that slavery had "its dark side as well as its bright side." In the preceding pages, Keckley has recounted a beating she received as a young girl, the permanent separation of her parents, and her impressions of the first slave sale that she ever witnessed; she has also recalled that her master's "heart" softened over time. Do these events place her uncle's suicide on slavery's dark or bright side? It is difficult to know, but in any case, she does not condemn his act of self-destruction or assign to it negative spiritual consequences.[117]

The lack of negative assessments of slave suicide can also be seen in the oral histories of ex-slaves and their children who were interviewed by the WPA in the 1930s. Those individuals did not express alarm or shame when relating stories of ancestors who had chosen self-destruction as an alternative to enslavement, nor did they appear to believe that self-killing had negative spiritual consequences. For example, Fannie Berry recounted her Aunt Nellie's suicide. Nellie had been badly beaten by her master and ran away. Patrollers then found and whipped her; afterward, she went to the barn and "hid in the hay" until dark. Although Berry said that she didn't think Nellie was going to "kill herself," she also recollected that after the patrollers had beaten Nellie, she declared that she "done had" her last "whipping" and was going to God. Nellie ultimately ran to the woods and threw herself down a mountain. Berry noted that when they found her body, a basket of food lay nearby, an echo, perhaps, of ritual bundles that some newly imported African in the eighteenth century had used to accompany their suicides.[118] In a second example, when Ida Blackshear Hutchinson's aunt killed herself before patrollers could beat her, Hutchinson noted triumphantly that "they didn't get Lucy."[119] Similarly, William Henry Towns related the story of three enslaved men who attempted to escape. They were caught, but only two of them were brought back because the third, as Towns recalled, jumped in the "creek and drown." That man, Towns concluded, "went to the land of sweet dreams."[120] Like the slave narrators of the antebellum period, the ex-slaves and children of slaves interviewed in the 1930s expressed no condemnation—from earthly or heavenly figures—of enslaved men and women who died in difficult and tragic circumstances by suicide.

Since the early eighteenth century, stories of slave suicide and the illustrations that accompanied them galvanized political debates over slavery. Accounts of suicide by enslaved people, particularly as written by former slaves and antislavery activists, helped to change American attitudes toward slavery. Did those reports also change attitudes toward suicide? Perhaps it was only coincidence that Thomas Jefferson, a Virginia slave owner, was among the first American politicians to argue for the elimination of state-imposed penalties for self-murder. As part of his project to revise common law and bring it into conformity with republican principles in the wake of revolution, Jefferson argued that suicides did no damage to the state, and forfeiture was a fruitless deterrent to them. Can we suppose, he queried, that one willing to "calmly determine to renounce life" could be "susceptible of influence from the losses to his family by confiscation?" Suicide, in

Jefferson's view, one shared by Enlightenment progressives, was a secular "disease" rather than a religious sin.[121] Jefferson's embrace of Enlightenment science and knowledge of Locke and Montesquieu certainly shaped his views on suicide.

Jefferson's views were also possibly the product of his familiarity with slave suicide—unless, like other slave owners, he compartmentalized his understanding of suicide and disarticulated it from slavery, choosing to believe that slaves were not fully enough evolved to fall victim to the complex psychological and emotional exigencies that fostered suicide.[122] From the late eighteenth-century forward, others argued that slaves had no mental capacity for suicide.[123] Certainly it was the case that some proslavery advocates flatly denied that slaves died by suicide. In 1844, a prominent South Carolina politician and planter averred that he had "never known or heard of a single instance of deliberate self-destruction," a fact, he argued, that cast doubt on the abolitionist portrayals of the "abject misery" of slavery.[124] As late as 1860, an attorney argued that an enslaved woman simply lacked the will to kill herself. Suicide, he claimed, sprang from various motives: to avoid disgrace, express patriotism or avoid a crueler fate; or from motives of honor and valor. An enslaved woman, he asserted, lacked all of these reasons for killing herself.[125]

The postscript from the *Pennsylvania Evening Herald* in 1785, discussed earlier, reported that whites were adopting the beliefs of "*refined* negroes" regarding suicide and conveyed anxiety over the dangers of cultural contamination by these beliefs.[126] The writer for the *Herald* certainly seemed to believe that this was the case, but the extent to which slaves' views actually held sway with whites is unclear. At the same time, attitudes toward suicide were modernizing across the United States and Europe. Did attitudes change in part because of the widespread depiction of suicidal slaves in antislavery literature? Certainly, acts of suicide, most of them by free persons, were routinely recounted in eighteenth-century newspapers and marked the onset of the medical model for understanding suicide as the consequence of psychological or emotional troubles rather than as the product of sin. Despite this evidence, measuring the broader impact of suicide by slaves on attitudes toward suicide generally remains, still, a matter of suggestion and conjecture.

In antislavery literature, the power to die was founded on the assertion that slaves had a natural right and religious dispensation to kill themselves in response to the arbitrary power and capricious cruelty that they suffered as bondpeople. Tracts drew on this Revolutionary inheritance, choosing the liberty of death over the tyranny of slavery. Alongside that powerful philosophy, the idea that slavery was a greater sin than suicide allowed antislavery advocates and ex-slaves to transform suicide into a tragic but a moral and particularly a political act, even though the terms of these politics differed significantly for enslaved men and women. Seen from the perspective of antislavery poetics and slave narratives from the American Revolution to the Civil War, then, liberty was measured not simply by the contrast between slavery and freedom, but, for men, by access to natural rights and patriarchal privileges and, for women, by their ability to protect their sexual virtue and their children, and to take up their roles as dependents. The power to die could also be, more simply, the power to renounce a life of enslavement and the ability to recast suicide as virtuous, justifiable, and, above all, political. This heroic interpretation, however, should be tempered by the fundamentally tragic finality of such acts. Enslaved people's deaths by suicide exposed the many contradictions of slavery and and became a focus of international and national debate across the Anglo-Atlantic and the early United States. In radically reframing the political implications and cultural meanings of suicide and slavery for early Americans, the power to die was nothing short of revolutionary.

EPILOGUE

Suicide, Slavery, and Memory in American Culture

> Long as I can remember . . . I've been hearing about that. Lots of slaves what was brung over from Africa could fly. There was a crowd of them working in the field. They don't like it here and they think they go back to Africa. One by one they fly up in the air and all fly off and gone back to Africa.
>
> —Jack Tattnall, Georgia Writers' Project Interview, 1930[1]

In the interviews of ex-slaves conducted by the Federal Writers' Project in the 1930s, the subject of suicide rarely surfaced. However, several ex-slaves from the South Carolina and Georgia Sea Islands, like Jack Tattnall, discussed an account of suicide in some detail, an event that has given rise to the regional folklore of the "flying Africans."[2] Stories of suicide were part of the history and culture of slavery. The memory of suicide in slavery was used to indict the institution of slavery and the history of white prejudice, to keep alive the injustices of slavery in the past to fuel the politics of the present historical moment. In these recollections, African Americans asserted authority over national history; remembrance was a means for them to interpret the past of slavery on their own terms, although these testimonies were often "highly mediated."[3] Stories of self-destruction in slavery were central to an African American cultural politics that stretched into the twentieth century, long after slavery had ended. By focusing on the by gone tragedies of suicide, competing and distinct visions of the useable past of slavery were served up as lessons and reminders for the present national moment.

Ida Blackshear Hutchinson, born in Alabama in 1865, observed in 1938 that "they say negroes won't commit suicide."[4] Exactly who she meant by "they" and whether she was referencing the slave past or the present moment is unclear, but she continued on to contradict "them" by relating the story of Lucy, an enslaved woman who killed herself in antebellum Alabama.[5] The story of Lucy is a window into the memory of suicide in slavery. Hutchinson heard the account of Lucy's suicide from her father, Isom, and much of Hutchinson's interview relates his personal history. Isom was a fieldhand, mechanic, and occasional runaway. She described his escapes in detail; like other slaves, he periodically absconded in response to punishment. On one occasion he ran because he had attempted to protect his wife from a whipping and then endured the lash himself; on another he escaped after having been falsely accused of theft, tied up, and whipped for two days. Running away, the interview makes clear, was his way of coping with punishment and confinement; it was also his means of enforcing his own code of plantation justice. In both instances, he was able to tip the scales in his favor: as Hutchinson relates the story, he felt vindicated when his master admitted that Isom had been treated unfairly.

Lucy's suicide reflects another route of escape from punishment. Like Isom, she was a repeat truant; she liked to go to dances at night and had managed to consistently elude patrollers. Because they could never catch her out at night, one day they came to the plantation in order to thrash and make an example of her. Lucy ran, and when they set after her, she "went on down to the slough and drowned herself rather than let them beat her, and mark her up." Hutchinson concluded with the telling statement, "They didn't get Lucy."[6] Just as Isom enjoyed vindication, Lucy too found a kind of victory in her escape through death. Echoing accounts found in nineteenth-century slave narratives, Lucy's suicide was not condemned by Hutchinson, who framed her act of self-destruction as an acceptable alternative to the brutality of the patrollers.

Yet not every death in slavery was a vindication, and in a chilling tale that followed the story of Lucy's suicide, Hutchinson recalled the alarming avarice of her former owners and recounted their drive to exploit the full capacity of their laborers. Because enslaved mothers might "lose time walking backward and forward nursing," their infants were brought to the field with them and placed in a trough. One day a torrential rainstorm separated the laborers from their offspring; when the storm subsided, the trough had filled up with water and all of the babies were drowned. Hutchinson assessed this tragic event through the grim financial calculus of slavery. She remarked of these deaths that the owners got "nary a lick of labor" and "nary a red penny" for "any one of them babies."[7] In summoning the economies of work, including the labor of nursing, Hutchinson laid the blame for these sixty deaths squarely at the feet of those who sought to profit from the labor of the mothers and their children.

In the three stories contained within her interview—her father's escapes, Lucy's suicide, and the deaths of sixty infants—Hutchinson juxtaposed the resilience of slaves against the injustices of slave owners. In her history of slavery, slaves might be vindicated, like Isom, through stories of escape and masters' apologies, or they might achieve a tragic victory through suicide, like Lucy. The full meaning of slavery's inhumanity was measured by situating the resourcefulness of Hutchinson's father's escape and the courage with which Lucy chose death against the greed of slave owners who caused the needless demise of sixty infants.

Hutchinson related the story of Lucy in the early twentieth century, but memories of suicide in slavery began to appear in the nineteenth century, as African American writers used stories of slave suicide to indict white prejudice and keep alive the memory of slave suffering. Charles W. Chesnutt wrote a short story, "Dave's Neckliss," about a slave who succumbed to madness and killed himself. Chesnutt believed that this story, which was published in *The Atlantic Monthly* in 1889, was "the best" in his series centered on an aged ex-slave, Uncle Julius. According to both Chesnutt and his critics, the story was pivotal in his career and emphatically attacked white supremacy.[8] Although Uncle Julius conforms to racial stereotypes and speaks in dialect, the story he relates is heavily laden with complexity as he recounts the suffering and eventual suicide of Dave.[9] As the story unfolds, Dave is falsely accused of stealing bacon and given forty lashes; as an ingenious punishment, his owner wrapped a ham in wire cloth and ordered a blacksmith to fasten it to an iron chain that was also wound around Dave's neck. These punishments, and particularly the ham necklace, made Dave the object of derision. Eventually he lost his mind, believed that he was becoming a ham, and hung himself in a row of curing meat in the smokehouse.[10]

The story powerfully illustrates the psychological and emotional pain of slavery, as Uncle Julius's memory of suicide exposes the suffering of slaves and the racism that were central to the institution. As critics note, the story is a "vigorous, outraged, and particularly clear condemnation of slavery and its effects."[11] In Uncle Julius's memory, Dave's suffering takes several forms. Once falsely accused of theft and saddled with the ham necklace, he was deprived of the former respect he had enjoyed from the plantation community, rejected by the woman he loved, and ostracized by his fellow slaves. His pain is at once brutally corporal (lashes, the necklace), deeply psychological (in his identification with the ham), and emotional (rejection and isolation), a deadly combination that leads to his act of self-destruction.

For Chesnutt, the memory of Dave's suicide was intended to outrage readers by reminding them of the multiple ways in which slavery and racism assaulted the individual. Ultimately, Dave's battering led to the obliteration of his identity. This is measured by his identification with an object, the ham, an image that resurrects the person-property divide that was central to the law and commerce of slavery. Dave's psychological crisis, and eventual suicide, rests on this divide. Dave's belief that he is becoming a ham indicates his "metamorphosis" from a person into an object, a transformation from a tragic figure into an irreparably alienated thing.[12] In all senses, Dave is a consumable, expendable object; his madness ensues from his awareness of this subjectivity as a slave. Chesnutt's story of suicide is a powerful and evocative reminder of the legacy and enduring power of slavery to shape race relations.

To remember "Dave's neckliss"—the dehumanization that fostered slave suicide—was to remind readers that the suffering produced in the past by slavery remained paramount and present in American culture. Similar themes related to self-destruction are also found in the work of twentieth- and twenty-first-century African American literary and visual artists. As part of the research for his Pulitzer Prize- and National Book Award–winning *Roots: The Saga of an American Family* (1976), for instance, Alex Haley sought to simulate the experience of the Middle Passage. After visiting Africa, he boarded a ship bound for Florida. For two nights he climbed down into the hold, stripped, and lay down on his back. On the third night, extremely ill and plagued with self-doubt, he went instead to the stern of the ship. As he gazed into the water, he was struck by the "startling" but not "frightening" notion that he could simply "step through the rail and jump into the sea" and cure his troubles.[13] In *Song of Solomon* (1977), Nobel laureate Toni Morrison is more equivocal on the subject of self-destruction. The title of the book in part refers to its protagonist's great-grandfather, an enslaved African who "just stood up in the fields one day, ran up some hill, spun around a couple of times, and was lifted up in the air [and] went right on back to wherever it was he come from."[14] His flight was magical and triumphant, but Morrison also describes it as ambiguous and disturbing. His escape from slavery—whether obtained through mythical flight or actual suicide—left behind the living to cope with loneliness and loss. Suicide might be a triumphal gesture of love or rebellion, but it also was an act that fostered despair for survivors.[15] Similarly, the character of Sethe, from Morrison's Pulitzer Prize–winning novel *Beloved* (1987), is literally haunted by the daughter she murdered, although her intent was to destroy herself as well as her children. In contrast, Kara Walker's silhouettes offer less ambivalent depictions of self-destruction in slavery. In *Cut* and *Burn*, both produced in 1998, Walker explores the violent power dynamics of slavery in which suicide is an act of "bliss and defiance," at once empowering and transgressive. Both images portray in particular the stoicism of young enslaved women who endure great physical harm—one cuts her wrists, the other sets fire to her dress—as a means of asserting "ownership of their deaths" and rebelling against their bondage.[16] In this way, Walker uses suicide to visualize and memorialize both the violence of slavery and the triumph of resistance.

Outside of North America as well, artists like Cuba's Manuel Mendive grapple with the legacy and memory of slavery. For instance, in *Barco Negrero* (1976), Mendive reimagines the experience of the slave ship and, utilizing imagery derived from Yoruban and Santería religions, meditates on themes of death, rebirth, and resurrection. Much of his work is driven by a desire to "free enslaved African spirits" so that they can "fly freely home to their ancestral land."[17] These themes can be seen in *Barco Negrero*, which presents the viewer with a cross-section of the hold of a slave ship, not unlike the famous antislavery image of the *Brooks* (1788). In contrast to that earlier image, however, Mendive's slaves, while chained together, look directly outward, engaging the viewer. The ship's rail is lined with skulls that represent the pervasive mortality of the Atlantic crossing and highlight the ubiquity of death and disease in the slave trade. Simultaneously, however, the hold is also a space of transformation. The vibrant red and deep black signals that those chained together below deck are in a liminal space, a crossroads where outcomes are uncertain. Some of the bodies of slaves undulate, caught between death and life, in distinction to the rigidly packed bodies of the *Brooks*. One figure on the left has plunged overboard—a suicide?—the body black and grey, both alive and dead. Yet the ocean itself is a space alive with deities and the force of potential transformation, a place where the material and spiritual worlds cross. The diving figure on the left balances ascending fish on the right; other marine-like figures on both sides of the ship similarly rise up into the sky. In the upper corners of the painting, human figures hover, symbols of resurrection and rebirth that suggest that the spirits of formerly captive Africans have taken flight.[18]

Perhaps the most lasting and powerful memories of suicide and slavery lie in African American folklore from the Georgia and South Carolina Sea Islands. Interviewed in the 1930s and 1940s, ex-slaves and their children related stories, similar to that of Jack Tattnall's, of Africans who literally

7.1. Ebos Landing, Dunbar Creek, St. Simon's Island, Glynn County, Georgia. Photo by the author.

had the power to take flight to escape enslavement. The flying African folktale probably has its historical roots in an 1803 collective suicide by newly imported slaves. A group of Igbo (variously, Ebo or Ibo) captives who had survived the Middle Passage were sold near Savannah, Georgia, and reloaded onto a small ship bound for St. Simon's Island. Off the coast of the island, the enslaved cargo, who had "suffered much by mismanagement," "rose" from their confinement in the small vessel and revolted against the crew, forcing them into the water, where they drowned. After the ship ran aground, the Igbos "took to the marsh" and drowned themselves—an act that most scholars have understood as a deliberate, collective suicide. The site of their fatal immersion was named Ebos Landing (figure 7.1).[19]

The fate of those Igbo in 1803 gave rise to a distinctive regional folklore and a place name, but both individual and collective suicide were also part of the general history of North American slavery. Reaching beyond the immediate experience and perception of the act of self-destruction, ex-slave memories also reconfigured the intersections of slavery and suicide. Flying African folklore, in particular, illustrates how distinct cultural communities chronicled, compressed, and remembered the experience of self-destruction in slavery. Stories of flying Africans, like the types of African

American folklore that were explored by Lawrence W. Levine and Sterling Stuckey, served didactic purposes. Using Saidiya V. Hartman's argument that memory is not simply an inventory of what went before, but is instead a bridge from the past to the present that redresses the wrongs of history, the stories can also be seen as corrective measures.[20] In this sense, flying African folklore demonstrates the power of cultural memory to reshape past tragedies, transforming stories of suicide into stories of strength and propelling them into the future.

> My daddy use to tell me all the time about folks what could fly back to Africa. They could take wing and just fly off. . . . Lots of time he tell me another story about a slave ship 'bout to be caught by a revenue boat. The slave ship slip through back river into creek. There was about fifty slaves on board. The slave runners tie rocks 'round the slaves' necks and throw them overboard to drown.
>
> —Paul Singleton, Georgia Writers' Project interview, 1930[21]

In coastal Georgia and South Carolina, ex-slave memories of the 1803 Igbo suicide are often intertwined with versions of the flying African folktale and other memories of slavery. Historians, literary scholars, and folklorists have noted the power of flying African folklore to transform an "experience of mass suicide into a tale of mythical transmigration." The folklore redresses the dislocations caused by slavery, as captives literally rise above their enslavement, transcending the natal alienation of the Middle Passage and returning to Africa. Because they serve as a form of reparation, the reliability of the memories is less important than their function as a bridge between the living and the dead. The folklore ultimately reflects one means of reshaping the memory of suicide in slavery.[22]

The ex-slaves interviewed by the Federal Writers' Project in the 1930s focus in part on the dislocations that newly imported slaves faced and reflect the circumstances that shaped their attempts at self-destruction. Many ex-slaves recall flying Africans as unseasoned slaves who did not comprehend the language, authority, or labor system of their captors. Mose Brown retold the story of a man and his wife "brung from Africa"; Carrie Hamilton spoke about another couple that was "fooled" onto a slave ship; and yet another ex-slave recalled that the flying Africans were not "climatize[d]." According to the interviewees, the flying Africans could not understand New World language or labor systems. As one informant recalled, "They can't understand your talk and you can't understand their talk" and "they did not know how to 'work right.'" Informants' stories also focused on the shock of slavery's brutality: one noted that "wild" Africans were chained in a house until they were "tame."[23] Ex-slave memories do not mention any of the elements that captive Africans used in ritual preparation for suicide (such as singing, bundled clothing, or food), but several of their accounts explain that there was often a collective ritual shout as a prelude to flight. Hamilton mentioned shouts of "goodie bye," but another slave remembers the words as "quack, quack, quack."[24]

While we do not know the gender composition of the captive Igbo in 1803, gender figures importantly in ex-slave memories of flying Africans. In the ex-slave telling, no single leader is remembered; instead, they refer to a couple, a man and wife, and it is the ritual magic performed collectively—by men and women together—that channels the power to escape enslavement and fly back to Africa. In the version of the story remembered by Hamilton, the couple ("this man and his wife") together decides "we going back home." In contrast, the WPA interviewers' rendering of the flying Africans as well as folktales published in the 1940s focus on one central male figure that empowers other slaves to fly. The Georgia Writers' Project interviewers, for example, describe the 1803 Igbo as a group of slaves who were "led by their chief" as they deliberately walked into the water to their deaths. In one version of the flying African tale published in the 1940s, a woman "took her breast with her hand and threw it over her shoulder that the child might suck and be content" as she labored in the master's fields. Her child continues to nurse, even after taking flight, as do all of the children who "laughed and sucked as their mothers flew and were not afraid." Added to the sense of power that is conveyed by the ability to literally fly away from slavery is the power represented by African American women suckling over their shoulders—an image with deep and troublesome roots in the European imagination.[25] Taken together, these folkloric elements address the dislocations of slavery, reflect the ecology of slave suicide, and imagine the restoration of family and community.

The memories of the ex-slaves interviewed in the 1930s reveal the complex intersections of folklore, slavery, and suicide. It is at just such a confluence, David Blight has noted, that historians may best be able to "write the history of memory." The coastal ex-slaves interviewed during the 1930s may have joined together separate discursive events. Paul Singleton, for example, summons the story of the slave smugglers who murdered their human cargo rather than face arrest immediately after he recounts the story of the flying Africans. Other informants similarly associated place and personal names with their stories.

A further clue to this compression of memory can be found in the connection of the 1803 Igbo collective suicide, flying Africans, and a person called "Mr. Blue." The boat that carried the Igbo ran ashore on St. Simon's Island at a plantation owned by multiple generations of the Butler family. A written account of the event lists the surname Patterson for the captain of the ship and Roswell King (overseer of Butler plantation) as the person who recovered the bodies of the drowned Igbo. None of those names appear in any of the ex-slave interviews; instead, Mr. Blue was the overseer mentioned by Wallace Quarterman in connection with the flying Africans. "Well, at that time Mr. Blue he was the overseer and Mr. Blue put them in the field but he couldn't do nothing with them. They gabble, gabble, gabble, and nobody could understand them and they didn't know how to work right. Mr. Blue he go down one morning with a long whip for to whip them good." When the interviewers asked if Mr. Blue was a hard overseer, Quarterman replied that "he ain't hard, he just can't make them understand. They's foolish acting. He got to whip them, Mr. Blue. . . . He whip them good."[26]

Alexander Blue was, in fact, the manager of the Butler estate from 1848 to 1859. Quarterman was born in 1844 and his recollection of Mr. Blue—more than a coincidence, surely—makes sense. As the last manager of the Butler plantation before the end of slavery, Blue's name would have been most prominent in the memories of ex-slaves who were interviewed in the 1930s, especially because he was the overseer—the immediate symbol of domination for most slaves.

The figure of Alexander Blue also exemplifies how ex-slaves may have connected stories of suicide with their own experiences of separation, interweaving their knowledge of flying Africans and the Igbo in the transatlantic slave trade with their personal memories of domestic sale. That connection developed simultaneously with Blue's role in the sale of slaves for the Butler plantation. Living in Philadelphia and managing his Georgia estates in absentia, Pierce Butler was, by 1855, in serious financial trouble. Four years later, he sold 436 slaves (approximately half of the estate's holdings) in what became known as the largest slave sale in history. Those who supervised the sale separated the Butler slaves, packed them into railroad cars, and shipped them to a racetrack outside of Savannah where they were sold over a period of four days. Some of the former Butler slaves still remained on St. Simon's Island in 1863, and they remembered the "great sale" as the "weeping time" and recalled, according to Col. Robert Gould Shaw, that a steady rain accompanied the sale of their "sons and daughters" and their "children and grandchildren."[27] Alexander Blue likely oversaw the sorting of human property for the momentous sale on those rainy days. By attaching

Blue's name to the flying African tale, the ex-slave Wallace Quarterman forged a connection between himself, the captive Africans who arrived—and died by suicide—in 1803, and the Butler plantation slaves who were sold and dispersed in 1859. In that confluence, water symbolically links memory and experience. The fatal immersion of the Igbo has its parallel in the rain that fell on the great sale, and water joins both the experience of the African-born Igbo and native-born Christianized slaves' notions of the spiritual and redemptive qualities of baptism. Water creates a bridge between the Igbo, the flying Africans, and the ex-slaves in the 1930s; it also bridges suicide, sale, and the power to escape to home. In 1803, the Igbo chanted as they marched into the water—an element that is reconfigured in the flying African myth as a vocalization of the joy of return (whether "goodie bye, goodie bye" or "quack, quack, quack"). Such expression stands in stark contrast, however, to the sorrow of separation invoked by the idea of a "weeping time." If the flying African folklore provides a "reprieve from domination" for the Igbo as they fly back to Africa rather than drown, the reprieve is tempered by one ex-slave's recollection of Mr. Blue, whose figure loomed large over the dispersal of families and communities in Quarterman's own experience in slavery.[28] The great sale was not a suicide, of course, but the separation it engendered paralleled the permanence of a mythical return to Africa. Like many of those who were dispersed in the great sale, flying Africans were never seen again by those who watched and remembered their departure.

The flying African stories lie at the crossroads of memory and history. The tales are an attempt at some restoration of the losses from suicide and separation that were precipitated by the slave trade. The stories assert the power of culture to maintain community in the face of its forcible dislocation. Sullen stubbornness and sentimental despair—characteristic of accounts of slave suicide in the early modern, early Republic, and antebellum eras—have no role in the tales, although the ecology of slave suicide is present in the form of refusals, brutality, labor regimes, and separation. Flying African folklore allows for the possibility of escaping slavery through the supernatural power of refusal rather than through self-destructive violence. Like both the African- and North American-born slaves who contemplated or sought self-inflicted death, flying Africans also made a choice. Collective memory conferred upon them the power to fly—to escape slavery and to return home. Ex-slave memories and folklore perform the cultural work of remaking the history of the self, the family, and the community within slavery, ultimately transforming the crossroads of despair, suicide, and separation into an intersection of power, transcendence, and reunion.

Studying Slave Suicide: An Essay on Sources

In the seventeenth century, an agent aboard slave ships reported that Akan and Gold Coast Africans were "headstrong" in their commitment to death. By the late 1700s, a slave owner described suicide as "not uncommon" among enslaved men and women in the West Indies. And in the three decades before the Civil War, two former slaves depicted self-destruction as more "frequent" than was "generally supposed," while a third asserted that "thousands" of enslaved people in the United States had died by their own hands.[1] Despite the apparent constancy of suicide throughout slavery's history suggested by these remarks, however, the sources for its study remain fragmentary, particularly if the focus, as it is here, is eighteenth-century British America and the early United States. In order to study the significance of suicide in slavery, I have pulled together fragments of evidence from legal sources, private correspondence and diaries, and a wide range of early modern printed materials, ranging from seventeenth-century treatises on suicide to antebellum slave narratives. In addition to this essay, readers should consult the Select Bibliography of Primary Sources that follows the notes.

Like other historians of self-destruction, I have consulted coroner's inquests. For my purposes, those from selected southern colonies and states, primarily North Carolina, South Carolina, and Virginia, have been subjected to systematic study. While helpful, these legal records of course do not exclusively—or even largely, in many cases—address self-destruction by slaves. Even in jurisdictions with a slave majority, inquests on whites dominate the archive. Coroner's juries were charged with determining the causes of all unexplained deaths, but in North American slave societies, official postmortem examinations of slaves appear to have occurred largely at the discretion or request of their owners. While inquests provide evidence of self-killing by enslaved people, like many other documents, they underrepresent the numbers of deaths by suicide.

In addition, coroner's inquests often reveal little, if anything, about any individual reasons for suicide. These inquiries were designed to determine the manner and cause of unexplained deaths. Jurors were sworn under oath to render truthful verdicts that were legally binding; those verdicts could establish proof of criminal acts or be used as evidence in civil litigation. Occasionally inquests are accompanied by testimony from those familiar with the victim's state of mind, but this is rarely the case for slaves. Coroner's inquests are useful sources in documenting the timing, place, and method of suicide. Inquests include a statement of where—in a barn, at the bottom of a hill, near a stream—the body was found. Examiners often described wounds or marks, if any, that appeared on the corpse. They also assessed the size and value of any instrument used in the act of self-destruction: knives and ropes were often measured, for instance, and assigned a monetary value. The precise determination of the cause of death was documented, then, as the outcome of a methodical and rational process. In the early American South, inquests often employed formulaic language to describe the act of suicide; the subjects were routinely described as lacking a "fear of God" and their deaths attributed to the "instigation of the Devil."

Despite these limitations, however, the systematic review of coroner's inquests was necessary in this study in order to establish the legal response to slave suicide in the context of British North America. I consulted nearly one thousand (N = 999) coroners' inquests from jurisdictions in colonial and early national North Carolina, South Carolina, and Virginia. On average, verdicts of accidental death (37%) and homicide (23%) predominated in this sample. In contrast 13% (N = 127) of inquests determined suicide as a cause of death; of these 28% (N = 35) were inquests on the suicides of enslaved men and women. The inquests varied by county and date; some counties have surviving inquests for the seventeenth century, while others remain only for the nineteenth century; many records exist in broken sequences. I utilized all of the extant inquests on suicide from each county from their earliest date through 1840 with an occasional foray beyond. Most of these exist in manuscript form; many of them seem to have never been previously opened. Because of erratic early American record keeping, the lack of, until the twentieth century, any systematic attention to filing inquests, the probable existence of unfiled inquests interleaved in court records, and the chronological gaps in the surviving records, my sampling of the inquests should not be understood to be complete. Despite this caveat, however, those interested in completing a comparative analysis of accident, suicide, and homicide in the early South would be well served by these records. Because these inquests offer data on suicide by both enslaved and free people, they provide a window into the local context of and legal responses to self-destruction. They thus form one of the evidentiary foundations for this study.

Statuary and legislative sources have also provided evidence for this study. In the jurisdictions considered here, the traditions of English statutory and common law initially shaped the legal disposition of suicide, while newly enacted colonial statutes governed the institution of slavery. These separate legal entities came together uniquely in the colony's legislative houses and courts, particularly when slaves accused of felonies killed themselves before they were taken into custody. The conjoining of the law of suicide and the criminal justice of slavery is especially well documented in Virginia, where slave owners petitioned the government for compensation when their slaves killed themselves after allegedly committing capital crimes. Like inquests, these surviving petitions document the timing and method of suicide. However, as they were calculated to benefit slave owners and address a variety of situations, they are less formulaic and better elaborated than coroner's inquests. More importantly, they also often contain narratives—sequences of events, snippets of conversation, a fragment of personal history—that offer clues to enslaved people's motives for killing themselves.

An entirely different vein of eighteenth-century legislative sources comes not from those who supported slavery, but rather from those who opposed it. In late eighteenth-century England, witnesses in a Parliamentary investigation into the slave trade were repeatedly questioned about suicide by slaves in British American plantations; even those who were not directly questioned about it testified that captives leapt from ships and starved themselves in response to slavery. While much of the testimony addressed the experience of newly arrived Africans in the Caribbean, substantial sections also document suicide on the Middle Passage. In addition, the passage of the Dolben Act in 1788 required that slave ships retain surgeons on board to provide medical attention to captive Africans and keep accurate logs of shipboard mortality.[2] These too provide examples of slave suicide along the Middle Passage. These sources are not, of course, unproblematic. Surgeons (and ship captains) had incentives to underreport suicide. Moreover, for eighteenth-century antislavery advocates, as this book relates, accounts of slave suicide were one of the most immediate if summary condemnations of the slave trade, a profound and moving measure of the human losses that it caused. Witness after witness testified to the frequent mention of self-destruction by enslaved people, using these accounts as primary political weapons in the Parliament investigation.

If legal sources are foundational to any understanding of suicide in North American slavery, this study was also enriched by a wide array of manuscript sources. Private correspondence and diaries in particular offer evidence of attitudes toward suicide in the slave societies of early North America. Yet here too, as in the legal records, I have consulted those that addressed acts of self-destruction, regardless of whether they were exclusively suicides of enslaved people. Like the legal documents, the majority of private sources reference suicide by Anglo-Americans; only rarely do these documents directly address suicide by enslaved men and women. In addition, these sources, many of which came from the pens of planters and overseers, reflect patterns of beliefs toward suicide among the slave owning classes and attitudes toward slave death—by whatever means—more generally.

Although legal and private sources were essential to this study, printed materials that circulated in the early modern Anglo-Atlantic were indispensible for viewing the cultural politics of suicide from a transatlantic perspective. Many of the earliest printed sources directly referencing slave suicide came from the pens of mariners and planters who controlled the trade and shaped the law and practice of slavery. Whether these documents were formulated as histories of colonial ventures, as repositories of medical advice for planters, or even, as improbable as it may seem, as poetry, suicide by slaves was a consistent touchstone in them.

Eighteenth-century newspapers and periodicals provided another resource for studying suicide: they popularized the debate over the criminalization of suicide and published accounts of actual acts of self-destruction. Here again the focus on European subjects is disproportional relative to stories of slave suicide. I have systematically studied all accounts of suicide in the *Virginia Gazette* from 1736–1776 and used accounts from other papers and magazines anecdotally. Yet another printed source for studying slave suicide can be found in seventeenth- and eighteenth-century fiction and drama, as well as in the earliest slave narratives, such as those by Job Ben Soloman and William Ansah Sessarakoo that appeared in the 1750s, before the emergence of organized antislavery advocacy. These sources reveal a range of often competing attitudes toward slave suicide, providing an unparalleled corpus of evidence of the cultural politics of slave suicide that antedated antislavery materials. Indeed, one insight garnered from this material is the power of early modern print to shape antislavery consciousness prior to organized activism.

A major source of evidence for this study comes of course from antislavery printed literature that emerged in the 1770s. These materials very deliberately moved accounts and images of slave suicide that had long existed at the margins of culture to the very center of politics. The contradictions of suicide in slavery first arose across colonial British America, but by the late eighteenth century slaves, ex-slaves, and abolitionists wove them into the very fabric of antislavery politics, where they would remain through the antebellum period. Printed sources reflect the changing aims, approaches, and values of antislavery activism over time. Perhaps this is best seen in the rise of narratives that, among other things, document suicide as it was contemplated and experienced by enslaved people. The earliest antislavery poetics spoke for their enslaved subjects; slaves, particularly enslaved men, were positioned as protagonists who died heroically, a motif that grew out of fiction and drama. In contrast, in slave narratives, which I have selectively consulted here, men and women who had thought about suicide or had observed it directly or indirectly, that is, through stories told by other slaves, provide a more authentic, if politically motivated, perspective on slave self-destruction. That the narrator lives to tell their story, however, lends these mostly antebellum narratives a force of authenticity—a witnessing—that differs greatly from the poetics of the era of the American Revolution.

The final corpus of evidence used in this study is found in oral histories and folklore. Interviews of former slaves were conducted by the Federal Writers' Project of the Works Progress Administration in the 1930s; they were subsequently published and today are available digitally at the Library of Congress. The histories themselves are not unproblematic; the interviewers were predominantly white and the subjects were black; and as the Library of Congress website notes, the interviews were shaped by the inequalities of race in early twentieth-century America.[3] Along with folklore, however, they form a valuable part of this study. They do not so much allow me to reflect on the lived experience of slavery, although there is some of that. Rather, their power lies in their ability to reveal the meaning of slavery in modern memory. As Laura F. C. Holloway has argued, "black death," and in this case death by suicide, is a persistent theme in twentieth-century African American cultural memory and politics.[4] It is reminder of the continuing relevance of slavery to understandings of race in the contemporary United States.

ABBREVIATIONS

BL	British Library, London.
GWP	Georgia Writers' Project, *Drums and Shadows: Survival Stories among the Georgia Coastal Negroes* (Athens: University of Georgia Press, 1986).
Hening	W. W. Hening, *The Statutes At Large, Being a Collection of all the Laws of Virginia, From the First Session of the Legislature in the Year 1619* (Charlottesville, VA: Published for the Jamestown Foundation of the Commonwealth of Virginia by University Press of Virginia, 1969).
HCSP	Shelia Lambert, ed., *House of Commons Sessional Papers* (Wilmington, DE: Scholarly Resources, 1975). Note that because these volumes carry multiple page numbers, my citations refer to the editor's pagination numbers found at the bottom of the page.
HL	Huntington Library, San Marino, California.
JHB	H. R. McIllwaine, *Journals of the House of Burgesses* (Richmond, VA: Colonial Press, E. Waddley Co., 1905–1915). Citations to *JHB* include a range of years, indicating the volume.
LOV	Library of Virginia, Richmond.
NCSA	North Carolina State Archives, Raleigh.
SCDAH	South Carolina Department of Archives and History, Columbia.
VG (Hunter)	Hunter's *Virginia Gazette* (Williamsburg).
VG (Parks)	Parks's *Virginia Gazette* (Williamsburg).
VG (Pickney)	Pickney's *Virginia Gazette* (Williamsburg).
VG (P&D)	Purdie and Dixon's *Virginia Gazette* (Williamsburg).
VHS	Virginia Historical Society, Richmond.
YCDOW	York County Deeds, Orders, Wills, Library of Virginia.

NOTES

PROLOGUE

1. Jesse Torrey, *A Portraiture of Domestic Slavery, in the United States, With Reflections on the Practicability of Restoring the Moral Rights of the Slave Without Impairing the Legal Rights of His Possessor* (Philadelphia, 1817), illustration caption, n.p. Torrey does not give Anna's name; however, E. A. Andrews' 1836 interview refers to her as Anna. See E. A. Andrews, *Slavery and the Domestic Slave Trade in the United States* (Boston, 1836), 128–133.
2. Torrey, *A Portraiture of Domestic Slavery*, 43 (quotation), 42–44; Allen C. Clark, "James Heighe Blake, the Third Mayor of the Corporation of Washington [1813–1817]," *Records of the Columbia Historical Society, Washington, D.C.*, ed., John B. Larner, vol. 24 (Washington, D.C.: Published by the Society, 1922), 136–163.
3. Torrey, *A Portraiture of Domestic Slavery*, 43.
4. For Torrey's account of Anna for the congressional investigation, see Jesse Torrey "To the Honorable John Randolph," April 29, 1816, "Select Committee to inquire into the existence of an inhumane and illegal traffic in slaves . . . in the District of Columbia," HR14A-C17.4, Committee Reports and Papers, RG 233, US House of Representatives 14th Congress, 1816, National Archives, Washington, DC. See also George Miller's account of Anna and defense of himself, "To the Public," *City of Washington Gazette*, 11 May 1819, 3. For the account of the citizen's refusal and the designation of the site as "historic," see W. Bryan, "A Fire in an Old Time F Street Tavern and What It Revealed," *Records of the Columbia Historical Society, Washington, D.C.*, vol. 9 (Washington, DC: Published for the Society, 1906), 195, 201. For other accounts, of Anna's leap, see Andrews, *Slavery and the Domestic Slave Trade in the United States*, 112–113, 128–133; John Davis, "Eastman Johnson's *Negro Life at the South* and Urban Slavery in Washington, DC," *Art Bulletin* 80 (March 1998), 77; and Robert H. Gudmestad, *A Troublesome Commerce: The Transformation of the Interstate Slave Trade* (Baton Rouge: Louisiana State University Press, 2003), 35–37, 61.
5. This image (fig. 00.1 in this volume) appears in Torrey, *A Portraiture of Domestic Slavery*, unnumbered between pages 42 and 43.
6. On suicide in early America, see Richard Bell, *We Shall Be No More: Suicide and Self-Government in the Newly United States* (Cambridge, MA: Harvard University Press, 2012), 43–80.

7. On commodification and slavery, see Walter Johnson, *Soul by Soul: Life Inside the Antebellum Slave* Market (Cambridge, MA: Harvard University Press, 1999), 19–44, 58; Stephanie Smallwood, "Commodified Freedom: Interrogating the Limits of Anti-slavery Ideology in the Early Republic," *Journal of the Early Republic* 24 (Summer 2004), 289–298; Amy Dru Stanley, "Wages, Sin and Slavery: Some Thoughts in Free Will and Commodity Relations," *Journal of the Early Republic* 24 (Summer 2004), 279–288; and Edward B. Rugemer, "The Development of Mastery and Race in Comprehensive Slave Codes of the Greater Caribbean during the Seventeenth Century," *William and Mary Quarterly*, 3d ser., 70 (July 2013), 454–457.
8. Torrey, *A Portraiture of Domestic Slavery*, 43.
9. Deposition of Francis S. Key of Georgetown, "Select Committee to inquire into the existence of an inhumane and illegal traffic in slaves . . . in the District of Columbia"; Torrey, *A Portraiture of Domestic Slavery*, 44–45.
10. Torrey, "To the Honorable John Randolph," Select Committee to inquire into the existence of an inhumane and illegal traffic in slaves . . . in the District of Columbia."
11. John Randolph's speech in *Debates and Proceedings of the Congress of the United States, Fourteenth Congress, First Session* (Washington, DC: Gales and Seaton, 1854), 1115. The phrase "Negro Bastille" is attributed to William P. Gardner; see "To The Public," *City of Washington Gazette*, 11 May 1819, 3.

INTRODUCTION

1. *South Carolina Gazette*, 5 May 1759, 3.
2. *South Carolina Gazette*, 5 May 1759, 3. The initial notice was dated 12 December 1758; it included only the physical description of Caesar, the guesses at his owner's name, and the location of Caesar's capture; these details were reprinted in each issue of the paper through 10 March 1759. The additional detail on the unnamed slave's suicide was added to the 5 May edition of the notice, which was reprinted through 23 June 1759.
3. Michael MacDonald and Terence R. Murphy, *Sleepless Souls: Suicide in Early Modern England* ([1990]; Oxford, UK: Oxford University Press, 2000), 16–21, 31–41, 44–57.
4. Henry Hammond, *A Practical Catechism* (London: R Norton, 1677), 126. On the publication of *A Practical Catechism*, see Hugh de Quehen, "Hammond, Henry (1605–1660)," *Oxford Dictionary of National Biography* (Oxford, UK: Oxford University Press, 2004; online ed., January 2008 [http://www.oxforddnb.com.huntington.idm.oclc.org/view/article/12157, accessed 14 November 2014]).
5. Michael Dalton, *The Countrey Justice: Containing the Practice of the Justices of the Peace out of their Sessions* (London, 1635), 235, HL.
6. John Sym, *Life's Preservative Against Self-Murder* (London: R. Flesher, 1637), 269. HL.
7. Dalton explained, "Their dead bodies (for the terror of others) are drawne out of the house & c. with ropes, by a horse, to a place appointed for punishment, or shame, where the dead body is hanged upon a Gibbet; And none may take downe the body, but by the authority of the Magistrate." Dalton, *Countrey Justice*, 235.
8. For evidence on burial practices in Europe, see MacDonald and Murphy, *Sleepless Souls*, 15–41, 121–125; Alexander Murray, *Suicide in the Middle Ages: The Curse on Self-Murder*, vol. 2 (Oxford, UK: Oxford University Press, 2000), 152–188; Georges Minois, *History of Suicide: Voluntary Death in Western Culture*, trans. Lydia G. Cochrane (Baltimore: Johns Hopkins University Press, 1999), (Baltimore: Johns Hopkins University Press, 1999), 74–76, 135–138; and Clare Gittings, *Death, Burial and the Individual in Early Modern England* (London: Croom Helm, 1984), 72–73. Such

punishments were evident in early America, but David Silkenat argues that in antebellum North Carolina, while suicide was "damned" as one of the "most deplorable acts that an individual could commit," there is "no evidence" that these prejudices extended to burial practices; see *Moments of Despair: Suicide, Divorce, and Debt in Civil War Era North Carolina* (Chapel Hill: University of North Carolina Press, 2011), 11, 13.

9. Major Thomas Massie to Cap. Henry Massie, 20 July 1819, Massie Family Papers, VHS; and T. L. Scott to Oscar George, 26 July 1832, George Family Papers, VHS.

10. On the use of dismemberment to punish slave suicide, see Vincent Brown, "Spiritual Terror and Sacred Authority: The Power of the Supernatural in Jamaican Slave Society," in Edward E. Baptist and Stephanie M. H. Camp, eds., *New Studies in the History of American Slavery* (Athens: University of Georgia Press, 2006), 180–182.

11. Slaves' attitudes toward suicide are addressed in Sylvia R. Frey and Betty Wood, *Come Shouting to Zion: African American Protestantism in the American South and British Caribbean to 1830* (Chapel Hill: University of North Carolina Press, 1998), 35–37; John Thornton, "Cannibals, Witches, and Slave Traders in the Atlantic World," *William and Mary Quarterly*, 3d ser., 60 (2003), 273–294; Michael A. Gomez, *Exchanging Our Country Marks: The Transformation of African Identities in the Colonial and Antebellum South* (Chapel Hill: University of North Carolina Press, 1998), 114–128; Daniel E. Walker, "Suicidal Tendencies: African Transmigration in the History and Folklore of the Americas," *The Griot* 18 (1999), 10–19; and William D. Pierson, "White Cannibals, Black Martyrs: Fear, Depression, and Religious Faith as Causes of Suicide among New Slaves," *Journal of Negro History* 62 (1977), 147–159; and Sally E. Hadden, "The Fragmented Laws of Slavery in the Colonial and Revolutionary Eras," in Michael Grossberg and Christopher Tomlins, eds., *The Cambridge History of Law in America*, vol. 1 (New York: Cambridge University Press, 2008), 284–285.

12. Gomez, *Exchanging Our Country Marks*, 116–128; John Thornton, "Religious and Ceremonial Life in the Kongo and Mbundu Areas, 1500–1700," in Linda M. Heywood, ed., *Central Africans and Cultural Transformation in the American Diaspora* (New York: Cambridge University Press, 2002), 80–81; Thornton, "Cannibals, Witches, and Slave Traders in the Atlantic World," 273–294; and Louis A. Pérez, Jr., *To Die in Cuba: Suicide and Society* (Chapel Hill: University of North Carolina Press, 2005), 8.

13. For slaves' desires for death and thoughts of suicide, see, for instance, Olaudah Equiano, *The Life of Olaudah Equiano or Gustavas Vassa, The African* (London: Dawson's of Pall Mall, 1969), vol. 1, 50–51, 56-57, 73, 74, 80, 81–82; Mary Prince, *The History of Mary Prince, a West-Indian Slave* (London, 1831) in *Six Women's Slave Narratives* (New York: Oxford University Press, 1988), 8–9. On the prominence of suicide in ex-slave narratives, see Silkenat, *Moments of Despair*, 14–22; for a discussion of abolitionism and slave suicide, see Mark S. Schantz, *Awaiting the Heavenly Country: The Civil War and America's Culture of Death* (Ithaca, NY: Cornell University Press, 2008), 126–162, and Richard Bell, *We Shall Be No More: Suicide and Self-Government in the Newly United States* (Cambridge, MA: Harvard University Press, 2012), 201–246.

14. Kevin Dawson, *Enslaved Water People in the Atlantic World, 1444–1888: The Cultural Meanings of Water, Swimming, Surfing, and Canoeing in Atlantic Africa and the African Diaspora* (Philadelphia: University of Pennsylvania Press, forthcoming).

15. William Dusinberre, *Them Dark Days: Slavery in the American Rice Swamps* (New York: Oxford University Press, 1996), 128–131.

16. On African understandings of death and the afterlife in the context of the slave trade, see, for instance, Vincent Brown, *The Reaper's Garden: Death and Power in the World*

of Atlantic Slavery (Cambridge, MA: Harvard University Press, 2008), 143; Thornton, "Religious and Ceremonial Life in the Kongo and Mbundu Areas, 1500–1700," 80–81; and Jason R. Young, *Rituals of Resistance: African Atlantic Religion in Kongo and the Lowcountry South in the Era of Slavery* (Baton Rouge: Louisiana State University Press, 2007), 146–182.

17. It is possible that his master deliberately ignored the runaway notice, leaving Caesar to the horrors of the workhouse in order to punish his insubordination. Six months was a long time to go without a prime laborer, one evidently strong enough to sever a head from a lifeless body.
18. Timothy Williams, "Suicides Outpacing War Deaths for Troops," *New York Times*, 8 June 2012 (http://www.nytimes.com/2012/06/09/us/suicides-eclipse-war-deaths-for-us-troops.html?_r=0); see also print version, 9 June 2012, A10. More recently, the *Los Angeles Times* reported that a slight majority of troops who committed suicide while on active duty were never deployed to Afghanistan or Iraq; see Alan Zarembo, "Their Battle Within," *Los Angeles Times*, 16 June 2013, A1, A16–A17.
19. S. E. Sproutt, *The English Debate on Suicide, From Donne to Hume* (LaSalle, IL: Open Court, 1961), 94-158; MacDonald and Murphy, *Sleepless Souls*, 109-143; Howard I. Kushner, *Self-Destruction in the Promised Land: A Psychocultural Biology of American Suicide* (New Brunswick, NJ: Rutgers University Press, 1989), 27–34; Bell, *We Shall Be No More*, 15–23.
20. For instance, attempted suicide continued to be a crime, although a largely unenforced one, in many U.S. jurisdictions well into the twentieth century: North Carolina ruled an attempted suicide to be a misdemeanor offense as late as 1961. In most countries and states it is a felony to aid, advise, or encourage another person to die by suicide; at this writing, five of the fifty United States have laws that permit some form of physician-assisted suicide. In the 1997 case, *Washington v. Glucksberg*, the Supreme Court majority opinion averred that "opposition to and condemnation of suicide . . . are consistent and enduring themes in our philosophical, cultural, and legal heritages" and ruled that the personal rights guaranteed by the Fourteenth Amendment do not encompass the right to end one's life. Of course, any attempt or act of suicide that also causes others to die—such as suicide bombing—remains a criminal offense, and suicide continues to be an issue in civil litigation, such as in insurance claims. See Richard S. Kay, "Causing Death for Compassionate Reasons," *American Journal of Comparative Law* 54 [*American Law in the 21st Century: U.S. National Reports to the XVIIth International Congress of Comparative Law*] (Fall 2006), 696 (quotation), 693–696 (inclusive); Robert I. Simon, James L. Levenson, and Daniel W. Shuman, "On Sound and Unsound Mind: The Role of Suicide in Tort and Insurance Litigation," *Journal of the American Academy of Psychiatry and the Law Online* 33 (June 2005), 176–182; R. E. Shulman, "Suicide and Suicide Prevention: A Legal Analysis," *American Bar Association Journal* 54 (September 1968), 855–856; *Washington v. Glucksberg*, 521 U.S. 702 (1997).
21. This is an elaboration of Vincent Brown's concept of "mortuary politics." See Brown, *The Reaper's Garden*, 5.
22. Erik R. Seeman, *Death in the New World: Cross-Cultural Encounters, 1492–1800* (Philadelphia: University of Pennsylvania Press, 2010), 2–8.
23. Well into Reconstruction, for instance, blacks were understood to be more prone to mania and less prone to melancholia because of their alleged mental inferiority; see Silkenat, *Moments of Despair*, 50–51.
24. See for instance, Henry Laurens to Peter Funnell, 6 September 1755, in Philip M.

Hamer, George C. Rogers, Jr., and Peggy J. Wehage, eds., *The Papers of Henry Laurens*, vol. 1 (Columbia: University of South Carolina Press, 1970), 331.

25. David M. Walker, *The Oxford Companion to Law* (Oxford, UK: Oxford University Press, 1980), 833; Bryan A. Garner, *Black's Law Dictionary*, 7th ed. (St. Paul: West Group, 1999), 999; Jeannine Marie DeLombard, *In the Shadow of the Gallows: Race, Crime, and American Civic Identity* (Philadelphia: University of Pennsylvania Press, 2012), 6–11, 28–33, 51–86; and Jeannine Marie DeLombard, *Slave Narratives and U.S. Legal History*, "Slave Narratives and U.S. Legal History," in John Ernest, ed., *The Oxford Handbook of the African American Slave Narrative* (New York: Oxford University Press, 2014), 67–88. At the moment of death, enslaved people gained the force of subjects: as Achille Mbembe argues, the human being becomes a subject in the confrontation with death; for slaves, this was doubly true. See Achille Mbembe, "Necropolitics," trans. Libby Meintjes, *Public Culture* 15 (2003), 14.
26. John Wood Sweet, *Bodies Politic: Negotiating Race in the American North* (Philadelphia: University of Pennsylvania Press, 2003), 72.
27. Walter Johnson, *Soul by Soul: Life Inside the Antebellum Slave Market* (Cambridge, MA: Harvard University Press, 1999), 19–20.
28. In England, the literary campaign against slavery originated in the seventeenth century. As Wylie Sypher argued long ago, objections to slavery gained force after 1725 and emerged as an active opposition in the early 1770s; see Sypher, *Guinea's Captive Kings: British Anti-slavery Literature of the XVIIIth Century* (Chapel Hill: University of North Carolina Press, 1942), 1–10. More recent studies of British and America print campaigns against slavery include Bell, *We Shall Be No More*, 201–247; Jeannine Marie DeLombard, *Slavery on Trial: Law, Abolitionism, and Print Culture* (Chapel Hill: University of North Carolina Press, 2007); Brycchan Carey, *British Abolitionism and the Rhetoric of Sensibility: Writing, Sentiment, and Slavery, 1760–1807* (New York: Palgrave Macmillian, 2005); and Philip Gould, *Barbaric Traffic: Commerce and Antislavery in the Eighteenth-Century Atlantic World* (Cambridge, MA: Harvard University Press, 2003).
29. David Blight, "If You Don't Tell It Like It Is, It Can Never Be as It Ought to Be," in *Slavery and Public History: The Tough Stuff of American Memory*, ed. James Oliver Horton and Lois E. Horton (New York: New Press, 2006), 26.
30. *Born in Slavery: Slave Narratives from the Federal Writers' Project, 1936–1938*, Library of Congress (http://memory.loc.gov/ammem/snhtml/, accessed 11 July 2014).
31. Thornton, "Cannibals, Witches, and Slave Traders in the Atlantic World," 273–294; Gomez, *Exchanging Our Country Marks*, 114–128; Walker, "Suicidal Tendencies," 10–19; Frey and Wood, *Come Shouting to Zion*, 35–37; and Pierson, "White Cannibals, Black Martyrs," 147–159.
32. Louis A. Pérez, Jr., *To Die in Cuba: Suicide and Society* (Chapel Hill: University of North Carolina Press, 2005).
33. Schantz, *Awaiting the Heavenly Country*; Bell, *We Shall Be No More*; Silkenat, *Moments of Despair*; and Terri L. Snyder, "Suicide, Slavery, and Memory in North America," *Journal of American History* 97, no. 1 (June 2010), 39–62. Other important treatments of suicide in American history include Diane Miller Sommerville, "'A Burden Too Heavy to Bear': War Trauma, Suicide and Confederate Soldiers," *Civil War History* 59 (December 2013), 453–491; Shannon Doyle, "'They Found Their Freedom in Death'—An Examination and Consideration of African and African-American Slave Suicide in Pre-Civil War America" (unpublished undergraduate dissertation), University of Glasgow, 2013; Kushner, *Self-Destruction in the Promised Land*; Donna

Merwick, *Death of a Notary: Conquest and Change in Colonial New York* (Ithaca, NY: Cornell University Press, 1999); and Roger Lane, *Violent Death in the City: Suicide, Accident, and Murder in Nineteenth-Century Philadelphia*, 2nd ed. (Columbus: Ohio State University Press, 1999). Studies of suicide in medieval and early modern England and Europe include S. E. Sprott, *The English Debate on Suicide from Donne to Hume* (LaSalle, IL: Open Court, 1961); MacDonald and Murphy, *Sleepless Souls*; Alexander Murray, *Suicide in the Middle Ages*, vol. 1, *The Dead Against Themselves* (Oxford, UK: Oxford University Press, 1998); and Alexander Murray, *Suicide in the Middle Ages*, vol. 2, *The Curse on Self-Murder* (Oxford, UK: Oxford University Press, 2000); Minois, *History of Suicide*; Jeffrey R. Watt, *Choosing Death: Suicide and Calvinism in Early Modern Geneva* (Kirksville, MO: Truman State University Press, 2001); Jeffrey R. Watt, ed., *From Sin to Insanity: Suicide in Early Modern Europe* (Ithaca, NY: Cornell University Press, 2004); R. A. Houston, *Punishing the Dead? Suicide, Lordship, and Community in Britain, 1500–1830* (Oxford, UK: Oxford University Press, 2010); and Kelly McGuire, *Dying to Be English: Suicide Narratives and National Identity, 1721–1814* (London: Pickering and Chatto, 2012). For a documentary history of suicide in England, see Paul Seaver, ed., *The History of Suicide in England, 1650–1850*, 4 vols. (London: Pickering and Chatto, 2012).

34. Edward E. Baptist, *The Half Has Never Been Told: Slavery and the Making of American Capitalism* (New York: Basic Books, 2014, xxv.
35. Brown, *The Reaper's Garden*; Seeman, *Death in the New World*; Karla FC Holloway, *Passed On: African American Mourning Stories: A Memorial Collection* (Durham, NC: Duke University Press, 2002); and Drew Gilpin Faust, *This Republic of Suffering: Death and the American Civil War* (New York: Knopf, 2008).
36. See, for instance, Gomez, *Exchanging Our Country Marks*, 120; Eric Robert Taylor, *If We Must Die: Shipboard Insurrections in the Era of the Atlantic Slave Trade* (Baton Rouge: Louisiana State University Press, 2006), 37.
37. *HCSP*, vol. 73, 114–115.
38. Jesse Torrey, *A Portraiture of Domestic Slavery, in the United States, With Reflections on the Practicability of Restoring the Moral Rights of the Slave Without Impairing the Legal Rights of His Possessor* (Philadelphia, 1817), 42–44.
39. Jennifer L. Morgan, *Laboring Women: Reproduction and Gender in New World Slavery* (Philadelphia: University of Pennsylvania Press, 2004), 167.
40. Walter Johnson, "On Agency," *Journal of Social History* 37 (Fall 2003), 113–114.
41. See for instance, Inquest on Sampson, Slave to William Potter, 17 May 1765, Granville County, North Carolina, CR Box 04.913.1, Coroners Folder, NCSA.
42. Inquest on James, 15 July 1828, Charlotte County Coroners' Inquests, 1770–1870, Miscellaneous Records/Bonds/Commissions/Oaths/Estrays (1774–1885), Box 141, LOV.
43. Inquest on Quamey, 19 September 1770, Hanover County, North Carolina, Coroner's Inquisitions, Series, SSXVII, Box 1, Folder 1770, NCSA.
44. Karla FC Holloway, *Passed On: African American Mourning Stories: A Memorial Collection* (Durham, NC: Duke University Press, 2002), 91.
45. Inquest on Rose, 1 February 1813, Coroner's Inquisitions, 1800-1911, Series L35189, South Carolina Court of General Sessions, Marlboro County, SCDAH.
46. Inquest on Booker, 30 March 1823, Coroner's Inquisitions, 1803-1908, Series L 42164, South Carolina Court of General Sessions, Spartenburg County, SCDAH.
47. *The Story of Mattie J. Jackson; A True Story*, written and arranged by Dr. L. S. Thompson (1866), in *Six Women's Slave Narratives* (New York: Oxford University Press, 1988), 6.

48. See for instance, Inquest on Henry, 17 September 1829, Coroner's Inquisitions, 1806–1869, Series L44163, South Carolina Court of General Sessions, Union District, SCDAH; Inquest on Delia, 12 July 1861, Iredell County Slave Records, Folder: Coroners' Inquests Concerning Slave Deaths, NCSA.

49. Records also reflect the local tensions between slave owners and the juries who made final rulings. When an enslaved woman named Rachel died of a blow to her head in 1834, for example, the jurors "rest[ed] their suspicion" on her owner Thomas Preay. Inquest on Rachel, 18 February 1834, Box 1, Series L 20149, Coroners' Inquests, Fairfield County, South Carolina Court of General Sessions, SCDAH. On the greater attention to punishing crimes against slaves, see Eugene Genovese, *Roll, Jordan, Roll: The World the Slaves Made* (New York: Vintage, 1976), 37–41; Peter Kolchin, *American Slavery, 1619–1877*, rev. ed. (New York: Hill and Wang, 2003), 111–122.

50. The "not uncommon" remark was by Henry Hew Dalrymple, *HCSP*, vol. 73, 312. Testimony on slave suicide can be found throughout *HCSP*, vols. 68–73 and 82.

51. Marcus Rediker, *The Slave Ship: A Human History* (New York: Viking, 2007), 291.

52. Although an imperfect comparison, in 2012, according to the American Association for Suicidology, suicide ranked tenth in causes of death in the United States, accounting for less than 2% of all mortalities across all age and racial groups, and less than 1% for African Americans, see http://www.suicidology.org/Portals/14/docs/Resources/FactSheets/2012datapgsv1d.pdf; see also http://www.cdc.gov/nchs/fastats/deaths.htm. According to the Centers for Disease Control and Prevention, this rate is understood to be rising among middle-aged adults in the United States, an increasing public health concern, see http://www.cdc.gov/mmwr/preview/mmwrhtml/mm6217a1.htm; and Emily Greenhouse, "The Neglected Suicide Epidemic," *New Yorker*, 13 March 2014 (http://www.newyorker.com/news/news-desk/the-neglected-suicide-epidemic); http://www.suicidology.org/Portals/14/docs/Resources/FactSheets/2012datapgsv1d.pdf. On eighteenth-century statistics, see David Eltis, *The Rise of African Slavery in the Americas* (New York: Cambridge University Press, 2000) 157n73. His conclusions are drawn from data from Richard H. Steckel and Richard A. Jenson, "New Evidence on the Causes of Slave and Crew Mortality in the Atlantic Trade," *Journal of Economic History* 46 (March 1986), 57–77. A sample of suicide in the Dutch trade suggests that rates were lower than those given by Eltis, accounting for nearly one percent of slave deaths in the Middle Passage; see Johannes Menne Postma, *The Dutch in the Atlantic Slave Trade, 1600–1815* (New York: Cambridge University Press, 1990), 241. On contemporary statistics, see "10 Leading Causes of Death by Age Group, United States-2010," National Vital Statistics System, National Center for Health Statistics, WISQARS, Center for Disease Control and Prevention (http://www.cdc.gov/injury/wisqars/index.html and http://webappa.cdc.gov/cgi-bin/broker.exe, accessed 9 June 2014); and "National Suicide Statistics, Fact Sheet, U.S.A. Suicide 2011 Official Final Data," American Association of Suicidology (http://www.suicidology.org/resources/facts-statistics-current-research/suicide-statistics, accessed 12 July 2014).

53. "Law Report, Trinity Term, 1785, *Jones Against Small*," *The Times*, 1 July 1785, p. 3, col. 1; James Oldham, "Insurance Litigation Involving the *Zong* and Other British Slave Ships, 1780–1807, *Journal of Legal History* 28 (July 2007), 309–310; Rediker, *The Slave Ship*, 291; Geoffrey Clark, *Betting on Lives: The Culture of Life Insurance in England, 1695–1775* (Manchester, UK: Manchester University Press, 1999), 16–17 (refers to the case as "Jones v. Schmoll").

54. Journal of James Matthew Morley, 1788–1789 ("suddenly," "sulkiness") from

"Extracts of Such Journals of the Surgeons Employed in Ships Trading to the Coast of Africa, Since the 1st of August 1788, as have been transmitted to the Custom House in London," House of Lords Papers, 3 May 1792, Slave Trade Papers, Shelf Number: HL/PO/JO/10/7/920, Parliamentary Archives, Houses of Parliament, London, England. See also Log of the *Union* (drowned, missing); Journal of the *Percival*, 1796 (jumped overboard); Log of the *Diana*, 1795 (six slaves died, no reason given), "Logbooks, etc. of slave ships, 1791–7, House of Lords Papers, 17–19 June, 1799," Shelf Number: HL/PO/JO/10/7/1104, Parliamentary Archives, Houses of Parliament. See also Rediker, *The Slave Ship*, 291.

55. Rediker, *The Slave Ship*, 291. On the methodological problems of studying the history of suicide, see Silkenat, *Moments of Despair*, 221–223.
56. Pérez, *To Die in Cuba*, 9.

CHAPTER ONE

1. P. E. H. Hair, Adam Jones, and Robin Law, eds., *Barbot on Guinea: The Writings of Jean Barbot on West Africa 1678–1712*, vol. 2 (London: Hakluyt Society, 1992), 639–640. Barbot identifies her homeland as "Aquambo" or the Akwamu state, which likely meant that she was Akan-speaking; see Ray A. Kea, "'When I Die, I Shall Return to My Own Land': An 'Amina' Slave Rebellion in the Danish West Indies, 1733–1734," in John Hunwick and Nancy Lawler, eds., *The Cloth of Many Colored Silks: Papers on History and Society, Ghananian and Islamic in Honor of Ivor Wilks* (Evanston, IL: Northwestern University Press, 1996), 160.
2. Marcus Rediker, *The Slave Ship: A Human History* (New York: Viking, 2007), 17–19.
3. Barbot's account was originally written in French; an English-language version was posthumously published and enjoyed wide circulation. On the composition and publication history of Barbot's manuscripts, see Hair, Jones, and Law, *Barbot on Guinea*, vol. 1, xxv–xxxvi, lii–liii.
4. Hair, Jones, and Law, *Barbot on Guinea*, vol. 2, 639.
5. See, for instance, Michael MacDonald and Terence R. Murphy, *Sleepless Souls: Suicide in Early Modern England* ([1990]; Oxford, UK: Oxford University Press, 2000); and Georges Minois, *History of Suicide: Voluntary Death in Western Culture*, trans. Lydia G. Cochrane (Baltimore: Johns Hopkins University Press, 1999).
6. Kelly McGuire, *Dying to Be English: Suicide Narratives and National Identity, 1721–1814* (London: Pickering and Chatto, 2012).
7. Hair, Jones, and Law, *Barbot on Guinea*, vol. 2, 639–640. On the use of death to measure early modern cultural difference, see Erik R. Seeman, *Death in the New World: Cross-Cultural Encounters, 1492–1800* (Philadelphia: University of Pennsylvania Press, 2010), 2–8.
8. Marcus Rediker describes this as a "language of action"; see *The Slave Ship*, 285 and also 284–291.
9. Joseph C. Miller, *Way of Death: Merchant Capitalism and the Angolan Slave Trade, 1730–1830* (Madison: University of Wisconsin Press, 1988), 42; Eric Robert Taylor, *If We Must Die: Shipboard Insurrections in the Era of the Atlantic Slave Trade* (Baton Rouge: Louisiana State University Press, 2006), 28–39.
10. John Thornton, "Cannibals, Witches, and Slave Traders in the Atlantic World," *William and Mary Quarterly*, 3d ser., 60 (2003), 273–294; William D. Pierson, "White Cannibals, Black Martyrs: Fear, Depression, and Religious Faith as Causes of Suicide among New Slaves," *Journal of Negro History* 62 (1977), 147–150; Daniel E. Walker, "Suicidal Tendencies: African Transmigration in the History and Folklore of the

Americas," *The Griot* 18 (1999), 10–19. Melancholy and nostalgia were frequently used to explain slave suicide in Latin America, but as discussed later in this chapter, they were also used to describe slave suicide in the British Caribbean. See Adrian López Denis, "Melancholia, Slavery, and Racial Pathology in Eighteenth-Century Cuba, *Science in Context*, 18 (2005), 179–199; and Mary C. Karasch, *Slave Life in Rio de Janeiro, 1808–1850* (Princeton, NJ: Princeton University Press, 1987), 316–320.

11. Hair, Jones, and Law, *Barbot on Guinea*, vol. 2, 639.
12. Henry Laurens to Henry Brith, 3 October 1769, in George Rogers, Jr., David R. Chesnutt, and Peggy J. Clark, eds., *The Papers of Henry Laurens*, vol. 7 (Columbia: University of South Carolina Press, 1979), 192; Henry Laurens to Peter Furnell, 6 September 1755, in Philip M. Hamer, George C. Rogers, Jr., and Peggy J. Wehage, eds., *The Papers of Henry Laurens*, vol. 1 (Columbia: University of South Carolina Press, 1970), 331; Elizabeth Donnan, *Documents Illustrative of the History of the Slave Trade to America* (Washington, DC: Carnegie Institution of Washington, 1935), vol. 4, 316–317n3; and Henry Laurens to Devonsheir, Reeve, and Lloyd, 22 May 1755 in Hamer, Rogers, and Wehage, *The Papers of Henry Laurens*, vol. I, 252.
13. Testimony of George Baillie in *HCSP*, vol, 73, 204.
14. David Brion Davis, *The Problem of Slavery in the Age of Revolution, 1770–1823* (New York: Oxford University Press, 1999), 32; William M. Wiecek, *The Sources of Antislavery Constitutionalism in America, 1760–1848* (Ithaca, NY: Cornell University Press), 70–83; James Walvin, *England, Slaves, and Freedom, 1776–1838* (Jackson: University of Mississippi Press, 1986), 97–122.
15. Philippe Ariès, *The Hour of Our Death*, trans. Helen Weaver (New York: Knopf, 1981; reprint New York: Oxford University Press, 1991), xvi. See also MacDonald and Murphy, *Sleepless Souls*, 46; S. E. Sprott, *The English Debate on Suicide from Donne to Hume* (LaSalle, IL: Open Court Publishing, 1961); Alexander Murray, *Suicide in the Middle Ages*, 2 vols. (Oxford, UK: Oxford University Press, 1998-2000); Minois, *History of Suicide*; Jeffrey R. Watt, *Choosing Death: Suicide and Calvinism in Early Modern Geneva* (Kirksville, MO: Truman State University Press, 2001); Jeffrey R. Watt, ed., *From Sin to Insanity: Suicide in Early Modern Europe* (Ithaca, NY: Cornell University, Press, 2004); R. A. Houston, *Punishing the Dead? Suicide, Lordship, and Community in Britain, 1500–1830* (Oxford, UK: Oxford University Press, 2010); and Paul Seaver, ed., *The History of Suicide in England, 1650–1850*, 4 vols. (London: Pickering and Chatto, 2012).
16. On deathways and the colonization of North America, see Seeman, *Death in the New World*; and David Stannard, *The Puritan Way of Death: A Study in Religion, Culture, and Social Change* (New York: Oxford University Press, 1979), 3–30. See also Karla F. C. Holloway, *Passed On: On African American Mourning Stories: A Memorial Collection* (Durham, NC: Duke University Press, 2002); Mark S. Schantz, *Awaiting the Heavenly County: The Civil War and America's Culture of Death* (Ithaca, NY: Cornell University Press, 2008), and Drew Gilpin Faust, *This Republic of Suffering: Death and the American Civil War* (New York: Knopf, 2008).
17. Pierson, "White Cannibals, Black Martyrs", 151; Samuel Johnson, *The History of the Yorubas: From the Earliest Times to the Beginning of the British Protectorate* (London: Routledge and Paul, 1921; reprint, 1966), 54–57; and Basil Davidson, *African Slave Trade: Precolonial History 1450–1850* (Boston: Little, Brown, 1921), 236.
18. Michael A. Gomez, *Exchanging Our Country Marks: The Transformation of African Identities in the Colonial and Antebellum South* (Chapel Hill: University of North Carolina Press, 1998), 133 ("abomination"), 117 ("unthinkable), 116–120, 127–134

(inclusive discussion). See also Elizabeth Isichei, *Voices of the Poor of Africa* (Rochester, NY: University of Rochester Press, 2002), 37. On the issue of African ethnicity, see David Eltis, *The Rise of African Slavery in the Americas* (Cambridge, UK: Cambridge University Press, 2000), 224–257.

19. Melville J. Herskovits, *Dahomey, An Ancient West African Kingdom* (Evanston, IL: Northwestern University Press, 1967), vol. 1, 397.
20. Gomez, *Exchanging Our Country Marks,* 133; and Jack Goody, *Death, Property, and Ancestors: A Study of the Mortuary Customs of the LoDagaa of West Africa* (London: Tavistock Press, 1962), 151–155.
21. Jerome S. Handler, "A Prone Burial from a Plantation Slave Cemetery in Barbados, West Indies: Possible Evidence for an African-Type Witch or Other Negatively Buried Person," *Historical Archaeology* 30 (1996), 81–82.
22. Gomez, *Exchanging Our Country Marks,* 116–120, 127–134. See also Isichei, *A History of the Igbo People.*
23. For accounts of slaves who attempted suicide after initial loading onto ships, see Alexander X. Byrd, *Captives and Voyagers: Black Migrants across the Eighteenth-Century British Atlantic World* (Baton Rouge: Louisiana State University Press, 2008), 41.
24. Gomez, *Exchanging Our Country Marks,* 133–134; Pierson, "White Cannibals, Black Martyrs," 152–154; Walker, "Suicidal Tendencies," 10–19; and Sylvia R. Frey and Betty Wood, *Come Shouting to Zion: African American Protestantism in the American South and British Caribbean to 1830* (Chapel Hill: University of North Carolina Press, 1998), 28.
25. John Thornton, "Religious and Ceremonial Life in the Kongo and Mbundu Areas, 1500–1700," in Linda Heywood, ed., *Central Africans and Cultural Transformations in the American Diaspora* (New York: Cambridge University Press, 2002), 75.
26. Thornton, "Religious and Ceremonial Life in the Kongo and Mbundu Areas," 79–80.
27. Gomez, *Exchanging Our Country Marks,* 117, 120–121, 130–134.
28. Sally E. Hadden, "The Fragmented Laws of Slavery in the Colonial and Revolutionary Eras," in Michael Grossberg and Christopher Tomlins, eds., *Cambridge History of Law in America,* vol. 1 (New York: Cambridge University Press, 2008), 285.
29. Olaudah Equiano, *The Life of Olaudah Equiano or Gustavus Vassa, the African,* vol. 1, ed. Paul Edwards (London: Dawsons of Pall Mall, 1969), 80–81. The veracity of Equiano's account of his African birth and, therefore, his experience of the Middle Passage, has been called into question, but his account seems remarkably accurate with regard to the trauma of enslavement and the nature of the slave trade. See Vincent Carretta, *Equiano, the African: Biography of a Self-Made Man* (Athens: University of Georgia Press, 2007), 1-39; Paul E. Lovejoy, "Autobiography and Memory: Gustavus Vassa, alias Olaudah Equiano, the African," *Slavery and Abolition* 27 (2006), 317–347; Alexander X. Byrd, "Eboe, Country, Nation, and Gustavus Vassa's *Interesting Narrative,*" *William and Mary Quarerly,* 3d ser., 58 (2006), 123–148; and Gregory E. O'Malley, *Final Passages: The Intercolonial Slave Trade of British America, 1619–1807* (Chapel Hill: University of North Carolina Press, 2014), 32–35.
30. Fredrika Bremer, *The Homes of the New World: Impressions of America,* trans. Mary Howitt, vol. 2 (New York: Harper & Brothers Publishers, 1853), 332.
31. Elizabeth Keckley, *Behind the Scenes, or, Thirty Years a Slave and Four Years in the White House* (New York: G. W. Carleton, 1868), 30 (http://docsouth.unc.edu/neh/keckley/keckley.html, accessed 7 April 2015).
32. Letter from Frederick Douglass, 5 September 1850, *Frederick Douglass: Selected Speeches and Writings,* Philip S. Foner, ed. (Chicago: Lawrence Hill Books, 1999), 162.

33. Charles Ball, *Slavery in the United States: A Narrative of the Life and Adventures of Charles Ball, A Black Man* (New York: John S. Taylor, 1837), 70 (http://www.docsouth.unc.edu/neh/ballslavery/ball.html, accessed 2 June 2013).
34. David Daube, "The Linguistics of Suicide," *Philosophy and Public Affairs* 1 (1972), 419–429.
35. Early modern missionaries who worked among the Iroquois also linked permissiveness in childrearing to suicide, suggesting the influence of Catholicism in their interpretations; see J. F. Lafitau, *Moeurs de Sauvages Americquains* (1724), as translated by and cited in William N. Fenton, "Iroquois Suicide: A Study in the Stability of a Cultural Pattern," *Bureau of American Ethnology Bulletin*, no. 128, Anthropological Papers, no. 14 (Washington, DC, 1941), 107.
36. John Sym, *Life's Preservative Against Self-Murder* (London, 1637), A3, HL.
37. William Blackstone, *Commentaries on the Law of England*, 4 vols. (London, 1809), 4: 189–190.
38. Leonard W. Levy, *License to Steal: The Forfeiture of Property* (Chapel Hill: University of North Carolina Press, 1996), 31–37.
39. MacDonald and Murphy, *Sleepless Souls*, 126–132.
40. On desecration practices, see MacDonald and Murphy, *Sleepless Souls*, 44–51; Minois, *History of Suicide*, 200–202; Machiel Bosman, "The Judicial Treatment of Suicide in Amsterdam," in Watt, ed., *From Sin to Insanity: Suicide in Early Modern Europe*, 18–23; Craig M. Koslofsky, "Controlling the Body of the Suicide in Saxony," in Watt, *From Sin to Insanity*, 52–56; and Elizabeth G. Dickenson and James M. Boyden, "Ambivalence toward Suicide in Golden Age Spain," in Watt, *From Sin to Insanity*, 100–105. In an interesting variation, Koslofsky reports that in early modern Germany, a suicide's clothing was used to strengthen livestock, the hands and skull of a suicide were understood to have healing capacities, and soil from a suicide's grave was believed to have magical powers; see Koslofsky, "Controlling the Body," 52.
41. Gomez, *Exchanging Our Country Marks*, 117; Louis A. Pérez, Jr., *To Die in Cuba: Suicide and Society* (Chapel Hill: University of North Carolina Press, 2005), 34–38.
42. Hair, Jones, and Law, *Barbot on Guinea*, vol. 2, 639–640.
43. Quoted in Thornton, "Cannibals, Witches, and Slave Traders," 274.
44. Johannes Menne Postma, *The Dutch in the Atlantic Slave Trade, 1600–1815* (Cambridge, UK: Cambridge University Press, 1990), 242.
45. Taylor, *If We Must Die*, 33.
46. *HCSP*, vol. 69, 126.
47. Log of *Le Jeune Louis*, French Clandestine Slave Trade Collection, 1822–1828, HL.
48. Alexander Falconbridge, *An account of the slave trade on the coast of Africa, by Alexander Falconbridge, Late Surgeon in the African Trade* (London, 1788), 33-41.
49. Account of J. B. Romaigne, 1819, in George Francis Dow, ed., *Slave Ships and Slaving* (Salem, MA: Marine Research Society, 1927), xxx.
50. *HCSP*, vol. 72, 274.
51. Captain Theophilus Conneau, *A Slaver's Log Book or 20 Years Residence in Africa*, Howard S. Mott, ed. (London: Robert Hale Limited, 1977), 208; and Malcolm Cowley, *Adventures of an African Slaver: Being a True Account of the Life of Captain Theodore Canot* (London: George Routledge, 1928), 264. The accounts disagree in particulars: the former calls the ship the *Venus* and notes that the suicides made Conneau uneasy; while the latter identifies the vessel as *La Estrella* and indicates that "the officers" were uneasy. The editor of the 1977 version asserts that it is a more

authentic transcription; see Conneau, *A Slaver's Log Book*, iii–iv. On Conneau, see Daniel P. Mannix and Malcolm Cowley, *Black Cargoes: A History of the Atlantic Slave Trade, 1518–1865* (New York: Viking, 1962), 235, 294.

52. Conneau, *A Slaver's Log Book*, 208.
53. Dow, *Slave Ships and Slaving*, xxx–xxxi.
54. "Law Report, Trinity Term, 1785, Jones Against Small, *The Times*, 1 July 1785, p. 3, col. 1; see also Rediker, *The Slave Ship*, 291; Taylor, *If We Must Die*, 165–166. On women as leaders in shipboard revolts, see Deborah Grey White, *Ar'nt I a Woman: Female Slaves in the Plantation South* (New York: W. W. Norton, 1985), 63–65.
55. Pierson, "White Cannibals, Black Martyrs," 147–150; Taylor, *If We Must Die*, 25–26; Miller, *Way of Death*, 413, n. 134.
56. Hair, Jones, and Law, *Barbot on Guinea*, vol. 2, 550; Pierson, "White Cannibals, Black Martyrs," 148–150.
57. Thornton, "Cannibals, Witches, and Slave Traders in the Atlantic World," 275; Pierson, "White Cannibals, Black Martyrs," 147–149.
58. T. Aubrey, M.D., *The sea-surgeon, or the Guinea man's vade mecum* (London : printed for John Clarke at the Bible under the Royal-Exchange, 1729), 128. *Eighteenth Century Collections Online*. On other instances of suicide in the trade, see Rediker, *The Slave Ship*, 284–291.
59. *HCSP*, vol. 72, 274; Mannix and Cowley, *Black Cargoes*, 121.
60. *HCSP*, vol. 72, 274–275; see also Mannix and Cowley, *Black Cargoes*, 119–121; and Denis, "Melancholia, Slavery, and Racial Pathology in Eighteenth-Century Cuba."
61. *HCSP*, vol. 72, 300.
62. [Thomas Phillips], "The Voyage of the Ship *Hannibal* of London, in 1693"; extracted in Dow, *Slave Ships and Slaving*, 62–63.
63. John Stewart, *A View of the Past and Present State of the Island of Jamaica With Remarks on the Moral and Physical Condition of the Slaves and on the Abolition of Slavery in the Colonies* (Edinburgh, 1823), 280-281.
64. James Oldham, "Insurance Litigation Involving the *Zong* and Other British Slave Ships, 1780–1807," *Journal of Legal History* 28 (2007), 299–300, 310–318; Jonathon Levy, *Freaks of Fortune: The Emerging World of Capitalism and Risk in America* (Cambridge, MA: Harvard University Press, 2012), 47–49; Rediker, *The Slave Ship*, 240; Ian Baucom, *Specters of the Atlantic: Finance Capital, Slavery, and the Philosophy of History* (Durham, NC: Duke University Press, 2005), 128–135.
65. Stephanie E. Smallwood, *Saltwater Slavery: A Middle Passage from Africa to American Diaspora* (Cambridge, MA: Harvard University Press, 2007), 34.
66. *HCSP*, vol. 73, 88; see also *HCSP*, vol. 72, 277.
67. Postma, *The Dutch in the Atlantic Slave Trade, 1600–1815*, 241.
68. Linda A. Newson and Susie Minchin, *From Captive to Sale: The Portuguese Slave Trade to Spanish South America in the Early Seventeenth Century* (Leiden, Netherlands: Brill, 2007), 120–121.
69. *HCSP*, vol. 73, 83 (throat cutting), 124 (child); for examples of self-starvation, see also *HCSP*, vol. 69, 125; vol. 73, 88,117, 138, 160, 375.
70. The officer was Paul Erdmann Isert, first a Royal Medical Officer for the Danish Hospital on the Gold Coast and, later, a medical officer on slave ships in the late eighteenth century. See Isidor Paiewonsky, *Eyewitness Accounts of Slavery in the Danish West Indies* (New York: Fordham University Press, 1989), 21.
71. Brig Sally's Account Book, 1764–1765, 69 (http://dl.lib.brown.edu/repository2/repoman.php?verb=render&id=1161038386638650); *HCSP*, vol. 72, 279–280.

72. On rails and nets, see *HCSP*, vol. 68, 270; Hair, Jones, and Law, *Barbot on Guinea*, vol. 2, 639–640; Equiano, *The Life of Olaudah Equiano or Gustavas Vassa, the African*, vol. 1, 82. See also *HCSP*, vol. 68, 270; Rediker, *The Slave*; Taylor, *If We Must Die*; Smallwood, *Saltwater Slavery*; Thornton, "Cannibals, Witches, and Slave Traders," 273–294.
73. *HCSP*, vol. 68, 270.
74. *HCSP*, vol. 72, 281.
75. [Phillips], "The Voyage of the Ship *Hannibal*," 62–63.
76. Dow, *Slave Ships and Slaving*, xxx–xxxi.
77. Pierson, "White Cannibals, Black Martyrs," 154–155.
78. Kevin Dawson, *Enslaved Water People in the Atlantic World, 1444–1888: The Cultural Meanings of Water, Swimming, Surfing, and Canoeing in Atlantic Africa and the African Diaspora* (Philadelphia: University of Pennsylvania Press, forthcoming).
79. [Phillips], "The Voyage of the Ship *Hannibal*," 63.
80. Public health researcher Richard Seiden, for instance, cites an example from mid-twentieth-century England, where nearly half of suicides died by self-asphyxiation in coal-gas ovens. Once Great Britain converted to the less toxic natural gas in the 1950s, however, the suicide rate plummeted by a third. See Seiden, "Where Are They Now? A Follow-up Study of Suicide Attempters from the Golden Gate Bridge," *Suicide and Life-Threatening Behavior* 8 (Winter 1978), 2, 13.
81. Scott Anderson, "The Urge to End It All," *New York Times Magazine*, July 6, 2008 (http://www.nytimes.com/2008/07/06/magazine/06suicide-t.html?pagewanted=1, accessed 13 August 2011).
82. Quoted in Taylor, *If We Must Die*, 38.
83. Taylor, *If We Must Die*, 37–39; Rediker, *The Slave Ship*, 288.
84. The unnamed Gold Coast woman who leapt from the ship, leaving her child behind, was an accomplished swimmer and put her skills to use. Although she was two hundred leagues from shore, Barbot tells us that she could not drown herself; she may have been attempting to swim to land. Leaving the child behind and possessing the ability to swim left open the possibilities for her or his future. Perhaps, rather than giving her life to escape slavery, she may have intended to escape with her life. On African women as swimmers, see Kevin Dawson, "Enslaved Swimmers in the Atlantic World," *Journal of American History* 92 (March 2006), 1327–1355.
85. Dawson, *Enslaved Water People in the Atlantic World, 1444–1888*.
86. See Thornton, "Cannibals, Witches, and Slave Traders," 274.
87. Hadden, "The Fragmented Laws of Slavery," 284–285.
88. James Field Stanfield, *Observations on a Guinea Voyage. In a Series of Letters Addressed to Rev. Thomas Clarkson* (London, 1788), 32–33.
89. *HCSP*, vol. 72, 304.
90. Equiano, *The Life of Olaudah Equiano or Gustavus Vassa, The African*, vol. 1, 81–82.
91. "Extract of a Letter from on board the *Prince of Orange* of Bristol, Capt. Japhet Bird, dated from St. Christophers, April 7," *Boston Weekly News Letter*, no. 1748, Sept. 8–15, 1737, page 1.
92. Quoted in Postma, *The Dutch in the Atlantic Slave Trade*, p. 241.
93. See Joseph E. Inikori and Stanley L. Engerman, eds., *The Atlantic Slave Trade: Effects on Economies, Societies, and Peoples in Africa, the Americas, and Europe* (Durham, NC: Duke University Press, 1992), 328.
94. Miller, *Way of Death*, 420.
95. Miller, *Way of Death*, 420.

96. See for instance, Postma, *The Dutch in the Atlantic Slave Trade*, 241; Mannix and Cowley, *Black Cargoes*, 118–119.
97. George Howe, "The Last Slave-Ship," *Scribner's Magazine* 8 (July 1890), 123–124.

CHAPTER TWO

1. William Byrd II, *The Secret Diary of William Byrd II of Westover, 1709–1712*, ed. Louis B. Wright and Marion Tinling (Richmond: Dietz Press, 1941), 24 June–2 July 1710, 195–198.
2. African imports to Virginia rose sharply in the first decade of the eighteenth century, increasing the likelihood that the unnamed woman was a recent import; see Philip D. Morgan, *Slave Counterpoint: Black Culture in the Eighteenth-Century Chesapeake and Lowcountry* (Chapel Hill: University of North Carolina Press, 1998), 80–81.
3. Thomas Clarkson, *An Essay on the Slavery and Commerce of the Human Species* (London: Joseph Crukshank, 1785), 93.
4. On seasoning, see Paul Finkelman and Joseph C. Miller, eds., *Macmillian Encyclopedia of World Slavery*, vol. 2 (New York: Macmillian, 1999), 792; Joseph E. Inikori and Stanley L. Engerman, eds., *The Atlantic Slave Trade: Effects on Economies, Societies, and Peoples in Africa, the Americas, and Europe* (Durham, NC: Duke University Press, 1992), 352. For seasoning of blacks and whites, see Edmund Morgan, *American Slavery, American Freedom: The Ordeal of Colonial Virginia* (New York: Norton, 1975); and David Galenson, *White Servitude in Colonial America: An Economic Analysis* (New York: Cambridge University Press, 1981), 266–267.
5. Alexander X. Byrd, *Captives and Voyagers: Black Migrants Across the Eighteenth-Century British Atlantic World* (Baton Rouge: Louisiana State University Press, 2008), 61.
6. Brenda E. Stevenson, *Life in Black and White: Family and Community in the Slave* South (New York: Oxford University Press, 1996), 167–168.
7. Dr. Collins, *Practical Rules for the Management and Medical Treatment of Negro Slaves in the Sugar Colonies* (London: J. Barfield, 1811; reprint 1971), 44–53.
8. Stephanie E. Smallwood, *Saltwater Slavery: A Middle Passage from Africa to American Diaspora* (Cambridge, MA: Harvard University Press, 2007), 184.
9. Betty—as she was eventually named—ran away a total of nine times between June and November 1710: 25 June, 1 July, 2 July, 8 July, 15 July, 19 July, 10 August, 6 November, 12 November. See Byrd, *Secret Diary*, 196–197, 199, 202, 205, 206, 215–216, 254, 257.
10. Jason R. Young, *Rituals of Resistance: African Atlantic Religion in Congo and the Lowcountry South in the Era of Slavery* (Baton Rouge: Louisiana State University Press, 2007), 13.
11. Byrd, *Secret Diary*, 31 December 1710, 279–280; similarly, later when he was brought word that "one of my new negroes was in danger," Byrd was silent on the source of this harm. Byrd, *Secret Diary*, 27 January 1711, 293.
12. Byrd, *Secret Diary*, 31 December 1710, 279–280.
13. Hans Sloane, *A Voyage to the Islands of Madera, Barbados, Nieves, S. Christophers and Jamaica*, vol. 1 (London: Printed by B.M. for the Author, 1707), xlviii, BL, Shelfmark 38.f.4.
14. Kevin J. Hayes, *The Library of William Byrd of Westover* (Madison, WI: Madison House, 1997), 42–43. However, the volume is not listed as part of the library. For the letter, see Marion Tinling, ed., *The Correspondence of the Three William Byrds of Westover, 1684–1776*, vol. 1 (Charlottesville: University of Virginia Press, 1977), 274–275.

15. Young, *Rituals of Resistance*, 12–13.
16. On scrambles and slave sales, see Byrd, *Captives and Voyagers*, 60–62; Gregory E. O'Malley, *Final Passages: The Intercolonial Slave Trade of British America, 1619–1807* (Chapel Hill: University of North Carolina Press, 2014), 35-39; and Sean Kelley, "Scrambling for Slaves: Captive Sales in Colonial South Carolina," *Slavery and Abolition* 34 (August 2012), 1–21.
17. Olaudah Equiano, *The Life of Olaudah Equiano or Gustavus Vassa the African*, vol. 1 (London: Dawsons of Pall Mall, 1969), 86–87.
18. *HCSP*, vol. 73, 88; *HCSP*, vol. 72, 307–308.
19. *HCSP*, vol. 72, 308; Byrd, *Captives and Voyagers*; O'Malley, *Final Passages*, 35–39.
20. Edward Littleton, *Groans of the Plantations* (London: Clark, 1698), 19; Larry Gragg, "Littleton, Edward (*bap.* 1625, *d.* 1702)," in *Oxford Dictionary of National Biography*, ed. Lawrence Goldman (Oxford, UK: Oxford University Press, http://www.oxforddnb.com.huntington.idm.oclc.org/view/article/16782, accessed 30 December 2013); Vincent Brown, *The Reaper's Garden: Death and Power in the World of Atlantic Slavery* (Cambridge, MA: Harvard University Press, 2008), 50–54.
21. Testimony of Thomas Woolrich, in *HCSP*, vol. 73, 276.
22. Morgan, *Slave Counterpoint*, 444–445.
23. Morgan, *Slave Counterpoint*, 446.
24. Brown, *The Reaper's Garden*, 45.
25. Littleton, *Groans of the Plantations*, 20.
26. *HCSP*, vol. 82, 85.
27. These petitions are treated in detail in chapter 4.
28. Jerome S. Handler, "Life Histories of England Africans in Barbados," *Slavery and Abolition* 19 (April 1998), 132–133.
29. Brown, *The Reaper's Garden*, 44–46.
30. Handler, "Life Histories of England Africans in Barbados," 133; Smallwood, *Saltwater Slavery*, 205.
31. *HCSP*, vol. 69, 122.
32. "Petition of an African Slave, to the Legislature of Massachusetts," from *The American Museum, or Repository of Ancient and Modern Fugitive Pieces, Prose and Poetical*, June 1787, vol. 1, no. 6 (Philadelphia: Mathew Carey, 1787).
33. Morgan, *Slave Counterpoint*, 446.
34. *HCSP*, vol. 73, 277–278.
35. Petition of Peter Richeson, in *JHB*, 418; rejected. Although he did not specify that these slaves were newly imported, in years between 1730 and 1740 Virginia imported "more slaves than ever before or again in its history," and their collective suicide suggests the likelihood that they were new to the Americas; see Morgan, *Slave Counterpoint*, 81.
36. John S. Bassett, *Slavery in North Carolina* (Baltimore: Johns Hopkins University Press, 1899), 92–93. In the nineteenth century, in the Caribbean eleven slaves in Cuba hanged themselves collectively, while fourteen slaves in Jamaica went into the woods and cut their throats together. Louis A. Pérez, *To Die in Cuba: Suicide and Society* (Chapel Hill: University of North Carolina Press, 2005), 37; William D. Pierson, "White Cannibals, Black Martyrs: Fear, Depression, and Religious Faith as Causes of Suicide among New Slaves," *Journal of Negro History* 62 (1977), 152–153. Collective suicide seems to have occurred alongside enslavement across the world. English officers reported from the Malabar Coast of India that half of the ten men

transported to St. Helena to serve as slaves "soon after their arrival desperately hanged themselves," while the survivors, referred to as "desperate fellows," threatened to destroy themselves rather than submit to any kind of work." Dispatch, 11 November 1757, *Madras Dispatches, 28 November 1753–7 December 1757*, 814–814, Indian Office Records and Private Papers, IOR/Z/E/4/34/S53, BL.

37. George C. Rogers, Jr., David R. Chesnutt, and Peggy J. Clark, eds., *The Papers of Henry Laurens*, vol. 7 (Columbia: University of South Carolina Press, 1979), 192.
38. *Charleston Courier*, 7 January 1807. For the suicide of a child, see *HCSP*, vol. 82, 50.
39. *HCSP*, vol. 69, 122.
40. *HCSP*, vol. 82, 65.
41. *HCSP*, vol, 73, 278.
42. On Simon Overzee, see *Virginia Magazine of History and Biography* 3 (January 1896), 323–324; *Archives of Maryland*, ed. J. Hall Pleasants (Baltimore: Maryland Historical Society, 1937), vol. 41, 499–500; Alexa Silver Cawley, "A Passionate Affair: The Master-Servant Relationship in Seventeenth-Century Maryland," *The Historian* 61 (Summer 1999), 751–762; and Whittington B. Johnson, "The Origin and Nature of African Slavery in Maryland," *Maryland Historical Magazine* 73 (September 1978), 239.
43. Stephanie M. H. Camp, *Closer to Freedom: Enslaved Women and Everyday Resistance in the Plantation South* (Chapel Hill: University of North Carolina Press, 2004), 7. As Camp points out, the phrase originated with Edward Said, but she applies it specifically to slavery in the antebellum U.S.
44. Morgan, *Slave Counterpoint*, 446.
45. Note: I have regularized spelling and capitalization in the quotations from this episode. Overzee was tried because Tony "died under his correction." See *Attorney General v. Symon Overzee*, in Bernard Christian Steiner, ed., *Archives of Maryland* (Baltimore: Maryland Historical Society, 1922), vol. 41, 204 (charge); see also 190–191, 204–205.
46. Depositions of Hannah Littleworth and William Hewes, *Attorney General v. Symon Overzee*, 190–191.
47. Deposition of Job Chandler, *Attorney General v. Symon Overzee*, 205–6.
48. Deposition of Hannah Littleworth, *Attorney General v. Symon Overzee*, 190.
49. Elaine Forman Crane argues that the depression caused by pain elicits suicidal ideation; see "'I Have Suffer'd Much Today': The Defining Force of Pain in Early America," in Ronald Hoffman, Mechal Sobel, and Fredrika J. Teute, eds., *Through a Glass Darkly: Reflections on Personal Identity in Early America* (Chapel Hill: University of North Carolina Press, 1997), 385.
50. Deposition of Job Chandler, *Attorney General v. Symon Oversee*, 205–206.
51. Deposition of Hannah Littleworth, *Attorney General v. Symon Overzee*, 190.
52. Deposition of William Hewes, *Attorney General v. Symon Overzee*, 191.
53. Edward Long, *The History of Jamaica. Or, General Survey of the Antient and Modern State of that Island: With Reflections on Its Situation, Settlements, Inhabitants, Climate, Products, Commerce, Laws, and Government* (London: T. Lowndes, 1774), vol. 2, 304.
54. The slave later died from his injuries. See *HCSP*, vol. 82, 76.
55. Michael A. Gomez, *Exchanging Our Country Marks: The Transformation of African Identities in the Colonial and Antebellum South* (Chapel Hill: University of North Carolina Press, 1998), 135.
56. Byrd, *Captives and Voyagers*, 63.
57. No other unnamed slave is mentioned as having gone missing in this period, which is why, despite the editors' interpolations, it seems that all of the entries about the

unnamed enslaved woman and the woman that Byrd named Betty, refer to the same person. All interpolations are those of Wright and Tinling. The entries are as follows: Byrd, *Secret Diary*, 195, 24 June 1710, "I found all well except that a negro woman and seven cattle were gone away"; 196–197, 25 June 1710, "My people could not find the negro woman but found her hoe by the church land"; 28 June 2010, "The negro woman was found again that they thought had drowned herself"; 199, 1 July 1710, "The negro woman ran away again with the [bit] in her mouth"; 2 July 1710, "The negro woman ran away again with the [bit] in her mouth and my people could not find her"; 202, 8 July 1710, "The negro woman was found and tied but ran away again in the night"; 205, 15 July 1710, "About 7 o'clock the negro boy [or Betty] that ran away was brought home"; 206, 19 July 1710, "My negro boy [or Betty] ran away again but was soon caught. I was angry with John G-r-l for losing the screw of the [bit]"; 215–216, 10 August 1710, "My cousin's John brought home my negro G-l [girl?] that ran away three weeks ago"; 254, 6 November 1710, "The negro woman ran away again; and 257, 13 November 2010, "I had a letter from home which told me all was well except a negro woman who ran away and was found dead".

58. Although many scholars assume that assigning names to newly imported Africans was the master's domain, Jerome S. Handler and JoAnn Jacoby caution that this was not always the case; see "Slave Names and Naming in Barbadoes," *William and Mary Quarterly*, 3d ser., 53 (October 1996), 692; see also David Barry Gaspar, *Bondmen and Rebels: A Case Study of Master-Slave Relations in Antigua* (Baltimore: Johns Hopkins University Press, 1985), 131.
59. Byrd, *Secret Diary*, 202, 205–206.
60. Byrd, *Secret Diary*, 254 (6 November 1710 departure); 257 (13 November 2007 discovery of body).
61. Byrd, *Secret Diary*, 265 (30 November 1710).
62. Douglas B. Chambers, *Murder at Montpelier: Igbo Africans in Virginia* (Oxford: University of Mississippi Press, 2009), 67–74.
63. Inquest at Mr. John Foster's, 2 May, 1754, Craven County Coroner's Reports, Series SSXVIII, Box 1, Folder 1754; Inquest Taken at the Cypress Swamp, 6 May 1759, Craven County Coroner's Reports, Series SSXVIII, Box 1, 1759; Inquest on Hannah, Randolph County 27 October 1812, Box: CR 081.928.4, Folder: Coroners, 1808–29, NCSA. Representative examples from Kershaw County, South Carolina, include the Inquest on the body of negro man slave to Darling Jones, 13 March 1824 (verdict: accidentally fell and drown), and the Inquest on Bob a negro slave, 18 February 1823 (verdict: death by exposure). Kershaw District, Kershaw County Court General Sessions, Coroner's Inquisitions, 1801–1911, South Carolina Court of General Sessions (Kershaw) Series L28183, SCDAH.
64. In 1805, a South Carolina coroner's jury was ordered to go "into the woods, then and there to inquire upon the view of a Body, of a certain person then hanging and how and in what manner he came to his death." Inquest on Unknown Negro, 26 June 1805, Kershaw District, Kershaw County Court General Court Sessions, Coroner's Inquisitions, 1801–1911, Box 1, Stack Location 273L04, SCDAH. The enslaved man Henry was ruled to have hung himself accidentally by "swinging by a rope used for suspending a wagon body." Inquisition on Henry, 17 September 1829, Coroner's Inquests, 1806–69, Union County Court General Sessions, Box 1, Stack Location 268J02, SCDAH.
65. *The Story of Mattie J. Jackson; A True Story*, in *Six Women's Slave Narratives* (New York: Oxford University Press, 1988), 6.

66. Kevin Dawson, *Enslaved Water People in the Atlantic World, 1444–1888: The Cultural Meanings of Water, Swimming, Surfing, and Canoeing in Atlantic Africa and the African Diaspora* (Philadelphia: University of Pennsylvania Press, forthcoming).
67. Mary C. Karasch, *Slave Life in Rio de Janeiro, 1808–1850* (Princeton, NJ: Princeton University Press, 1987), 319; Dawson, *Enslaved Water People in the Atlantic World, 1444–1888*.
68. Dawson, *Enslaved Water People in the Atlantic World 1444–1888*; Karasch, *Slave Life in Rio de Janeiro*, 319–320.
69. Smallwood, *Saltwater Slavery*, 183–186; Pérez, *To Die in Cuba*, 37–38.
70. Winfield Scott, *Memoirs of Lieut.-General Scott, LL.D, Written By Himself*, vol. 1 (New York: Sheldon and Co., 1864), 23–24.
71. Bassett, *Slavery in North Carolina*, 92–93.
72. Dawson, *Enslaved Water People in the Atlantic World, 1444–1888*.
73. Smallwood, *Saltwater Slavery*,183–186; William D. Pierson, *Black Yankees: The Development of an Afro-American Subculture in Eighteenth-Century New England* (Amherst: University of Massachusetts Press, 1988), 75; Dawson, *Enslaved Water People in the Atlantic World, 1444–1888*.
74. Pierson, *Black Yankees*, 75.
75. Sloane, *A Voyage to the Islands of Madera, Barbados, Nieves, S. Christophers and Jamaica*, vol. 1, xlviii.
76. See Dawson, *Enslaved Water People in the Atlantic World, 1444–1888*; Aimery P. Caron and Arnold R. Highfield, trans. and eds., *The French Intervention in the St. John Slave Revolt of 1733–34* (Charlotte Amalie, St. Thomas, Virgin Islands: Bureau of Libraries, Museums, and Archaeological Services, Department of Conservation and Cultural Affairs,1981), 51n.13; Ray A. Kea, "When I Die, I Shall Return to My Own Land: An 'Amina' Slave Rebellion in the Danish West Indies, 1733–1734," in John Hunwick and Nancy Lawler, eds., *The Cloth of Many Colored Silks: Papers on History and Society Ghanaian and Islamic in Honor of Ivor Wilks* (Evanston, IL: Northwestern University Press 1997), 159–160.
77. Pierson, *Black Yankees*, 75.
78. John Stewart, *A View of the Past and Present State of the Island of Jamaica With Remarks on the Moral and Physical Condition of the Slaves and on the Abolition of Slavery in the Colonies* (Edinburgh, 1823), 280–281.
79. Postscript-Saturday Evening, *Pennsylvania Evening Herald*, 18 June 1785, vol. 1, issue 42, 2.
80. Pierson, "White Cannibals, Black Martyrs," 154–155.
81. See, for instance, the essays collected in Jeffrey R. Watt, ed., *From Sin to Insanity: Suicide in Early Modern Europe* (Ithaca, NY: Cornell University Press, 2004); and Philip J. Schwarz, *Slave Laws in Virginia* (Athens: University of Georgia Press, 1996), 72–73.
82. Pierson, "White Cannibals, Black Martyrs," 154–155; Vincent Brown, "Spiritual Terror and Sacred Authority: The Power of the Supernatural in Jamaican Slave Society," in Baptist and Camp, eds., *New Studies in the History of American Slavery*, 179–184; and Dawson, *Enslaved Water People in the Atlantic World, 1444–1888*.
83. The planter's mask was an idea inspired by Bertram Wyatt-Brown, who wrote extensively about masks and slaves; see "The Mask of Obedience: Male Slave Psychology in the Old South," *American Historical Review* 93 (December 1988): 1228–1252.
84. Inquest on Teena, 11 January 1796," Coroners' Inquisitions, 1784–1799, Series L49076, South Carolina Court of General Sessions, Camden County, SCDAH.

85. John W. Blassingame, ed., *Slave Testimony: Two Centuries of Letters, Speeches, Interviews, and Autobiographies* (Baton Rouge: Louisiana State University Press, 1977), 285; see also 165n19.
86. *St. Bernard Alexandre Ville v. Perry*, 5 October 1741, in Heloise H. Cruzat, trans. and ed., "Records of the Superior Council of Louisiana, XXXVII," *Louisiana Historical Quarterly* 11 (January 1928), 141. See also *Ritchie v. Wilson* (1825), 3 Mart. (n.s.) 585, 1825 La. LEXIS 82. Seaman William Snelgrave noted that insurrections aboard ships were caused by "sailors' ill-usage" of their human cargo, and it seems reasonable that others would attribute suicide on plantations to the same cause. William Snelgrave, *New Account of Some Parts of Guinea and the Slave Trade* (London, 1734), 162–165.
87. See for instance the account of Betty and that of Jenny, who ran into the James River. Byrd, *The Secret Diary*, 195-199, and 15, and Jack P. Greene, ed., *The Diary of Colonel Landon Carter of Sabine Hall, 1752 to 1752–1778* (Charlottesville: University of Virginia Press, 1965), vol. 1, 119.
88. See chapter 4.
89. Deposition of William Beverley in *HCSP*, vol. 82, 217. Beverley testified that the slave population of Virginia was replacing itself naturally, rather than through imports and suggested that a cessation of the transatlantic slave trade would have little effect on slaves in the United States; see *HCSP*, vol. 82, 216–218. For testimony on numbers of slave suicides, see *HCSP*, vol. 82, 35, 49, 65, 71–74, 85, 196, 204, 211, 229, 230. For other testimony that seasoned slaves were not at all prone to suicide, see *HCSP*, vol. 82, 85, 172.
90. William was the son of Robert and Maria Carter Beverley, one of the most powerful families in early Virginia; see Brent Tarter, "Robert Beverley," in John T. Kneebone, J. Jefferson Looney, Brent Tarter, and Sandra Gioia Treadway, eds., *Dictionary of Virginia Biography* (Richmond: Library of Virginia, 1998), vol. 1, 473–474.
91. *HCSP*, vol. 73, 194–195.
92. Snelgrave, *A New Account of Some Parts of Guinea and the Slave Trade*, 162–165.
93. Henry Laurens to Peter Furnell, 6 September 1755, in Philip M. Hamer, George C. Rogers, Jr., and Peggy J. Wehage, eds., *The Papers of Henry Laurens*, vol. 1 (Columbia: University of South Carolina Press, 1970), 331.
94. *HCSP*, vol. 73, 204; Collins, *Practical Rules for the Management and Medical Treatment of Negro Slaves in the Sugar Colonies*, 37.
95. Gomez, *Exchanging Our Country Marks*, 114–153.
96. Elizabeth Donnan, *Documents Illustrative of the History of the Slave Trade to America* (Washington, D.C.: Carnegie Institution of Washington, 1965), vol. 4, 316–317. Virginians were not, however, dissuaded from Igbo imports, which constituted almost 38 percent of all slaves brought into Virginia in the eighteenth century. See Gomez, *Exchanging Our Country Marks*, 115; see also the discussion, 114–133.
97. James Grainger, "A History of Sugar Cane, from a Poem called Sugar Cane," *Gentleman's Magazine* (October 1764), 487, and later published as *The Sugar Cane: A Poem in Four Books* (London: Printed for R. and J. Dodsley, 1764), Book 4, 129, 130. On James Grainger and the popularity of the poem, see John Gilmore, *The Poetics of Empire: A Study of James Grainger's The Sugar Cane* (London: Athlone Press, 2000), 1–85; and David Shields, *Oracles of Empire: Poetry, Politics, and Commerce in British America, 1690–1750* (Chicago: University of Chicago Press, 1990), 72–78. For one of the latest printings of the quoted lines, see *Debow's Review, Agricultural, Commercial,*

Industrial Progress and Resources 9, no. 6 (1850), 668. "The Moco-nation" probably referred to a diverse range of peoples shipped from Western Africa; see Philip D. Curtin, *The Atlantic Slave Trade: A Census* (Madison: University of Wisconsin Press, 1969), 188.

98. Grainger, *The Sugar Cane*, 128–129.
99. William Mayo to John Perratt, 17 August 1731, VHS.

CHAPTER THREE

1. *VG* (Hunter), 10 July 1752, 3. For other discussions of this incident, see Alex Bontemps, *The Punished Self: Surviving Slavery in the Colonial South* (Ithaca, NY: Cornell University Press, 2001), 88–92; and Rhys Isaac, "On Explanation, Text, and Terrifying Power in Ethnographic History," *Yale Journal of Criticism* 6 (1993), 217–218.
2. On the timing and emergence of slave societies, see Ira Berlin, *Many Thousands Gone: The First Two Centuries of Slavery in North America* (Cambridge, MA: Belknap Press of Harvard University, 1998), 7–9.
3. The items were not given equal space. The Reverend Davies's disquisition on melancholy ran more than one hundred lines and extended over portions of two columns—the printer noted that a pamphlet was a "more proper vehicle" for these sentiments—while the other accounts ran fewer than twenty lines, with the advertisement for the sale of enslaved people and the notice of the unnamed man's suicide occupying the least amount of text. The editor's insertion was a not-so-subtle indication that the paper was modernizing as well; see *VG* (Hunter), 10 July 1752, 3.
4. Attempts were made to revive suicides; for an instance of a slave who attempts to kill himself but is saved through the efforts of a surgeon, see *VG* (Pinkney), 14 September 1775, 3.
5. Walter Johnson, "On Agency," *Journal of Social History* 37 (Fall 2003), 113–114, 118.
6. Group reading and reading out loud were common in early America. Reading, discussing, and debating newspapers in public venues was a typical occurrence at the coffeehouses, pubs, and commercial exchanges that often supplied newspapers. See Reinhard Wittmann, "Was There a Reading Revolution at the End of the Eighteenth Century?" in Guglielmo Cavallo and Roger Chartier, eds., *A History of Reading in the West*, trans. Lydia G. Cochrane (Amherst: University of Massachusetts Press, 1999), 284–286, 291–293; R. M. Wiles, *Freshest Advices: Early Provincial Newspapers in England* (Columbus: Ohio University Press, 1965), 25–26; Jeffrey L. Pasley, *"The Tyranny of Printers": Newspaper Politics in the Early American Republic* (Charlottesville: University of Virginia Press, 2001), 7–8; and William J. Gilmore, *Reading Becomes a Necessity of Life: Material and Cultural Life in Rural New England, 1780–1835* (Knoxville: University of Tennessee Press, 1989), 193.
7. P. E. H. Hair, Adam Jones, and Robin Law, eds., *Barbot on Guinea: The Writings of Jean Barbot on West Africa 1678–1712*, vol. 2 (London: Hakluyt Society, 1992), 639.
8. Byrd's social capital was so influential that his death helped to preserve what was left of his fortune for his family. See A. G. Roeber, *Faithful Magistrates and Republican Lawyers: Creators of Virginia Legal Culture, 1660–1810* (Chapel Hill: University of North Carolina Press, 1981), 170; and Woody Holton, *Forced Founders: Indians, Debtors, Slaves, and the Making of the Revolution in Virginia* (Chapel Hill: University of North Carolina Press, 1999), 43.
9. Bertram Wyatt-Brown, *Southern Honor: Ethics and Behavior in the Old South* ([1983]; New York: Oxford University Press, 2007), 375.

10. Michael MacDonald and Terence R. Murphy, *Sleepless Souls: Suicide in Early Modern England* ([1990] Oxford, UK: Oxford University Press, 2000), 179–190 (code of male honor), 274–281 (upper classes), 281–300 (women and lower classes).
11. Catherine Molineux, *Faces of Perfect Ebony: Encountering Atlantic Slavery in Imperial Britain* (Cambridge, MA: Harvard University Press, 2012), 53.
12. *HCSP*, vol. 82, 50.
13. *HCSP*, vol. 82, 65.
14. *South Carolina Gazette*, 5 May 1759, 3.
15. Giraloma Benzoni, *History of the New World*, trans. and ed. W. H. Smyth (London: Hakluyt Society, 1857), vol. 21, 77–78; see also Bartolome de las Casas, *The Tears of the Indians*, trans. John Phillips (Stanford, CA: Academic Reprints, 1953), 16, 63; and *The Devastation of the Indies: A Brief Account*, trans. Bill M. Donovan (Baltimore: Johns Hopkins University Press, 1992), 46–47.
16. On indigenous suicide in early America, see *The Jesuit Relations and Allied Documents*, vol. 58, ed. Reuben Gold Thwaits, computerized transcription by Tomasz Mentrak (Cleveland: Burrows Brothers, 1902), 239 (http://puffin.creighton.edu/jesuit/relations/relations_58.html, accessed 24 February 2012); John Heckewelder, *The History, Manners, and Customs of the Indian Nations* ([1819]; Philadelphia: Historical Society of Philadelphia, 1876), in Edward Armstrong, ed., *Memoirs of the Historical Society of Pennsylvania*, vol. 12 (Philadelphia: McCarty and Davis, 1864), 258–259. Naturalists' accounts similarly agreed with these assessments. For instance, John Lawson reports that an Indian youth aged about twenty killed himself after his mother chastised him for drinking rum; see *A New Voyage to Carolina*, ed. Hugh Talmage Lefler (Chapel Hill: University of North Carolina Press, 1967), 211.
17. Heckewelder, *The History, Manners, and Customs of the Indian Nations*, 258–259. The Huron, for instance, appeared to make no distinction between suicides and natural deaths. Jesuit Brebeuf, for instance, writes that they honored "equally the internment" of the "the good and the bad, the virtuous and the vicious" deaths. William N. Fenton, "Iroquois Suicide: A Study in the Stability of a Cultural Pattern," *Bureau of American Ethnology Bulletin*, no. 128, Anthropological Papers, no. 14 (Washington, D.C. 1941), 134, 111; Thwaits, *The Jesuit Relations*, vol. 8, 121. At the same time, as Fenton points out, Brebeuf later contradicts himself, noting that "the souls of those who died in war form a band by themselves; the others fear them and do not permit them entry into their village, any more than to the souls of those who have killed themselves." See Fenton, "Iroquois Suicide," 133; and Thwaits, *The Jesuit Relations*, vol. 10, 145.
18. Bernard Romans, *A Concise History of East and West Florida* (New York, 1775), 88, 90, 105–106.
19. *American State Papers, Class II. Indian Affairs*, ed. Walter Lowrie and Matthew St. Clair Clarke, vol. 4 (Washington: Gales and Seaton, 1832), 141.
20. In addition to using Native informants, Fenton read deeply in the records of missionaries and attempts to show consistency between past and present Seneca attitudes toward suicide, so his remarks should be seen in this light. See Fenton, "Iroquois Suicide," 134.
21. On the relationship between the Naticks and the English, see Jean M. O'Brien, *Dispossession by Degrees: Indian Land and Identity in Natick, Massachusetts, 1650–1790* (New York: Cambridge University Press, 1997), 100–102. Isaac Nehemiah's suicide is reported in Samuel Sewall, *The Diary of Samuel Sewall, 1652–1730*, ed. M. Halsey Thomas (New York: Farrar, Straus, and Giroux, 1973), vol. 2, 801–802.
22. Daniel R. Mandell, *Behind the Frontier: Indians in Eighteenth-Century Eastern Massachusetts* (Omaha: University of Nebraska Press, 2000), 77.

23. Sewall, *The Diary of Samuel Sewall*, vol. 2, 801–802.
24. Erik R. Seeman, *Death in the New World: Cross-Cultural Encounters, 1492–1800* (Philadelphia: University of Pennsylvania Press, 2010), 4–6, 195–196; Vincent Brown, *The Reaper's Garden: Death and Power in the World of Atlantic Slavery* (Cambridge, MA: Harvard University Press, 2008), 5–10, 186–187.
25. *Coroner's Inquest on John Shorte*, Talbot County Court Proceedings, *Archives of Maryland*, ed. J. Hall Pleasants (Baltimore: Maryland Historical Society, 1937), vol. 54: 360–362; C. G. A. Oldendorp, *C. G. A. Oldendorp's History of the Mission of the Evangelical Brethren on the Caribbean Islands of St. Thomas, St. Croix, and St. John*, ed. Johann Jakob Bossard, trans. Arnold R. Highfield and Vladimir Barac (Ann Arbor, MI: Karoma Publishers, 1987), 244; William Byrd II, *The History of the Dividing Line*, in Louis B. Wright, ed., *The Prose Works of William Byrd of Westover: Narratives of a Colonial Virginian* (Cambridge, MA: Belknap, 1966), 315–316.
26. For a reference to the stubborn dispositions of newly imported slaves, see *HCSP*, vol. 82, 197.
27. Dateline New York, February 16, *New Hampshire Gazette*, vol. 13, no. 647, 3 March 1769, 2; *Connecticut Courant*, 20 February 1769, issue 218, 3.
28. Donald D. Wax, "Preferences for Slaves in Colonial America," *Journal of Negro History* 58 (October 1973), 371–401, 376 (quotations). On Antigua, see *New England Weekly Journal*, Dateline "New York, Febr. 28," no. 519, 15 March 1737, 1.
29. I have modernized spelling, capitalization, and punctuation from the inquests throughout these passages. Inquest on Thomas, servant to John Custis, Northampton County Deeds, Will, no. 7–8, 1655–1668, LOV.
30. Inquest on Walter Catford, 25 June 1661, YCDOW, 3, fol. 67, LOV; *Coroner's Inquest on John Shorte*, 360–362.
31. Juries were required to note the instrument of self-inflicted death; they often measured and valued the length of the belt, rope, or knife used in suicides. These details formed part of their official report to the Crown, and, like deodands, the instrument of death or its value was typically forfeited to the government's authorities. See Teresa Sutton, "The Deodand and the Responsibility for Death," *American Journal of Legal History* 18 (1997), 44–55; Elisabeth Cawthon, "New Life for the Deodand: Coroner's Inquests and Occupational Deaths in England, 1830–1846," *American Journal of Legal History*. 33 (1989), 137–147; and *Histories of Suicide: International Perspectives on Self-Destruction in the Modern World*, ed. John Weaver and David Wright (Toronto: University of Toronto Press, 2009), 116n83.
32. The only surviving coroners' reports for pre-1800 York County appear to be those for servants. For suicides, see YCDOW 3, fols. 10, 25, 46, 67, 74, 122, 133, 135, 183; YCDOW 4, fol. 116, LOV.
33. Dateline: "Ordinary of Newgate . . . Accounts of Malefactors Executed at Tyburn, Account of William Fleming," *The American Weekly Mercury*, no. 688, 28 February–6 March 1732–1733, 4 (quotations), 2–4 (inclusive).
34. Dateline: "*London Journal*," "True Greatness," *New England Weekly Journal*, no. 304, 15 January 1733, 1. According to one French writer in the early eighteenth century, suicide among the upper classes was in some instances pardonable and perhaps even glorious, provided that it was unsullied by "either brutality or despair." See A. F. Boreau Deslandes, *Dying Merrily; or Historical and Critical Reflexions on the Conduct of Great Men Who, in their Last Moments, Mock'd Death and Died Facetiously*, trans. T.W. (London, 1745); the first French edition appeared in 1714, quoted in MacDonald and Murphy, *Sleepless Souls*, 185.

35. Sewall, *The Diary of Samuel Sewall*, vol. 1, 163.
36. Sewall, *The Diary of Samuel Sewall*, vol. 2, 695.
37. Sewall, *The Diary of Samuel Sewall*, vol. 2, 1031, and 1, 177, respectively.
38. MacDonald and Murphy, *Sleepless Souls*, 247–250.
39. In North Carolina, for example, an inquest on the enslaved man Juno notes that he hanged himself from a dogwood tree with a "certain flaxen cord of the value of three pence." Inquest on Juno, a Negro Slave, 1823, Series CR, box 078.928.2, Folder Coroner's, 1796–1895, NCSA. For an account of an enslaved man who threw himself into a sugar mill, see John Homrn Interview, 1847, in John W. Blassingame, ed., *Slave Testimony: Two Centuries of Letters, Speeches, Interviews, and Autobiographies* (Baton Rouge: Louisiana State University Press, 1977), 257. On the use of the grinding stone, see Inquest on Walter Catford, 25 June 1661, YCDOW 3, fol. 67, LOV.
40. On class and suicide, see MacDonald and Murphy, *Sleepless Souls*, 184–216.
41. Benzoni, *History of the New World*, 78; Louis A. Pérez, Jr., *To Die in Cuba: Suicide and Society* (Chapel Hill: University of North Carolina Press, 2005), 3–4.
42. For North America, see Daniel Drake, "Diseases of the Negro," *Southern Medical and Surgical Journal* 1 (1845), 341; W. M. Carpenter, "Observations on the Cachexia Africana or the Habit and Effects of Dirt-Eating on the Negro Race," *New Orleans Medical Journal* 1 (1845), 154; and William Dosite Postell, *The Health of Slaves on Southern Plantations* (Baton Rouge: Louisiana State University Press, 1951), 82.
43. On early modern Western attitudes toward the healthfulness of dirt, see Kathleen M. Brown, *Foul Bodies: Cleanliness in Early America* (New Haven, CT: Yale University Press, 2009), 35–36; 155, 239. On geophagy, see Jennifer L. Fleissner, "Earth-Eating, Addiction, Nostalgia: Charles Chestnutt's Diasporic Regionalism," *Studies in Romanticism* 49 (Summer 2010), 313–336; Kenneth Morgan, "Slave Women and Reproduction in Jamaica, c. 1776–1834," *History* 91 (April 2006), 235–256 (231–253 inclusive); John S. Haller, Jr., "The Negro and the Southern Physician: A Study of Medical and Racial Attitudes, 1800–1860," *Medical History* 16 (August 1972), 238–253; and Robert W. Twyman, "The Clay Eater: A New Look at an Old Southern Enigma," *Journal of Southern History* 37 (August 1971), 439–448.
44. George Miller, "An Account of The *Cachexia Africana*," in Samuel L. Mitchill, M.D., and Edward Miller, M.D., *The Medical Repository*, 3d ed., vol. 2 (New York: T. & J. Swords, Printers to the Faculty of Physic of Columbia College, 1805), 265–266. In 1835, Scottish physician James Maxwell argued that dirt eating reflected the propensity of Africans who wished to return to their country for suicide; see "Pathological Inquiry Into the Nature of Cachexia Africana," *Jamaica Physical Journal* 2 (1835), 409–435. Later, in 1836, F. W. Cragin argued that the dirt eating among slaves in the Caribbean was definitely not related to melancholy; see Cragin, "Observations on Cachexia Africana or Dirt-Eating," *American Journal of the Medical Sciences* 17 (February 1836), 356–364.
45. R. S. Rattray, *The Tribes of the Ashanti Hinterland*, vol. 1 (Oxford, UK: Clarendon Press, 1932), 282; on the varieties of marriage and its relation to status in Dahomey, see Melville J. Herskovits, *Dahomey, An Ancient West African Kingdom*, (Evanston, IL: Northwestern University Press, 1967), vol. 1, 301–333, 338–341.
46. Francis Porteus Corbin Papers, Overseer's Account, Selsdon Quarter, 6 December 1712, Rare Book, Manuscript, and Special Collections Library, Duke University, Durham, NC.
47. Testimony of Reverend Robert Boucher Nicholls in *HCSP*, vol. 73, 335.
48. C. G. A. Oldendorp, *C. G. A. Oldendorp's History*, 243–244.

49. Note: I have modernized the spelling, capitalization, and punctuation from the inquest on John Shorte. The justices decreed that Shorte "ought not to have [a] Christian burial by law." See J. Hall Pleasants, ed. *Archives of Maryland* (Baltimore: Maryland Historical Society, 1937), vol. 54, 361–362.
50. A North American court case on cruelty as the cause of slave suicide took place in Louisiana in 1741. In *Viel v. Pery*, 1741, the plaintiff sought damages for the death of Francois, an enslaved carpenter who cut his throat "in despair, whether for ill-treatment or for other causes"; cited in Heloise H. Cruzat, trans. and ed., "Records of the Superior Council of Louisiana, XXXVII," *Louisiana Historical Quarterly* 11 (January 1928), 141.
51. Deposition of John Roys, *Coroner's Inquest on John Shorte*, 361.
52. Deposition of John Roys, *Coroner's Inquest on John Shorte*, 361; Deposition of Richard Fillinggam, *Coroner's Inquest on John Shorte*, 361–362; Deposition of Anthony Purss, *Coroner's Inquest on John Shorte*, 362.
53. Hening, vol. 2, 53; Seeman, *Death in the New World*, 99. For an example of a profane burial, see Westmoreland County Virginia Orders [25 August 1661], *William and Mary Quarterly*, 1st ser., 15 (January 1907), 39.
54. The denial of Christian burial was not consistently ordered for suicides of all British servants in early Maryland. For instance, no such directions were stipulated in two 1664 inquests in which one servant found to be a "causer of his own death by willfully drowning of himself" and another was determined to have "murdered her self with a bridal rein." *Inquest on John Constable*, in *Archives of Maryland*, ed. Bernard Christian Steiner (Baltimore: Maryland Historical Society, 1936), vol. 53, 502; *Inquest on Elisabeth Johnson*, in ibid., 501–502.
55. Westmoreland County Virginia Orders," 39.
56. Sewall, *The Diary of Samuel Sewall*, vol. 1, 179.
57. See the story of Ceasar, recounted in the introduction to this book; *South Carolina Gazette*, 5 May 1759, p. 3, column 3; and the account of London, in Ulrich B. Phillips, ed., *Plantation and Frontier, 1649–1863: Illustrative of the Industrial History in the Colonial and Antebellum South*, vol. 2 (Cleveland: A. H. Clark and Col, 1909), 94. Masters punished slaves who died accidentally, particularly if their deaths occurred as a result of disobeying orders. In December 1808, five slaves boarded a small dugout off the coast of Georgia in order to sail to nearby island, a privilege that, although recently forbidden by their overseer, they had traditionally enjoyed during the Christmas holiday. The seas were rough and the weather foul: the vessel overturned and they drowned. The overseer punished the dead and warned the living. He ordered slaves "to find the bodies and bury them like *dogs*, for not one of them should have a Coffin . . . and that the next got Drowned in violation of [Orders], [he] would sell the Bodies to be Cut to pieces by the Doctors." Roswell King to Major Butler, 31 December 1808, Butler Family Papers, Historical Society of Pennsylvania, Philadelphia; also quoted in William Dusinberre, *Them Dark Days: Slavery in the American Rice Swamps* (New York: Oxford University Press, 1996), 255.

CHAPTER FOUR

1. The first sentence of this passage is taken from the Petition of James Anderson to the South Carolina Assembly, General Assembly; the second sentence is taken from Jury of Inquest, Pendleton District Court, Petition of James Anderson to the South

Carolina Assembly, General Assembly, 19 November 1810, Legislative Petitions, Series S165015 Year 1810, Items 1810-0162 and 1801-0163, SCDAH.

2. Thomas D. Morris, *Southern Slavery and the Law, 1619–1860* (Chapel Hill: University of North Carolina Press, 1996), 10–14.

3. On the two systems of power enshrined in southern law, see Edward L. Ayers, *Vengeance and Justice: Crime and Punishment in the Nineteenth-Century American South* (New York: Oxford University Press, 1984), 135–136; Michael Meranze, "Penality and the Colonial Project: Crime, Punishment, and the Regulation of Morals in Early America," in Michael Grossberg and Christopher Tomlins, eds., *The Cambridge History of Law in America*, vol. 1 (New York: Cambridge University Press, 2008), 200–204. On the evolution of slave law, see Philip J. Schwarz, *Twice Condemned: Slaves and the Criminal Laws of Virginia, 1705–1865* (Baton Rouge: Louisiana State University Press, 1988), 6–58; Morris, *Southern Slavery and the Law*, 17–60; Michael Hindus, *Prison and Plantation: Crime, Justice, and Authority in Massachusetts and South* Carolina (Chapel Hill: University of North Carolina Press, 1980), 129–161. For an overview of the legalities of early American slavery, see Sally E. Hadden, "The Fragmented Laws of Slavery in the Colonial and Revolutionary Eras," in Grossberg and Tomlins, eds., *The Cambridge History of Law in America*, vol. 1, 253–287; Anthony S. Parent, *Foul Means: The Formation of a Slave Society in Colonial* Virginia (Chapel Hill: University of North Carolina Press), 105–196; Edmund S. Morgan, *American Slavery, American Freedom: The Ordeal of Colonial Virginia* (New York: Norton, 1975), 295–337; and Winthrop D. Jordan, *White over Black: American Attitudes toward the Negro, 1550–1812* (Chapel Hill: University of North Carolina Press, 1975), 44–98, 101–135; for an Atlantic perspective on the evolution of Anglo-American slavery, see see Michael Guasco, *Slaves and Englishmen: Human Bondage in the Early Modern Atlantic World* (Philadelphia: University of Pennsylvania Press, 2014), esp. 195-227.

4. Sodomy remained a capital crime in South Carolina until 1873; see Jonathan Ned Katz, *Gay/Lesbian Almanac: A New Documentary in Which Is Contained, in Chronological Order, Evidence of the True and Fantastical History of Those Persons Now Called Lesbians and Gay Men. . . .* (New York: Harper & Row, 1983), 128.

5. Petition of James Anderson, 19 November 1810, Item 1810-0162-07, SCDAH.

6. Bryan A. Garner, *Black's Law Dictionary*, 7th ed. (St. Paul: West Group, 1999), 37, 999; Jeannine Marie DeLombard, *In the Shadow of the Gallows: Race, Crime, and American Civic Identity* (Philadelphia: University of Pennsylvania Press, 2012), 54–64; and David M. Walker, *The Oxford Companion to Law* (Oxford, UK: Clarendon Press, 1980), 22, 833.

7. As Alexander Murray notes, in the medieval and early modern periods, a suicide was the "only criminal to bring punishment *exclusively*" on her or his family; see *Suicide in the Middle Ages: The Curse of Self*-Murder (Oxford, U.K.: Oxford University Press, 2000), vol. 2, 78 (quotation), 54–85 (disposition of suicide's property). For forfeiture in England, see Michael MacDonald and Terence R. Murphy, *Sleepless Souls: Suicide in Early Modern England* ([1990]; Oxford, U.K.: Clarendon Press, 2000), 78–86, 114–124; and R. A. Houston, *Punishing the Dead? Suicide, Lordship, and Community in Britain, 1500–1830* (Oxford, U.K.: Oxford University Press, 2010), 30–188. On the legalities of suicide in early America, see Keith Burgess-Jackson, "The Legal Status of Suicide in Early America: A Comparison with the English Experience," *Wayne Law Review* 29 (Fall 1982), 57–90; Terri L. Snyder, "What Historians Talk About When They Talk About Suicide," *History Compass* 5 (March, 2007), 658–674; and Howard I.

Kushner, *Self-Destruction in the Promised Land: A Psychocultural Biology of American Suicide* (New Brunswick, NJ: Rutgers University Press, 1989), 21–34. On forfeiture in early America and the United States, see Leonard W. Levy, *License to Steal: The Forfeiture of Property* (Chapel Hill: University of North Carolina Press, 1995), 21–38.

8. Burgess-Jackson, "Legal Status of Suicide," 61–76; and Kushner, *Self-Destruction in the Promised Land*, 21–34. Partly this had to do with local concerns: forfeiture of the personal property of a suicide ran the risk of impoverishing the household; surviving families might be forced to rely on the local government for relief. In southern colonies, forfeiture mattered to slavery because slaves were property. If intentional suicide was a felony that was to be punished, then when slave owners killed themselves, their slaves could be forfeited and sold. Any revenue from these sales would be placed into the hands of local representatives of the Crown, a possibility contrary to the interests of planters' families. In order to protect slaves' property from forfeiture or seizure, for instance, Virginia statutes in 1705 and 1727 defined slaves both as real estate and as personal property when it came to entails, endowing widows, and transmitting family wealth to heirs. In 1748, legislators made slaves personal property for all purposes. Parliament repealed both laws in 1752, which made the legal definition of slave property ambiguous, but in 1792 the now state of Virginia defined slaves as personal property; see Marylynn Salmon, *Women and the Law of Property in Early America* (Chapel Hill: University of North Carolina Press, 1986), 152–156; on the statutes, see Hening, vol. 3, 333; Hening, vol. 4, 223–228; and Hening, vol. 5, 432–433. On the repeal see *VG* (Hunter), 10 April 1752, p. 2, column 2.
9. Stanley N. Katz, ed., *Blackstone's Commentaries on the Laws of England* (Chicago: University of Chicago Press, 1979), vol. 2, 267, 499; vol. 4, 189–190.
10. Sir Edward Coke, *Third Part of the Institutes of the Laws of England* (London: M. Flesher, 1644) vol. 3, 54, HL; Michael Dalton, *The Countrey Justice: Containing the Practice of the Justices of the Peace out of their Sessions* (London, 1635), 235–236, HL.
11. MacDonald and Murphy, *Sleepless Souls*, 114–143; and Georges Minois, *History of Suicide: Voluntary Death in Western Culture*, trans. Lydia G. Cochrane (Baltimore: Johns Hopkins University Press, 1999), 137–147.
12. See for instance H. R. McIlwaine, ed., *Executive Journals of the Council of Colonial Virginia*, vol. 2, 1699–1705 (Richmond, 1925–), 20; and ibid., vol. 3 (1705–1721), 12,177, 328, 385, 490–491, 516–517.
13. Actually, Carter was arguing with Virginia's attorney general over who should be collecting the forfeiture. Carter, as the representative of the proprietor Lord Fairfax, thought it was owed to him while Virginia's attorney general disagreed and sought to collect the property for the Crown. Robert Carter to William Cage, 19 July 1725, *The Diary and Correspondence of Robert "King" Carter of Virginia, 1701–1732*, Edmund Berkeley, Jr., ed. (http://etext.virginia.edu, accessed 6 March 2011). See also Carter's letter of 28 July 1725.
14. See for instance, Hening, vol. 2, 406, 419; MacDonald and Murphy, *Sleepless Souls*, 24.
15. MacDonald and Murphy, *Sleepless Souls*, 247–248 (2:1 ratio given on 247); Howard I. Kushner, "Suicide, Gender, and the Fear of Modernity," in John Weaver and David Wright, eds., *Histories of Suicide: International Perspectives on Self-Destruction in the Modern* World (Toronto: University of Toronto Press, 2009), 33–38; Robert Lane, *Violent Death in the City: Suicide, Accident, and Murder in Nineteenth-Century Philadelphia*, 2nd ed. (Columbus: Ohio State University Press, 1999), 28–29.
16. MacDonald and Murphy, *Sleepless Souls*, 127–128.

17. See Burgess-Jackson, "Legal Status of Suicide," 61–62; Kushner, *Self-Destruction in the Promised Land*, 21–34; and MacDonald and Murphy, *Sleepless Souls*, 78–86; 114–123; 125–132.
18. On the easing of forfeiture penalties, Massachusetts juries returned 2.5 *felo de se* verdicts for each *non compos mentis* between 1731 and 1800; but between 1801 and 1828, they nearly reversed the ratio to 1 *felo de se* to 2 *non compos mentis*. See Kushner, *Self-Destruction in the Promised Land*, 29–30. Massachusetts appears to have been an outlier in this regard. In England in the early 1660s, fewer than 7 percent of suicides reported were *non compos mentis;* by the 1690s, the percentage rose to 30; and by the mid-eighteenth century, it exceeded 40 percent. In Norwich, for instance, by the 1720s over 90 percent of all suicides were ruled *non compos mentis*. See MacDonald and Murphy, *Sleepless Souls*, 114–116, 121–125. On forfeiture in England, Scotland, and Wales, see Houston, *Punishing the Dead?* 30–188.
19. MacDonald and Murphy, *Sleepless Souls*, 142–175.
20. Julian P. Boyd, ed., *The Papers of Thomas Jefferson* (Princeton, NJ: Princeton University Press 1950), vol. 2, 325, 496.
21. Ian Marsh, *Suicide: Foucault, History, and Truth* (Cambridge, UK: Cambridge University Press, 2010), 99; Kelly McGuire, *Dying to Be English: Suicide Narratives and National Identity, 1721–1814* (London: Pickering and Chatto, 2012), 2–3.
22. Weaver and Wright, eds., *Histories of Suicide: International Perspectives on Self-Destruction in the Modern World*, 3–11; Kushner, *Self-Destruction in the Promised Land*, 34–58; Richard Bell, *We Shall Be No More: Suicide and Self-Government in the* Newly United *States* (Cambridge, MA: Harvard University Press, 2012), 81–114.
23. David Silkenat, *Moments of Despair,: Suicide, Divorce, and Debt in Civil War Era North Carolina* (Chapel Hill: University of North Carolina Press, 2011), 11–14.
24. See chapter 3. MacDonald and Murphy, *Sleepless Souls*, 129–130; see also 109–218.
25. Machiel Bosman, "The Judicial Treatment of Suicide in Amsterdam," in Jeffrey R. Watt, ed., *From Sin to Insanity: Suicide in Early Modern Europe* (Ithaca, N.Y.: Cornell University Press, 2004), 21. See also Elizabeth G. Dickenson and James M. Boyden, "Ambivalence toward Suicide in Golden Age Spain," for a discussion of how a community exhumed the body of a woman who killed herself after refusing to cooperate with the Inquisition, ibid., 102–104. MacDonald and Murphy reach the same conclusion about England; see *Sleepless Souls*, 129–130. Felons who killed themselves were attainted of both chattels real and personal. Walker, *The Oxford Companion to Law*, 91–92; and Leon Radzinowicz, *A History of English Criminal Law* (New York: Macmillan, 1948), 197–198.
26. *Gentleman's Magazine* 5 (September 1735), 557–558; MacDonald and Murphy, *Sleepless Souls*, 130.
27. Bosman, "The Judicial Treatment of Suicide in Amsterdam," 22–23.
28. In another case, thousands of townspeople were gathered for an expected execution and the felon killed himself; jailers carried out his corpse and strung it up. See Bell, *We Shall Be No More*, 124–128.
29. Very occasionally coroners' reports list the value of slave-owned property to be forfeited. See for instance the inquest on the enslaved Sampson of Granville County, North Carolina; he hanged himself with a string of elm bark. The inquest noted that "the aforesaid Sampson . . . at the time of committing the murder on himself had no goods or chattels, lands or tenements in the county. . . ." Inquest on Sampson, 17 May 1754, Granville County, North Carolina, Coroner's Inquests, Folder 1755, Box 044.913.1, Series CR, NCSA.

30. Charles Ball, *Slavery in the United States: A Narrative of the Life and Adventures of Charles Ball, A Black Man* (New York, John S. Taylor, 1837), 325–227 (http://www.docsouth.unc.edu/neh/ballslavery/ball.html, accessed 2 June 2013).
31. Roswell King to Major Butler, 31 December 1808, quoted in William Dusinberre, *Them Dark Days: Slavery in the American Rice Swamps* (New York: Oxford University Press, 1996), 255.
32. Morris, *Southern Slavery and the Law,* 253–255; John Hudson, *The Oxford History of the Laws of England*, vol. 2, *871–1216* (Oxford, U.K.: Oxford University Press), 177–180.
33. Petition of William Wilson of Gloucester County to the Virginia Assembly, 23 December 1800, Legislative Petitions, Reel 65, Box 89, Folder 33, LOV.
34. Philip J. Schwarz, ed., *Gabriel's Conspiracy: A Documentary History* (Charlottesville: University of Virginia Press, 2012), xxi.
35. Hudson, *The Oxford History of the Laws of England*, II, 196–198, 414–415; Katz, *Blackstone's Commentaries on the Laws of England*, vol. 3, 283–284, vol. 4, 319–220. See also *Sharswood's Blackstone's Commentaries*, vol. 2 (Philadelphia, 1860), 190–191, 562–563.
36. Katz, *Blackstone's Commentaries*, vol. 4, 319–320.
37. Katz, *Blackstone's Commentaries*, vol 4, 320.
38. Meranze, "Penality and the Colonial Project," 200–204.
39. Virginia was the first North American colony to enact statutes regulating outlawed or outlying slaves; South and North Carolina followed suit, but all of these were modeled on Barbadian slave codes. See Hadden, "The Fragmented Laws of Slavery," 259–274; Donna J. Spindel, *Crime and Society in North Carolina, 1663–1776* (Baton Rouge: Louisiana State University Press, 1989), 133–134. On South Carolina, see Thomas J. Little, "The South Carolina Slave Laws Reconsidered, 1670–1700," *South Carolina Historical Magazine* 94 (April 1993), 98 (86–101, inclusive); on Barbados, see Richard S. Dunn, *Sugar and Slaves: The Rise of the Planter Class in the English West Indies, 1624–1730* (Chapel Hill: University of North Carolina Press, 1972), 238–262.
40. Hening, vol. 3, 86. The 1705 revision of the statute uses the same language, as do statutes in North and South Carolina.
41. Ayers notes that when southern justice found slaves guilty of crimes, punishments always focused on the body; see *Vengeance and Justice*, 136.
42. Hening, vol. 3, 460; see also Spindel, *Crime and Society in North Carolina*, 133–134.
43. The 1748 revision of the statute removed the phrase "he, she, or they"; see Hening, vol. 6, 110–111.
44. Slave owners were authorized to claim compensation from the state by two statutes enacted in 1705. The first allowed masters compensation for slaves who were killed because they were outlawed; the second compensated masters for slaves who were convicted and executed for felonies; see Hening, vol. 3, 269–270 (on compensation for felonious slaves); 460–461 (on outlying slaves). The statute was reauthorized in 1748; see Act for the Trial of Slaves, Hening, vol. 6, chapter 10, 107 (value of executed slaves paid by the public); chapters 21–22, 109–111 (masters of outlawed slaves who are killed in apprehension to be paid by the public). Little surprise that slave owners had all of the laws on their side, but despite the previous provisions, nothing barred them from suing anyone who, either directly or through negligence, killed one of their slaves. See also Hening, vol. 6, chapter 25, 111.
45. Hening, vol. 3, 460–461.
46. The statue was enacted in 1691 and revised in 1705 and 1748; see Hening, vol. 3,

269–270 (on compensation for felonious slaves), 460–461 (on outlying slaves), and n. 47 above. See also Schwarz, *Twice Condemned*, 11, 52–53.

47. Hening, vol. 3, 86, 460.
48. *State Records of North Carolina*, collected and edited by Walter Clark (Raleigh: P. M. Hale, 1886–1907), vol. 23, 64. See Spindel, *Crime and Society in North Carolina*, 133–134. On South Carolina, see Peter Wood, *Black Majority: Negroes in Colonial South Carolina from 1670 through the Stono Rebellion* ([1974] New York: Norton, 1996), 271–331. In Antigua, compensation rates exceeded the going prices for slaves, so compensation could be remunerative for masters. See David Barry Gaspar, "'To Bring Their Offending Slaves to Justice': Compensation and Slave Resistance in Antigua, 1669–1763," *Caribbean Quarterly*, 30:3/4 (September–December 1984), 45–59.
49. The North Carolina statute compensated owners for slaves "sentenced to death by the slave courts or who died as a result of punishments ordered by a court, or who were killed during their apprehension as outlaws or runaways or while committing some crime." Marvin L. Michael Kay and Lorin Lee Cary, *Slavery in North Carolina, 1748–1775* (Chapel Hill: University of North Carolina Press, 1995), 87. See also *State Records of North Carolina*, vol. 23, 64, 203, 488–489, 656 (laws of 1715, 1741, 1758, 1764). For South Carolina, see H. M. Henry, *The Police Control of the Slave in South Carolina* (Ph.D. diss., Emory and Henry College, 1914), 56–58.
50. This argument summarizes the extensive and important study of colonial compensation systems by Kay and Cary, *Slavery in North Carolina*, 73–89, esp. 87–88.
51. Kay and Cary, *Slavery in North Carolina*, table 3.2, 250–255.
52. Jack P. Greene, *The Diary of Colonel Landon Carter of Sabine Hall, 1752–1758* (Charlottesville: University Press of Virginia, 1965), vol. 1, 119.
53. Petition of William Southall, 5 May 1755, in *JHB, 1752–1758*, 239.
54. Petition of Peter Richeson, 5 June 1740, *JHB, 1727–1740*, 418. Joseph Hale's slave hanged himself, but the petition for compensation was rejected because it was not "sufficiently proved." See Petition of Joseph Hale, 7 November 1758, *JHB, 1752–1758*, 111, 138. Robert Adams' slave ran away and was outlawed and hung himself, but the petition was refused. See Petition of Robert Adams, 10 March 1752, *JHB, 1752–1758*, 27.
55. Petition of James Anderson, 19 November 1810, item 1810-162-03, SCDAH.
56. Petition of George Mason, 16 May 1755, *JHB, 1752–55*, 259.
57. Henry Summerson, "Suicide and the Fear of the Gallows," *Journal of Legal History* 21 (April 2000), 50.
58. Petition of George Mason, 16 May 1755, *JHB, 1752–55*, 239, 259.
59. Petition of George Mason, 16 May 1755, *JHB, 1752–58*, 259.
60. Petition of William Lightfoot, 9 May 1755, *JHB, 1752–58*, 248.
61. *VG* (P&D), 12 January 1769, 12 (suicide by thief); *VG* (P&D), 8 June 1769, 21 (suicide to avoid trial). On the double suicide of Tuscaroras held in jail, see H. R. McIlwaine, ed., *The Executive Journals of the Council of Colonial Virginia*, vol. 3 (Richmond: Virginia State Library, 1928), 172–174.
62. I have relied heavily on the phrase "shortly found dead" and have ruled out those deaths that might be better attributed to exposure.
63. For a modern perspective on "suicide-like" behaviors, see Karla FC Holloway, *Passed On: African American Mourning Stories* (Durham: Duke University Press, 2003), 91.
64. Petition of Benjamin Needler, 13 November 1738, *JHB, 1727–1740*, 338; Petition

of Lewis Willis, 13 March 1752, *JHB, 1752–1758*, 31, 43; and Petition of Edward Pegram, 22 November 1753, *JHB, 1752–1758*, 131.

65. *VG* (P&D), 23 December 1773.
66. No gender was specified for the remaining fourteen percent of certain suicides discussed in the House of Burgesses petitions for compensation. On sex ratios of slaves imported into pre-Revolutionary eighteenth-century Virginia, sixty-three percent were male and thirty-seven percent were female; for South Carolina, the percentages were sixty-five and thirty-five, respectively. See Philip D. Morgan, *Slave Counterpoint: Black Culture in the Eighteenth-Century Chesapeake and Lowcountry* (Chapel Hill: University of North Carolina Press, 1998), 71.
67. Six enslaved men attacked other slaves and two of these assaulted their wives; another four attacked masters, mistresses, or overseers. Petition of Joseph Peach, 20 August 1736, *JHB, 1727–1740*, 262; Petition of William Morris, 20 August 1736, *JHB, 1727–1740: 252;* Petition of Zachary Lewis, 12 May 1742, *JHB, 1742–49*, 14; Petition of Henry Wythe, 12 September 1744, *JHB, 1742–49*, 86; Petition of Moor Fauntleroy, 24 September 1744, *JHB, 1742–1749*, 104, 109; Petition of Robert Daniel, 9 November 1748, *JHB, 1742–1749*, 280; Petition of Joseph Hall/Haile, 7 November 1753, *JHB, 1752–1758*, 111, 138; Petition of Stephen Watkins, 19 May 1755, *JHB, 1752–1758*, 260; Petition of Kenneth MacKenzie, 21 May 1755, *JHB, 1752–1758*, 262; Petition of Elizabeth King, 10 March 1761 *JHB, 1758–1761*, 203, 210; and Petition of Thomas Patterson, 12 May 1774, *JHB, 1773–1776*, 92, 98.
68. Petition of Zachary Lewis, 12 May 1742, *JHB, 1742–1749*, 14; Petition of Elizabeth King, 10 March 1761, *JHB, 1758–1761*: 203, 210.
69. Petition of William Cox, 12 August 1736, *JHB, 1727–40*, 254; Petition of Stephen Ham, 8 May 1774, *JHB, 1773–1776*, 181–182, 204.
70. Hadden, "The Fragmented Laws of Slavery," 284–285.
71. Hadden, "The Fragmented Laws of Slavery," 284–285.
72. *VG* (Hunter), 17 October 1755, p. 3, column 1.
73. Trevor Burnard, *Mastery, Tyranny, and Desire: Thomas Thistlewood and His Slaves in the Anglo-Jamaican World* (Chapel Hill: University of North Carolina Press, 2004), 160–170, 176, 263-264. For jealousy as a motive for slave-on-slave violence, see Schwarz, *Twice Condemned*, 89–90, 153–154, 249–250.
74. Schwarz, *Twice Condemned*, 90, table 9 (p. 90), table 1 (p. 15).
75. *VG* (Parks) 25 Feb 1737, p. 4.
76. *VG* (P&D), 2 November 1728, p. 1; *VG* (P&D) 10 March 1774.
77. Petition of Thomas Lankford, for himself and Rebecca Collier, 8 November 1738, *JHB, 1727–1740*, 329.
78. Petition of John Evans, 3 November 1748, *JHB, 1742–1749*, 268.
79. Petition of John Carter, 6 November 1738, *JHB, 1727–1740*, 325.
80. *VG* (Pinkney), 14 September 75, p. 3.
81. Michel Foucault, *Discipline and Punish: The Birth of the Prison*, trans. Alan Sheridan (New York: Random House, 1977), 10–15; Meranze, "Penality and the Colonial Project," 203.
82. Ayers, *Vengeance and Justice*, 136.
83. Kay and Cary, *Slavery in North Carolina*, 81; Morris, *Southern Slavery and the Law*, 276–278; Schwarz, *Twice Condemned*, table 1 (p. 15).
84. Betty Wood, "Until He Shall Be Dead, Dead, Dead": The Judicial Treatment of Slaves in Eighteenth-Century Georgia," *Georgia Historical Quarterly*, vol. 81 (Fall 1987), 381-382.

85. Kirsten Fischer, *Suspect Relations: Sex, Race, and Resistance in Colonial North Carolina* (Ithaca, NY: Cornell University Press, 2002), 186.

86. Philip J. Schwarz, *Slave Laws in Virginia* (Athens: University of Georgia Press, 1996), 72-73; Douglas R. Egerton, "A Peculiar Mark of Infamy: Dismemberment, Burial, and Rebelliousness in Slave Societies," in *Mortal Remains: Death in Early America*, ed. Nancy Isenberg and Andrew Burstein (Philadelphia: University of Pennsylvania Press, 2003), 154-155; and Craig Thompson Friend, "Mutilated Bodies, Living Specters: Scalpings and Beheadings in the Early South," in Craig Thompson Friend and Lorri Glover, eds., *Death and the American South* (New York: Cambridge University Press, 2015), 34-35.

87. Such punishments could be fatal. For instance, in 1752, the enslaved Harry had been sentenced to whipping and had both of his ears cut off as a penalty for stabbing his mistress. He died from these punishments on his return to the plantation; see the Petition of Mary Jones, December 1752, *JHB, 1752–1758*, 182.

88. For examples of frostbite and jailed slaves, see Petition of Jacob Sellers, 29 November 1748, *JHB, 1742–1749*, 308–309; Petition of John Baskerville, 16 March 1759, *JHB, 1758–1761*, 96; Petition of Benjamin Grimes, 9 May 1774, *JHB, 1773–1776*, 81. Other slaves were simply reported to have died during confinement; see Petition of Francis Conway, 28 March 1761, *JHB, 1758–1761*, 236, 239. Still others burned to death in jail, some by fires they reportedly started; see Petition of Elizabeth Buchanan, 12 March 1761, *JHB, 1758–1761*, 210, 214; see also the Petition of John Martin, 15 June 1775, regarding a jailhouse fire in which three slaves perished, *JHB, 1773–1776*, 189, 222. The story of an unnamed slave who was frostbitten and, although not condemned to death, died as a result appears in Petition of Jacob Sellers, 29 November 1748, *JHB, 1742–1749*, 308. See also Petition of Peter Hay, whose slave died after a long confinement to jail and was so frostbitten that his "mortification ensued"; 7 November 1738, *JHB, 1727–1740*, 327.

89. Petition of Richard Randolph, 9 November 1738, *JHB, 1727–1740*, 335, 341; Petition of John Martin, 15 June 1775, *JHB, 1773–1776*, 189.

90. Petition of David Donnam, 15 June 1775, *JHB, 1773–1775*, 185. Accidental fire is mentioned in the Petition of George Brett, 25 February 1745, *JHB, 1742–1749*, 162; other petitions mention only that the prison burned, such as the Petition of John Scot, 11 May 1722, *JHB, 1712–1726*, 324. For claims that prisons were "fired," see Petition of Joseph Strother, 8 November 1748, *JHB, 1742–1749*, 279, 297.

91. *VG* (P&D), 23 December 1773, p. 1, columns 1–2.

92. See the story of Ceasar, discussed in the introduction to this book; *South Carolina Gazette*, 5 May 1759, p. 3. See also the account of London in Ulrich B. Phillips, ed. "Extract of a Letter of William Capers," *Plantation and Frontier, 1649–1863: Illustrative of the Industrial History in the Colonial and Antebellum South*, vol. 2 (Cleveland, OH: A. H. Clark and Col, 1909), 94.

93. Ball, *Slavery in the United States*, 69–70.

94. Morris, *Southern Slavery and the Law*, 182–188, 193–195.

95. Thomas Cooper and David J. McCord, *Statutes at Large of South Carolina*, vol. 7 ([1836]; reprint, Columbia: University of South Carolina, 1970), 411; *State Records of North Carolina*, vol. 23, 389–390.

96. For examples of prosecutions for cruelty to in early national South Carolina, see Hindus, *Prison and Plantation*, 136–137.

97. DeLombard, *In the Shadow of the Gallows*, 54 (quote), 54–64 (inclusive discussion). On *mens rea/actus rea*, see Walker, *The Oxford Companion to Law*, 22, 833; Garner, *Black's Law Dictionary*, 37, 999.

CHAPTER FIVE

1. "A Kind of Wild Tragedy" *The Spectator*, no. 215 (6 November 1711), in Donald F. Bond, ed., *The Spectator* (Oxford, UK: Clarendon Press, 1965), vol. 2, 339–340; later published as "The Two Negro Friends," *Virginia Almanack for 1775* (Williamsburg: Dixon and Hunter, 1775), n.p., Alderman Library, Small Special Collections, University of Virginia, Charlottesville.
2. Kelly McGuire, ed., "Introduction to Volumes 3 and 4," in *The History of Suicide in England, 1650–1850*, vol. 3 (London: Pickering and Chatto, 2012), vii.
3. Joseph Addison's *Cato* was performed by students of William and Mary in September 1736; see *VG* (Parks), 10 September 1736, p. 4. For the contents of Byrd's extensive library, see Kevin J. Hayes, *The Library of William Byrd of Westover* (Madison, WI: Madison House, 1997).
4. Toby L. Ditz cautions that many models of manhood prevailed in early America alongside Byrd's world, in which manhood was built on "aristocratic ideals . . . anchored in the claims of blood and honor"; see Toby L. Ditz, "Afterword: Contending Masculinites in Early America," in Thomas A. Foster, ed., *New Men: Manliness in Early America* (New York: New York University Press, 2011), 256. On manhood and honor in early modern England and America, see Alexandra Shepard, *Meanings of Manhood in Early Modern England* (Oxford, UK: Oxford University Press, 2006), 70–89; Thomas A. Foster, *Sex and the Eighteenth-Century Man: Massachusetts and the History of Sexuality in America* (Boston: Beacon Press), 7–100. The classic examination of honor and manliness in the South is Bertram Wyatt-Brown, *Southern Honor: Ethics and Behavior in the Old South* (New York: Oxford University Press, 1982), 1–116. See also his treatment of the male slave experience in *The Shaping of Southern Culture: Honor, Grace, and War, 1760s–1880s* (Chapel Hill: University of North Carolina Press, 2001), 3–30; and of changes in conceptions of honor during the American Revolution, 31–55.
5. By the 1730s, a propensity toward madness and suicide in particular were, more or less, seen as part of the English national character, see McGuire, *The History of Suicide in England*, vol. 3, viii (Cato), xiv–xv (connection to national character). Regardless of whether statistics would bear out the charge, according to the press, England reportedly witnessed a wave of suicides, mostly by men, in the wake of the economic disaster of the South Sea Bubble (1720). A 1751 news sheet was typical in asserting that suicide "seems to be on the increase," in England, see the *Derby Mercury*, 25 October 1751, p. 2. Similar statements persist well into and beyond the eighteenth century. For instance, the *Oxford Journal* asserted that suicide "is more common" among the English than "perhaps among any other people," see *Oxford Journal*, 26 December 1772, p. 1.
6. George Cheyne, *The English Malady; Or, A Treatise of Nervous Diseases of All Kinds* (London, 1733). On the connection between Byrd and Cheyne, see Hayes, *The Library of William Byrd of Westover*, 35.
7. McGuire, *The History of Suicide in England*, vol. 3, xvi. Images of suicide figured importantly into these debates as well. Ron M. Brown argues that visual representations of suicide changed dramatically in the eighteenth century, changes that began in the 1720s; see *The Art of Suicide* (London: Reaktion Books, 2001), 123–146.
8. Kevin Berland, Jan Kirsten Gilliam, and Kenneth A. Lockridge, eds., *The Commonplace Book of William Byrd II of Westover* (Chapel Hill: University of North Carolina Press, 2001), 124, 158, 166 for three suicide anecdotes.

9. Catherine Molineux, *Faces of Perfect Ebony: Encountering Atlantic Slavery in Imperial Britain* (Cambridge, MA: Harvard University Press, 2012), 85–87.
10. Addison writes that the events depicted in "A Kind of Wild Tragedy" occurred on the Leeward Islands in about 1699, but Bond notes that no written source has been discovered for this story, see Bond, *The Spectator*, 339n1. Similarly, Karina Williamson notes that the story has not been traced; see Karina Williamson, ed., *Contrary Voices: Representations of West Indian Slavery, 1657–1834* (Kingston, Jamaica: University of West Indies Press, 2008), 38.
11. On this point, see Philip Gould, *Barbaric Traffic: Commerce and Antislavery in the Eighteenth-Century Atlantic World* (Cambridge, MA: Harvard University Press, 2003), 10, 43–85.
12. Gould notes this to be the case for later antislavery literature; see *Barbaric Traffic*, 72–76.
13. Anonymous, *A Lamentable Ballad of the tragical End of a gallant Lord and a virtuous Lady, and the untimely End of their two Children, wickedly perform'd by a heathenish black-a-moor, their Servant, the like never heard of before* (Newcastle, 1760?), HL.
14. Molineux, *Faces of Perfect Ebony*, 67–69.
15. Paul Seaver, "Suicide and the Broadside Ballad," in Paul Seaver, ed., *The History of Suicide in England, 1650–1850*, vol. 1, 1650–1673 (London: Pickering and Chatto, 2012), 1–49.
16. Seaver, "Suicide and the Broadside Ballad," 3.
17. Molineux, *Faces of Perfect Ebony*, 70 (quote); 68–70 (inclusive).
18. Molineux, *Faces of Perfect Ebony*, 72.
19. On the popularity of *Oroonoko*, see Elizabeth Maddock Dillon, *New World Drama: The Performative Commons in the Atlantic World, 1649–1849* (Durham: Duke University Press, 2014), 54; Robert Jordan and Harold Love, eds., *The Works of Thomas Southerne*, vol. 2 (Oxford, UK: Clarendon Press, 1988), 90–92. They also note the publication date, despite what appears on the title page, as 1695; see 97. See also Susan B. Iwanisziw, *Oroonoko: Adaptations and Offshoots* (Burlington, VT: Ashgate, 2006), xi–xvii; Joanna Lipking, *Oroonoko* (New York: W. W. Norton, 1997), xi–xv; and Wylie Sypher, *Guinea's Captive Kings: British Anti-slavery Literature of the Eighteenth Century* (Chapel Hill: University of North Carolina Press, 1942), 116. For other studies of the novel, see Jane Todd, *The Secret Life of Aphra Behn* (New Brunswick, NJ: Rutgers University Press, 1996), 37–52; and Laura Brown, *Ends of Empire: Women and Ideology in Early Eighteenth-Century English* Literature (Ithaca, NY: Cornell University Press, 1993).
20. Joseph Addison, *Cato: A Tragedy, and Selected Essays*, ed. Christine Dunn Henderson and Mark E. Yellin (Indianapolis: Liberty Fund, 2004), 44.
21. Scholars debate the extent to which *Oroonoko* conveyed antislavery messages. For an indispensible overview of opposing interpretations, see Moira Ferguson, "*Oroonoko*: Birth of a Paradigm," *New Literary History* 23 (Spring 1992), 339–359, which claims that the novel set the paradigm for colonial and antislavery discourse until the early nineteenth century, 339. Robert Jordan and Harold Love, among others, point out that the novel objects to the enslavement of a prince, not slavery generally, as Oroonoko is a prince of a slave trading nation; see Jordan and Love, *The Works of Thomas Southerne*, vol. 2, 95–96. See also Iwanisziw, *Oroonoko*, xii–xiii; Charlotte Sussman, "The Other Problem with Women: Reproduction and Slave Culture in Aphra Behn's *Oroonoko*," in Heidi Hutner, *Rereading Aphra Behn: History, Theory, Criticism*

(Charlottesville: University Press of Virginia, 1993), 212–233; Ramesh Mallipeddi, "Spectacle, Spectatorship, and Sympathy in Aphra Behn's *Oroonoko,*" *Eighteenth-Century Studies* 45 (Summer 2012), 475–496; Molineux, *Faces of Perfect Ebony*, 73–85; Margaret Ferguson, "Juggling the Categories of Race, Class, and Gender: Aphra Behn's *Oroonoko,*" in Margo Hendricks and Patricia Parker, eds., *Women, "Race," and Writing in the Early Modern Period* (New York: Routledge, 1993), 209–224.

22. Aphra Behn, *Oroonoko: Or the Royal Slave. A True History* (1688), ed. Joanna Lipking (New York: W. W. Norton), 62–63 (quotations of disembowelment), 60 (quotation for Imoinda), 57–65 (inclusive).
23. Cato reportedly rent his abdomen and partially disemboweled himself but survived; when a physician was summoned to stitch up the wound, he was pushed away by Cato, who tore open the wound again and finished the process; see Addison, *Cato*, xx–xxi, 270–271.
24. *Oroonoko* was performed in New York City in 1832; see Dillon, *New World Drama*, 42 (quotatation), 43, 50–55, 165–167, 219–222.
25. Sussman, "The Other Problem with Women: Reproduction and Slave Culture in Aphra Behn's *Oroonoko,*" in Hutner, ed., *Rereading Aphra Behn: History, Theory, and Criticism*, 215 (quotation), 213–233 (inclusive).
26. Behn, *Oroonoko*, 60–61.
27. *Gentleman's Magazine* 19 (1749), 89–90; Wylie Sypher, "The African Prince in London," *Journal of the History of Ideas* 2 (April 1941), 241–242.
28. Byrd owned *The Spectator* (London: J. Tonson, 1723–1724), 9 vols.; see Hayes, *The Library of William Byrd of Westover*, 285.
29. McGuire, *The History of Suicide in England*, vol. 3, viii.
30. "A Kind of Wild Tragedy"; also reprinted in "The Two Negro Friends," *Virginia Almanack for 1775*, n.p.
31. "A Kind of Wild Tragedy," 340.
32. "A Kind of Wild Tragedy," 340.
33. Bond, *The Spectator*, no. 215, 6 November 1711, 339.
34. Trevor Burnard, *Mastery, Tyranny, and Desire: Thomas Thistlewood and His Slaves in the Anglo-Jamaican World* (Chapel Hill: University of North Carolina Press, 2004), 176.
35. Molineux, *Faces of Perfect Ebony*, 18–60.
36. Orlando Patterson, *Slavery and Social Death: A Comparative Study* (Cambridge, MA: Harvard University Press, 1982), 335–336.
37. Bond, *The Spectator*, no. 215, 6 November 1711, 339.
38. Gould describes the story as famous; see *Barbaric Traffic*, 68.
39. James Ramsey, "An Essay on the Treatment and Conversion of African Slaves in the British Slave Colonies" (1784), in Williamson, ed., *Contrary Voices: Representations of West Indian Slavery, 1657–1834*, 103–106.
40. Molineux, *Faces of Perfect Ebony*, 71.
41. "A Kind of Wild Tragedy," 440.
42. For Diallo's narrative, see Thomas Bluett, *Some Memoirs of the Life of Job, the Son of Solomon, the High Priest of Boonda* (London, 1734), 1–63 (http://docsouth.unc.edu/neh/bluett/bluett.html, accessed 11 September 2012); Daniel Domingues da Silva, "Ayuba Suleiman Diallo and Slavery," *Voyages: The Trans-Atlantic Slave Trade Database* (http://www.slavevoyages.org/tast/assessment/essays-solomon.faces, accessed 11 September 2012). The actual identity of the author of *The Royal African* is unknown; see Philip D. Curtin, ed., *Africa Remembered: Narratives by West Africans from the Era of the Slave Trade* (Madison: University of Wisconsin Press, 1967), 5. Vincent Carretta's

biography notes that *The Royal African* was anonymously published but treats it as a factual, if politically motivated biography; Carretta, "Sessarakoo, William Ansah," *Oxford Dictionary of National Biography* (New York: Oxford University Press, 2012, http://www.oxforddnb.com/view/article/97280, accessed 4 July 2013). See also Zachary Hutchins, "Summary," *The Royal African; or the Young Prince of Annamaboe* (London: W. Reeve, G. Woodfall, and J. Barnes, 1750, http://docsouth.unc.edu/neh/royal/summary.html). Wylie Sypher refers to *The Royal African* as a novel, but treats the account as an authentic one; see Sypher, "The African Prince," 240 (novel), 239n5 (assertion that the novel reflects true events). See also Pier M. Larson, "Horrid Journeying: Narratives of Enslavement and the Global African Diaspora," *Journal of World History* 19 (December 2008), 431–464.

43. Bluett, *Some Memoirs of the Life of Job*, 16.
44. *The Royal African*, 25, 36–52; Carretta, "Sessarakoo".
45. Curtin, *Africa Remembered*, 17.
46. Carretta, "Sessarakoo." Hutchins reports that the text appears to have gone through "at least three printings between 1749 and 1754"; see Hutchins, "Summary." Sypher details the press coverage of Sessarakoo; see "The African Prince in London," 240–244; see also the *Gentleman's Magazine and Historical Chronicle* 20 (June 1750), 272–273; and also Molineux, *Faces of Perfect Ebony*, 83. On Sessarakoo in context, see Randy J. Sparks, "Gold Coast Merchant Families, Pawning, and the Eighteenth-Century British Slave Trade," *William and Mary Quarterly* 70 (April 2013), 317–340.
47. Bluett, *Some Memoirs of the Life of Job*, 21, 34, 36.
48. *The Royal African*, 37, 43, 39.
49. *The Royal African*, 44.
50. Bluett, *Some Memoirs of the Life of Job*, 19–20.
51. The title page of Bluett's *Some Memoirs of the Life of Job* refers to Diallo as a "high priest".
52. *The Royal African*, 42–43.
53. Bond, *The Spectator*, no. 215, 6 November 1711, 339.
54. *The Royal African*, 44.
55. *The Royal African*, 43.
56. Bluett, *Some Memoirs of the Life of Job*, 59–60.
57. *The Royal African*, 48–50.
58. Hutchins, "Summary".
59. Henry Louis Gates, Jr., and William L. Andrews, eds., *Pioneers of the Black Atlantic: Five Slave Narratives from the Enlightenment, 1772–1815* (Washington, D.C.: Civitas, 1998), 5. The "Narrative of the Most Remarkable Particulars in the Life of James Albert Ukawsaw Gronniosaw, an African Prince, As Related by Himself," in *Unchained Voices: An Anthology of Black Authors in the English-Speaking World of the Eighteenth-Century*, ed. Vincent Carretta (Lexington: University of Kentucky Press, 2004), 32–58. For other narratives that similarly use suicide to reflect the crisis of Christian conversion, see "Narrative of the Lord's Wonderful Dealings with *John Marrant*, a Black," and "The Life, History, and Unparalleled Sufferings of *John Jea*, the African Preacher, Compiled and Written by Himself," in Gates and Andrews, *Pioneers of the Black Atlantic*, 61–82 and 367–439, respectively; see also the account of Ofodobendo Wooma, or Andrew the Moor, in Daniel B. Thorpe, "Chattel with a Soul: The Autobiography of a Moravian Slave," *Pennsylvania Magazine of History and Biography* 112 (July 1988), 433–451. Useful discussions of the Christianity in Black Atlantic writing include Carretta, *Unchained Voices*, 2-3, 8-10; Frank Lambert, "'I Saw the Book

Talk': Slave Readings of the First Great Awakening," *Journal of African American History* 87 (Winter 2002), 12–25; Tim Lockley, "David Margrett: A Black Missionary in the Revolutionary Atlantic," *Journal of American Studies* 46 (August 2012), 729–745; and James Sidbury, *Becoming African in America: Race and Nation in the Early Black Atlantic* (New York: Oxford University Press, 2007), 39–65.

60. The second paragraph puts an even finer point on the purpose of this life story, noting that this account will show the manner in which the Christian God will "deal with those benighted parts of the world where the gospel of Jesus Christ hath never reached"; see Carretta, *Unchained* Voices, 32–33.
61. Carretta, *Unchained Voices*, 34–35.
62. His master was Theodorus Jacobus Frelinghuysen, a New Jersey clergyman influential in the Great Awakening. Carretta, *Unchained Voices*, 55n36.
63. Carretta, *Unchained Voices*, 41. On melancholy and conversion, see John Owen King, III, *Iron of Melancholy: Structures of Spiritual Conversion in America From the Puritan Conscience to Victorian Neuroses* (Wesleyan, CT: Wesleyan University Press, 1983).
64. Sidbury, *Becoming African in America*, 39–44.
65. Gould, *Barbaric Traffic*, 6–8.

CHAPTER SIX

1. *VG* (P&D), 22 July 1773, 1. The notice first appeared in the London papers; see n7, below.
2. The first edition of the poem was published in 1773 as Thomas Day and John Bicknell, *The Dying Negro, a Poetical Epistle, supposed to be written by a black, (who lately shot himself on board a vessel in the River Thames;) to his intended Wife* (London, 1773). This quote is taken from a later edition, *The Dying Negro, a Poem* (London, 1775), 1; the poem can be found online at http://www.brycchancarey.com/slavery/dying.htm. Unless otherwise noted, all references are to the 1775 edition.
3. Brycchan Carey, *British Abolitionism and the Rhetoric of Sensibility: Writing, Sentiment, and Slavery, 1760–1807* (New York: Palgrave Macmillian, 2005), 75–84. See also Moira Ferguson, *Subject to Others: British Women Writers and Colonial Slavery, 1670–1843* (London: Routledge, 1992), 237; Wylie Sypher, *Guinea's Captive Kings: British Antislavery Literature of the Eighteenth Century* (Chapel Hill: University of North Carolina Press, 1942), 177–180; Philip Gould, *Barbaric Traffic: Commerce and Antislavery in the Eighteenth-Century Atlantic World* (Cambridge, MA: Harvard University Press, 2003), 72–74; and Richard Bell, *We Shall Be No More: Suicide and Self-Government in the Newly United States* (Cambridge, MA: Harvard University Press, 2012), 205–208.
4. These cases included those of Jonathan Strong (1767), John and Mary Hylas (1768), Thomas Lewis (1770), and James Somerset (1772). See David Brion Davis, *The Problem of Slavery in the Age of Revolution, 1770–1823* (New York: Oxford University Press, 1999), 471–489; F. O. Shyllon, *Black Slaves in Britain* (London: Oxford University Press, 1974), 17–23, 40–54; James Walvin, *England, Slaves and Freedom, 1776–1838* (Jackson: University Press of Mississippi, 1986), 26–45, 97–122; James Oldham, *The Mansfield Manuscripts and the Growth of English Law in the Eighteenth Century*, vol. 2 (Chapel Hill: University of North Carolina Press, 1992), 1221–1240; and Carey, *British Abolitionism*, 173–185.
5. On the contradictory status of slaves under English law, see William M. Wiecek, *The Sources of Antislavery Constitutionalism in America, 1760–1848* (Ithaca, NY: Cornell University Press, 1977), 23–39. Of those individuals seeking their freedom in

eighteenth-century England, James Somerset was the most famous; see Walvin, *England, Slaves and Freedom, 1776–1838*, 32–35, 40–44, 52–58.

6. Gretchen Holbrook Gerzina, *Black London: Life Before Emancipation* (New Brunswick, NJ: Rutgers University Press, 1995), 21-24.
7. See newspaper accounts from London and Virginia: *The Morning Chronicle and London Advertiser*, No. 253, 28 May 1773; *The General Evening* Post, No. 6181, 25–27 May 1773; *Lloyd's Evening* Post, 26–28 May 1773; *VG* (P&D), 22 July 1773. The notice that serves as epigraph to this chapter was also the epigraph to *The Dying Negro*; compare it to *The Dying Negro*, 24. See also Carey, *British Abolitionism*, 75, 82, 206n10; and Bell, *We Shall Be No More*, 207 (caption).
8. Although this was not the first poem about a slave, it "opened the campaign against slavery." Carey, *British Abolitionism*, 75–76.
9. Compare *The Dying Negro, A Poetical Epistle* (London: W. Flexney, 1773) and *The Dying Negro* (London, 1775); see also Carey, *British Abolitionism*, 82.
10. Paul Edwards, ed., *The Life of Olaudah Equiano or Gustavus Vassa, The African*, vol. 1 (London: Dawsons of Pall Mall, 1969), 18–189. See also Edwards' thorough discussion suggesting that Equiano may have combined lines from his memories of all three editions of *The Dying Negro* or modified his own manuscript as editions emerged; see lii–liii. Also see *Gould, Barbaric Traffic*, 74; and Bell, *We Shall Be No More*, 206.
11. Peter Williams, *An Oration on the Abolition of the Slave Trade; Delivered in the African Church, in the City of New York, January 1, 1808* (New York: Samuel Wood, 1808), 18; *The Interesting Life of Olaudah Equiano or Gustavus Vassa, The African*, vol. 1, ed. Paul Edward (London: Dawsons of Pall Mall, 1969), 80–81.
12. *The Dying Negro*, ix; Thomas Day, *Fragment of an Original Letter on the Slavery of the Negroes: Written in the Year 1776* (London, 1784), 33. Day's piece was written in 1776 but published later; see Carey, *British Abolitionism*, 81. Day's criticism was echoed in other critiques based on the natural rights claims of the Declaration of Independence; see David Armitage, *The Declaration of Independence: A Global History* (Cambridge, MA: Harvard University Press, 2007), 74–79.
13. Bell, *We Shall Be No More*, 203; and Mark S. Schantz, *Awaiting the Heavenly Country: The Civil War and America's Culture of Death* (Ithaca, NY: Cornell University Press, 2008), 139.
14. The classic statements on women and citizenship in the early Republic remain Linda K. Kerber, *Women of the Republic: Intellect and Ideology in Revolutionary America* (Chapel Hill: University of North Carolina Press, 1974); and Kerber, *No Constitutional Right to Be Ladies: Women and the Obligations of Citizenship in the United States* (New York: Hill and Wang, 1999). See also Mary Beth Norton, *Separated by Their Sex: Women in Public and Private in the Colonial Atlantic World* (Ithaca, NY: Cornell University Press, 2011).
15. See, for instance, Jeannine Marie DeLombard, *Slavery on Trial: Law Abolitionism, and Print Culture* (Chapel Hill: University of North Carolina Press, 2007); John Stauffer, *The Black Hearts of Men: Radical Abolitionists and the Transformation of* Race (Cambridge, MA: Harvard University Press, 2004); Erica L. Ball, *To Live an Antislavery Life: Personal Politics and the Antebellum Middle Class* (Athens: University of Georgia Press, 2012); Bell, *We Shall Be No More*, 233–246; and Richard S. Newman, *The Transformation of American Abolitionism: Fighting Slavery in the Early Republic* (Chapel Hill: University of North Carolina Press, 2002).
16. In contrast, in *The Spirit of the Laws* (1748), Montesquieu rejects suicide but maintains that slavery was an anathema to democracies, an idea that was widely circulated

among North American antislavery activists. On the popularity of Montesquieu in North America, see Winthrop D. Jordan, *White over Black: American Attitudes toward the Negro, 1550–1812* (Chapel Hill: University of North Carolina Press, 1968), 278–279. See also Montesquieu, *Persian Letters*, trans. John Ozell, vol. 2 (London, 1722), 12–14 (on suicide), 308 (Roxanna's suicide); Charles Montesquieu, *The Spirit of the Laws*, trans. and ed. Anne M. Choler, Basia C. Miller, and Harold Stone (Cambridge, UK: Cambridge University Press, 1989), 246–256. On *The Persian Letters*, see Anne M. Cohler, *Montesquieu's Comparative Politics and the Spirit of American Constitutionalism* (Lawrence: University Press of Kansas, 1988), 1–4; Diana J. Schaub, *Erotic Liberalism: Women and Revolution in Montesquieu's "Persian Letters"* (Lanham, MD: Rowan and Littlefield, 1995); Roxanne L. Euben, *Journeys to the Other Shore: Muslim and Western Travelers in Search of Knowledge* (Princeton, NJ: Princeton University Press, 2006), 134–170. See also Paul Merrill Spurlin, *Montesquieu in America, 1760–1801* (Baton Rouge: Louisiana State University Press, 1940).

17. John Locke, *Two Treatises of Government*, ed. Peter Laslett (New York: Cambridge University Press, 1960), 271; see also a parallel passage at 357. It is not my intention to detail Locke's attitude toward slavery, only to demonstrate how he uses slavery and suicide together to illustrate his ideas about the power and the role of government. Studies that find Locke in support of slavery include Robin Blackburn, *The Making of New World Slavery: From Baroque to Modern, 1492–1800* (London: Verso, 1997); Allan Gallay, *The Indian Slave Trade: The Rise of the English Empire in the American South, 1670–1717* (New Haven, CT: Yale University Press, 2002); David Armitage, "John Locke, Carolina, and *The Two Treatises of Government*," *Political Theory* 32, no. 5 (October 2004), 602–627; Wayne Glausser, "Three Approaches to Locke and the Slave Trade," *Journal of the History of Ideas* 51 (1990), 199–216; Robert Bernstein and Anika Maaza Mann, "The Contradictions of Racism: Locke, Slavery, and the Two Treatises," in Andrew Valls, ed., *Race and Racism in Modern Philosophy* (Ithaca, NY: Cornell University Press, 2005); and Peter Laslett's introduction in *The Two Treaties of Government*, ed. Peter Laslett (Cambridge, UK: Cambridge University Press, 1988), 105–107. Mary Nyquist offers an alternative reading of Locke's views on slavery, despotical power, and tyranny; see *Arbitrary Rule: Slavery, Tyranny, and the Power of Life and Death* (Chicago: University of Chicago Press, 2013), chapter 10. Holly Brewer argues that beginning in the 1690s, Locke attempted to undercut the development of slavery in substantial ways; see "Slavery, Sovereignty, and 'Inheritable Blood': The Struggle over Locke's Virginia Plan of 1698 in the Wake of the Glorious Revolution," unpublished paper, NYU Atlantic History Workshop, October 6, 2009.
18. Locke, *Two Treatises*, 284 (quote); 283–285 (discussion of slavery).
19. *The Dying Negro*, ix.
20. Equiano, *The Interesting Life of Olaudah Equiano or Gustavus Vassa, The African*, vol. 1, 187–188.
21. Frederick Douglass, *My Bondage and My Freedom*, ed. Philip S. Foner (New York: Dover, 1969), 284; Schantz, *Awaiting the Heavenly Country*, 138–139; and Bell, *We Shall Be No More*, 202–203, 236–239.
22. His theory also created a bifurcated understanding of suicide based on race. In Locke's formulation, slaves existed outside the social compact. In contrast, suicide by free persons remained unacceptable because of their inclusion in that compact. Locke, unwittingly perhaps, encouraged his audience to consider the legitimacy of suicide as dependent on one's status as free or enslaved. Since for early modern

Anglo-Americans, the most ready reference for a slave was an African-descended individual confined by law to a permanently inheritable enslaved status, Locke suggested that the validity of suicide depended upon race. In splitting off the suicide of black slaves from the suicides of free whites, Locke anticipated a separation that, as the *Philadelphia Evening Herald* with its reference to the suicides of *refined negroes* suggests, had far-reaching effects in American culture. See Terri L. Snyder, "Slavery, Suicide, and Memory in Early North America," *Journal of American History* 97 (June 2010), 29–62; and Bell, *We Shall Be No More*, 201–246.

23. On Locke and the American founding, see Pauline Maier, *American Scripture: Making the Declaration of Independence* (New York: Vintage, 1998); Jerome Huyler, *Locke in America: The Moral Philosophy of the Founding Era* (Lawrence: University Press of Kansas, 1995); Joyce Oldham Appleby, "The Social Origins of American Revolutionary Ideology," *Journal of American History* 64 (March 1978), 935–958.
24. "Letter from the Rev. Mr. George Whitefield to the Inhabitants of Maryland, Virginia, North and South Carolina," *Pennsylvania Gazette*, 17 April 1740, 1–2 (NewsBank/Readex, Database: America's Historical Newspapers, SQN: 1128F3B9D3EB5D80); reprinted in Thomas S. Kidd, ed., "Letter to the Inhabitants of Maryland, Virginia, North and South Carolina" (1740), *Encyclopedia Virginia*, Virginia Foundation for the Humanities, 18 January 2012, accessed 30 July 2013.
25. In the first full-length treatise on suicide, John Sym's exempted martyrs (who chose death over recantation), soldiers (who risked certain death in battle), children, and the insane from the category of self-murder, see John Sym, *Life's Preservative Against Self-Killing*, ed. Michael MacDonald (London: Routledge, 1988), xxxvi–xxxvii 2, 172–174; Michael MacDonald and Terence R. Murphy, *Sleepless Souls: Suicide in Early Modern England* ([1990]; Oxford, UK: Oxford University Press, 2000), 222. Only those over the age of 14 could be found guilty of felonious suicide, see Holly Brewer, *By Birth or Consent: Children, Law, and the Anglo-American Revolution in Authority* (Chapel Hill: University of North Carolina Press, 2005), 189–190, esp. n15.
26. Schantz, *Awaiting the Heavenly Country*, 144–152.
27. On sensibility, see Laura M. Stevens, *The Poor Indians: British Missionaries, Native Americans, and Colonial Sensibility* (Philadelphia: University of Pennsylvania Press, 2004); Sarah Knott, *Sensibility and the American Revolution* (Chapel Hill: University of North Carolina Press, 2009); G. J. Barker-Benfield, *The Culture of Sensibility: Sex and Society in Eighteenth-Century Britain* (Chicago: University of Chicago Press, 1992).
28. *VG* (P&D), 23 December 1773. For other antislavery items in the *Virginia Gazette*, see *VG* (P&D), 20 August 1772.
29. [Maurice Morgann?], "Memorandum on the Right of Englishmen Under the 7th Article of the Treaty to Withdraw Negroes from the United States," 1784, Shelburne Papers, vol. 87, 392, William L. Clements Library, University of Michigan, Ann Arbor. See also Simon Schama, *Rough Crossings: Britain, the Slaves, and the American Revolution* (London: BBC Books, 2005), 129–156; Sylvia R. Frey, *Water from the Rock: Black Resistance in a Revolutionary Age* (Princeton, NJ: Princeton University Press), 191–195; and Ellen Gibson Wilson, *The Loyal Blacks* (New York: Capricorn Books, 1976), 48–57.
30. Schama, *Rough Crossings*, 131.
31. Bell, *We Shall Be No More*, 212.
32. Postscript-Saturday Evening, *Pennsylvania Evening Herald*, 18 June 1785, vol. 1, issue 42, 2.

33. Philip Gould argues that in imaginative literature the convention of slave suicide works to allay fears of cultural degeneration; see *Barbaric Traffic*, 72–73.
34. David Brion Davis, *The Problem of Slavery in the Age of Revolution, 1770–1823* (New York: Oxford University Press, 1999), 275–285; Eric Slauter, *The State as a Work of Art: The Cultural Origins of the Constitution* (Chicago: University of Chicago Press, 2009), 169–214; and Christopher Leslie Brown, "The Problems of Slavery," in Edward G. Gray and Jane Kamensky, eds., *The Oxford Handbook of the American Revolution* (New York: Oxford University Press, 2012), 427–446.
35. Joanne Pope Melish, *Disowning Slavery: Gradual Emancipation and "Race" in New England, 1780–1860* (Ithaca, NY: Cornell University Press, 1998), 4 (quotation), 1–10.
36. See for instance, Petition of Frederick and Hampshire Counties to the House of Delegates of Virginia, 1786 and 1795, in J. H. Johnston, ed., "Antislavery Petitions Presented to the Virginia Legislature by Citizens of Various Counties," *Journal of African American History* 12 (October 1927) 671–673.
37. Davis, *The Problem of Slavery*, 303.
38. Gould notes that in imaginative antislavery literature like *The Dying Negro*, the appeal of the suicide of the enslaved subject lies in the fear of cultural contamination that might result if he lived; see *Barbaric Traffic*, 72–74.
39. *VG* (P&D), 22 July 1773: 1, column 2.
40. Carey, *British Abolitionism*, 70–80. Among its appearances are *Royal American Magazine* (February 1774), 71–72; *Pennsylvania Magazine* (January 1776), 36–38; *Universal Asylum and Columbian Magazine* (May 1790), 316–318. The poem is advertised in the *Boston Gazette*, 14 February 1791; the *Massachusetts Magazine* (January 1791); and the *Federal Gazette* 11 April 1792. The Delaware *Mirror of the Times and General Advertiser*, 20 April 1805, mentions it as a "noble poem" in an item reprinted from the *Richmond Enquirer*. The poem was also advertised in a collection in the *New York Evening Post*, 25 June 1821.
41. For songs that do not reference suicide or the poem's themes but utilize its title, see for instance *The Dying Negro: A Song*, London, Longman and Broderip, 1792; *The Dying Negro: A Much Admired Song, Mr. James Hook*; and *The Dying Negro, A Favorite Song sung by Mr. Clifford, at Vauxhall-Gardens*, Music Collections, BL. There is also a *Dying Negro* by Wm. Foster, set to the tune of "Indian Chief" that was published in *The Patrol* (Utica, NY), 2 October 1815, issue 39, p. 4.
42. See, for instance, "'The Dying Negro,' A Song Composed by Thomas Beilby, Organist of Scarbrough And by him humbly inscribed to Granville Sharpe Esq. and the other Gentlemen of the Committee formed for promoting Abolition of the Slave Trade" (London: Printed by Longman and Broderip No. 26 Cheapside and No.13 Haymarket, 1792), n.p. , BL 360.6.
43. For eighteenth-century former slave memoirs that discuss their African origins, see *A Narrative of the Most Remarkable Particulars in the Life of James Albert Ukawsaw Gronniosaw, an African Prince, as Related by Himself* (1770), Ottobah Cugoano, *Thoughts and Sentiments on the Evil of Slavery* (1787); and *The Interesting Life of Olaudah Equiano or Gustavus Vassa, the African* (1789). See also Chapter Five.
44. *VG* (P&D), 30 August 1773, 3.
45. *The Dying Negro*, 9 (quote), 7 (lust for gold).
46. Carey, *British Abolitionism*, 80.
47. Gould, *Barbaric Traffic*, 78–79.
48. *The Dying Negro, A Poem*, 22 and 24.

49. England ended profane burials for suicide in 1823 and outlawed forfeiture in 1870. France abolished postmortem desecration in 1770 and decriminalized suicide in 1791; Geneva acted similarly in 1732 and 1792, respectively; see MacDonald and Murphy, *Sleepless Souls*, 196–197, 346–347.
50. Keith Burgess-Jackson, "The Legal Status of Suicide in Early America: A Comparison with the English Experience," *Wayne Law Review* 29 (Fall 1982), 57–90.
51. *The Dying Negro*, 2, 4.
52. Derek A. Webb, "The *Somerset* Effect: Parsing Lord Mansfield's Words on Slavery in Nineteenth Century America," *Law and History Review* 32 (Aug. 2014), 455–490; William M. Wiecek, *The Sources of Antislavery Constitutionalism in America, 1760–1818* (Ithaca, NY: Cornell University Press, 1977), 28–30; William M. Wiecek, "Somerset: Lord Mansfield and the Legitimacy of Slavery in the Anglo-American World," *University of Chicago Law Review* 42 (Fall 1974), 86–146; and William M. Wiecek, "Somerset's Case," *Encyclopedia of the American Constitution*, vol. 4, Leonard W. Levy, Kenneth L. Karst, and Dennis J. Mahoney, eds. (New York: Macmillian, 1986), 1710. For an account of the case that includes the reaction of black Londoners, see Gerzina, *Black London*, 121–132.
53. Hening, vol. 3, 448.
54. Schama, *Rough Crossings*, 55.
55. Patricia Bradley, *Slavery, Propaganda, and the American Revolution* (Jackson: University of Mississippi Press, 1998), 66–80.
56. Wiecek, *The Sources of Antislavery Constitutionalism*, 35, 40–43.
57. Knott, *Sensibility and the American Revolution*, 4–7; Barker-Benfield, *The Culture of Sensibility*, 215–350.
58. *The Dying Negro*, 14.
59. Gould, *Barbaric Traffic*, 73.
60. Locke, *Two Treatises*, 283–284.
61. Bell, *We Shall Be No More*, 207 (caption); see Advertisement, *The Dying Negro* (1773).
62. Charles Ball relates the story of Paul in *Slavery in the United States: The Life and Adventures of Charles Ball, a Black Man* (New York: John S. Taylor, 1837), 335–337 (http://docsouth.unc.edu/neh/ballslavery/ball.html).
63. *Reflections on Slavery, With Recent Evidence of its Inhumanity. Occasioned by the Melancholy Death of Romain, a French Negro* (Philadelphia: Robert Cochran, 1803); the story of Romain is found in chapter 12, 14 (quotes), 12–17; Bell, *We Shall Be No More*, 212–215.
64. Bell, *We Shall Be No More*, 212–216.
65. Raynal retitled "A Kind of Wild Tragedy" as "The Legend of the Two Lovers"; see Abbé Raynal, *A Philosophical and Political History of the Settlements and Trade of the Europeans in the East and West Indies*, vol. 5 (Edinburgh: Mundell and Son, 1804), 29 (quotations), 28–29 (story). The story can also be found as "The Two Negro Friends" in the *Virginia Almanack for 1775* (Williamsburg: Dixon and Hunter, 1775) (transcribed by George Riser), Small Special Collections, Alderman Library, University of Virginia. For discussions of the various editions and reprintings of the story, see Sypher, *Guinea's Captive Kings*, 137–143.
66. Anonymous, "Scene in the West Indies," in James G. Basker, ed., *Amazing Grace: An Anthology of Poems about Slavery, 1660–1810* (New Haven, CT: Yale University Press, 2002), 280. Similarly, Elizabeth Knipe's poem recounts the story of two lovers who, rather than withstand the hold of the ship, leap to their deaths; see *Six Narrative Poems* (London, 1787).

67. Thomas Branagan, *Avenia or a Tragical Poem of the Oppression of the Human Species and Infringement of the Rights of Man* (Philadelphia: J. Cline, 1810), title page.
68. Norton, *Separated by their Sex*, 139.
69. Robert H. Gudmestad, "Slave Resistance, Coffles, and the Debates over Slavery in the Nation's Capital," in Walter Johnson, ed., *The Chattel Principle: Internal Slave Trades in the Americas* (New Haven, CT: Yale University Press, 2004), 72–73 (quotations), 72–90 (inclusive).
70. Jesse Torrey, *A Portraiture of Domestic Slavery*, 42–43.
71. Matthew Hale, *The History of Please of the Crown*, ed. Emlyn G. Wilson and T. Dogherty (London, 1800), I, 412.
72. Gudmestad, "Slave Resistance, Coffles, and the Debates over Slavery," 74–75.
73. *Debates and Proceedings of the Congress of the United States*, Fourteenth Congress, First Session, 4 December 1815 to 30 April, 1816 (Washington, DC, 1854), 1115–1117. See also Gudmestad, "Slave Resistance, Coffles, and the Debates over Slavery," 72–75.
74. Gudmestad, "Slave Resistance, Coffles, and the Debates over Slavery," 87–88. Richard Bell notes that Torrey's account of Anna "found its way to the hands" of Benjamin Lundy, William Lloyd Garrison, and Lydia Maria Child. See Bell, *We Shall Be No More*, 220.
75. Ball, *To Live an Antislavery Life*, 63 (quote) 70. On enslaved women's narratives, see Mary Prince, *The History of Mary Prince*, ed. Moira Ferguson (London: Pandora Press, 1987), introduction; Henry Louis Gates, Jr., "Foreword: In Her Own Write," *Six Women's Slave Narratives* (New York: Oxford University Press, 1988), vii–xxii, xxix–xli; Deborah M. Garfield and Rafia Zafar, *Harriet Jacobs and Incidents in the Life of a Slave Girl: New Critical Essays* (New York: Cambridge University Press, 1996); and the essays by Julie Winch, Anne M. Boylan, and Nell Irvin Painter in Jean Fagan Yellin and John C. Van Horne, eds., *The Abolitionist Sisterhood: Women's Political Culture in Antebellum America* (Ithaca, NY: Cornell University Press, 1994), 101–158.
76. On women's reform and abolitionism, see Bruce Dorsey, *Reforming Men and Women: Gender and the Antebellum City* (Ithaca, NY: Cornell University Press, 2002), 136–194; Shirley J. Yee, *Black Women Abolitionists: A Study in Activism, 1828–1860* (Knoxville: University of Tennessee Press, 1992), esp. 112–154; the essays collected in Yellin and Van Horne, ed., *The Abolitionist Sisterhood*; Beth A. Salerno, *Sister Societies: Women's Antislavery Organizations in Antebellum America* (DeKalb: Northern Illinois University Press, 2005), 9–24.
77. Wendy Hamand Venet, *Neither Ballots nor Bullets: Women Abolitionists and the Civil War* (Charlottesville: University Press of Virginia1991), 2–19; and Julie Roy Jeffrey, *The Great Silent Army of Abolitionism: Ordinary Women in the Antislavery* Movement (Chapel Hill: University of North Carolina Press, 1998), 14–32. On gender issues in antislavery politics, see William D. Pierson, *Free Hearts and Free Homes: Gender and American Antislavery Politics* (Chapel Hill: University of North Carolina Press, 2003).
78. Newman, *The Transformation of American Abolitionism*, 2 (quote), 16–86.
79. Newman, *The Transformation of American Abolitionism*, 13.
80. Newman, *The Transformation of American Abolitionism*, 124 (quote), 116 (quote), 105–130; Bell, *We Shall Be No More*, 201–246.
81. For a discussion of the changing representations of slave suicide in relationship to divisions and struggles within abolitionism, see Bell, *We Shall Be No More*, 203–246.
82. David Blight classifies the genre of slaves narratives into fiction, biography, and autobiography, including oral history, and notes that this last category is the largest;

see Blight, *A Slave No More: Two Men Who Escaped to Freedom Including Their Own Narratives of Emancipation* (New York: Harcourt, Inc., 2007), 11–12.

83. Charles T. Davis and Henry Louis Gates, Jr., *The Slave's Narrative* (New York: Oxford University Press, 1985), xv–xvi; William L. Andrews and Henry Louis Gates, Jr., *Slave Narratives* (New York: Library of America, 2000), 1008.

84. David W. Blight, "Introduction: 'A Psalm of Freedom,'" in *Narrative of the Life of Frederick Douglass, An American Slave: Written By Himself* (1845), ed. David W. Blight (Boston: Bedford Books, 1993), 16; also quoted in Dwight A. McBride and Justin A. Joyce, "Reading Communities: Slave Narratives and the Discursive Reader," in John Ernest, ed., *the Oxford Handbook of the African American Slave Narrative* (New York: Oxford University Press, 2014), 171. McBride and Joyce point out that the public demanded increasing sensationalism in the narratives as well; see 171. Because of white assumptions about black illiteracy and deviance, narratives often included testimonials from white abolitionists to lend veracity to the accounts. See Blight, *A Slave No More*, 12–13; Davis and Gates, *The Slave's Narrative*, xxxiv.

85. Blight, *A Slave No More*, 12–13.

86. Schantz, *Awaiting the Heavenly Country*, 143; Bell, *We Shall Be No More*, 225 (quote), 225–233 (inclusive discussion) (for challenges to these generic images, see ibid., 233–246); David Silkenat, *Moments of Despair: Suicide, Divorce, and Debt in Civil War Era North* Carolina (Chapel Hill: University of North Carolina Press, 2011), 14.

87. While women predominated as victims of sexual coercion, as Tom Foster reminds us, masters and mistresses sexually abused enslaved men as well. Those stories, however, were rarely addressed in connection with suicide in slave autobiographies. See Thomas A. Foster, "The Sexual Abuse of Black Men under Slavery," *Journal of the History of Sexuality* 20 (September 2011), 445–464.

88. On rape in slavery see Deborah Gray White, *Ar'nt I a Woman*: *Female Slaves in the Plantation* South (New York: Norton, 1975); 152–153, 174–175, 188–189; Daina Ramey Berry, *"Swing the Sickle for the Harvest is Ripe": Gender and Slavery in Antebellum* Georgia (Urbana: University of Illinois Press, 2010); 77–84; and Sharon Block, *Rape and Sexual Coercion in Early America* (Chapel Hill: University of North Carolina Press, 2006) 64–74, 100–101. On women in abolitionism, see for instance Julie Roy Jeffrey, *The Great Silent Army of Abolitionism: Women in the Anti-slavery Movement* (Chapel Hill: University of North Carolina Press, 1998); Stacey M. Robertson, *Hearts Beating for Liberty: Women Abolitionists in the Old Northwest* (Chapel Hill: University of North Carolina Press, 2010).

89. Solomon Northup, *Twelve Years a Slave: Narrative of Solomon Northup, a Citizen of New-York, Kidnapped in Washington City in 1841, and Rescued in 1853* (Auburn, Buffalo, and London, 1853), 189 (bribes), 258–259.

90. Harriett A. Jacobs, *Incidents in the Life of a Slave Girl, Written by Herself*, ed. Jean Fagan Yellin (Cambridge, MA: Harvard University Press, 1987), 61, 77–78.

91. Howard I. Kushner, "Suicide, Gender, and the Fear of Modernity," in John Weaver and David Wright, eds., *Histories of Suicide: International Perspectives on Self-Destruction in the Modern World* (Toronto: University of Toronto Press, 2009), 19–52; Kelly McGuire, *Dying to be English: Suicide Narratives and National Identity, 1721–1814* (London: Pickering and Chatto, 2012), 11–12.

92. Ball, *Slavery in the United States*, 336.

93. Austin Steward, *Twenty Two Years a Slave, and Forty Years a Freeman* (Rochester, NY: William Alling, 1857), 247–248 (http://docsouth.unc.edu/fpn/steward/steward.html).

94. Mary Prince, "*The History of Mary Prince, a West-Indian Slave*" (London, 1831), in *Six Women's Slave Narratives*, 8. There are important exceptions to this gendered representation of suicide found in slave narratives—for instance, in revolutionary San Domingue, where, according to Bernard Moitt, both men and women actively endorsed suicide rather than face execution or defeat by the French; see "Slave Women and Resistance in the French Caribbean," in David Barry Gaspar and Darlene Clark Hine, eds., *More Than Chattel: Black Women and Slavery in the Americas* (Bloomington: Indiana University Press, 1996), 239–258. Also, while discussions of suicide in WPA slave narratives are few, they focus more often on women than on men.
95. Jacobs, *Incidents in the Life of a Slave Girl*, 122.
96. Donald M. Jacobs, *Courage and Conscience: Black and White Abolitionists in Boston* (Bloomington: Indiana University Press, 1993), 92–93; Stanley J. Robboy and Anita W. Robboy, "Lewis Hayden: From Fugitive Slave to Statesman," *New England Quarterly* 46 (December 1973), 591–613.
97. Account of Lewis Hayden, in Harriet Beecher Stowe, *A Key to Uncle Tom's Cabin* (Boston, 1854), 303–304 (http://utc.iath.virginia.edu/uncletom/key/keyIII5t.html).
98. William Craft, *Running a Thousand Miles for Freedom, or, the Escape of William and Ellen Craft from Slavery* (London, 1860), 21.
99. *Ritchie v. Wilson* (1825), 3 Mart. (n.s.) 585, 1825 La. LEXIS 82.
100. Jacobs, *Incidents in the Life of a Slave Girl*, 22.
101. Jacobs, *Incidents in the Life of a Slave Girl*, 25.
102. Ball, *Slavery in the United States*, 37–38.
103. Ball, *Slavery in the United States*, 68.
104. Ball, *Slavery in the United States*, 37–38, 69.
105. Ball, *Slavery in the United States*, 69.
106. For a similar case of melancholy and uncertainty brought about by family separation, see David Silkenat's discussion of Moses Roper; Silkenat, *Moments of Despair*, 14–15.
107. Samuel Williams to John M. Williams, 14 December 1836, Paris, Kentucky, Samuel Williams Papers, 1836–1850, 87W3, Special Collections Library, University of Kentucky, Lexington.
108. Samuel Williams to John M. Williams, 14 December 1836 (reference to ten slaves); 25 December 1836 ("sad accident").
109. Samuel Williams to John M. Williams, 25 December 1836.
110. As Jeannine DeLombard has demonstrated, for the nineteenth century, thinking about slavery in legal terms had "far-reaching implications for the abolitionist movement"; see DeLombard, *Slavery on Trial*, 2.
111. *Thomason v. Dill* (January 1857), 30 Ala. 444, Ala LEXIS 121; see also Helen Tunnicliff Catterall, ed., *Judicial Cases Concerning American Slavery and the Negro*, vol. 3 (Washington, DC: Carnegie Institution of Washington, 1926–37), 216–217.
112. Ball, *Slavery in the United States*, 69. Similarly, William Wells Brown related the story of an unnamed woman aboard ship who jumped overboard after having been separated from her husband and children; she had "no desire to live without them." William Wells Brown, *Narrative of William Wells Brown*, in Andrews and Gates, *Slave Narratives*, 389–390.
113. Bell, *We Shall Be No More*, 234; Schantz, *Awaiting the Heavenly Country*, 143–152; Silkenat, *Moments of Despair*, 14–18.
114. Jacobs, *Incidents in The Lite of a Slave Girl*, 122 ("frequent occurrence"); Letter from Frederick Douglass, 5 September 1850, *Frederick Douglass: Selected Speeches and*

Writings, ed. Philip S. Foner (Chicago: Lawrence Hill Books, 1999), 162 (quote), 158–162 (inclusive).

115. Bell, *We Shall Be No More*, 233–246.
116. Ball, *Slavery in the United States*, 68–69; Jacobs, *Incidents in the Life of a Slave Girl*, 122.
117. Elizabeth Keckley, *Behind the Scenes, or, Thirty Years a Slave and Four Years in the White House* (New York: G. W. Carleton, 1868), 30 (http://docsouth.unc.edu/neh/keckley/keckley.html).
118. Interview with Fannie Berry in Charles L. Perdue, Jr., Thomas E. Barden, and Robert K. Phillips, eds., *Weevils in the Wheat: Interviews with Virginia Ex-Slaves* (Bloomington: Indiana University Press, 1980), 34. See also William Dusinberre, *Strategies for Survival: Recollections of Bondage in Antebellum Virginia* (Charlottesville: University of Virginia Press, 2009), 91, 133.
119. Interview with Ida Blackshear Hutchinson in *Born in Slavery: Slave Narratives from the Federal Writers' Project, 1936–1938*, 374 (http://lcweb2.loc.gov/ammem/snhtml/snhome.html, accessed 31 July 2013). The story of Lucy appears in the epilogue to this volume.
120. Interview with William Henry Towns, in *Born in Slavery* (http://memory.loc.gov/cgi-bin/ampage, accessed 2 January 2014).
121. Julian P. Boyd, ed., *The Papers of Thomas Jefferson* (Princeton, NJ: Princeton University Press 1950), vol. 2, 325, 496.
122. Todd Savitt, *Medicine and Slavery: The Diseases and Health Care of Blacks in Antebellum Virginia* (Urbana: University of Illinois Press, 1978), 284–249.
123. For instance, the Jamaican planter Bryan Edwards claimed that suicide among the enslaved in the Caribbean was much less frequent than among the "free-born, happy, and civilized inhabitants of Great Britain." Edwards revealed his belief that only more psychologically and emotionally advanced individuals fell prey to suicide. What had been associated with the stubbornness of the lower orders in the early modern period would come to be seen as a sign of sensibility and advancement in the nineteenth century. As Edwards put it, compared to slaves, suicide by "civilized" English men and women was frequent. In contrast, he wrote, slaves in the Caribbean were "far from courting death." See Bryan Edwards, *The History, Civil and Commercial, of the British Colonies in the West Indies*, 3rd ed., 3 vols. (London: Printed for John Stockdale, Picadilly, 1801), 105–106. Similarly, in 1801, Thomas Winterbottom claimed that slaves did not even understand mania and could only equate it with a moment when they "lose their head" in the "delirium of drunkenness." See Thomas Winterbottom, *An Account of the Native Africans* (1801), in Alan Bewell, ed., *Slavery, Abolition and Emancipation: Writings in the British Romantic* Period, vol. 7, *Medicine and the West Indian Slave Trade* (London: Pickering & Chatto Publishers, 1999), 247.
124. J. H. Hammond, "Slavery in the Light of Political Science" (1844), in *Cotton is King and Proslavery Arguments Comprising the Writings of Hammond, Harper, Christy, Stringfellow, Hodges, Bledsoe, and Cartwirght*, ed. E. N. Elliott (Augusta, GA: Pritchard, Abbott & Loomis, 1860), 655.
125. *Walker v. Hayes* (1860), in Catterall, *Judicial Cases Concerning American Slavery and the Negro*, vol. 2, 685; and Ariela J. Gross, *Double Character: Slavery and Mastery in the Antebellum Southern Courtroom* (Princeton, NJ: Princeton University Press, 2000), 150–151.
126. Postscript-Saturday Evening, *Pennsylvania Evening Herald*, 18 June 1785, vol. 1, issue 42, 2.

EPILOGUE

1. Interview with Jack Tattnall, in Georgia Writers' Project, *Drums and Shadows: Survival Stories among the Georgia Coastal Negroes,* intro. by Charles Joyner (Athens: University of Georgia Press, 1986), 108. Interviews in the *Drums and Shadows* collection, like others with African American informants in the 1930s, were often rendered in "negro dialect," which, as Rhys Isaac has pointed out, used spelling conventions that were developed for minstrel shows. Following the example of Isaac and others, I have regularized spelling without changing the syntax or the idiom of the informants' interviews. See Rhys Isaac, *Landon Carter's Uneasy Kingdom: Revolution and Rebellion on a Virginia Plantation* (New York: Oxford University Press, 2004), 193; and Timothy B. Powell, "Summoning the Ancestors: The Flying Africans' Story and Its Enduring Legacy," in *African American Life in the Georgia Lowcountry: The Atlantic World and the Gullah Geechee,* ed. Philip Morgan (Athens: University of Georgia Press, 2010), 259–262.
2. On the flying Africans, see Terri L. Snyder, "Suicide, Slavery, and Memory in Early North America," *Journal of American History* 97, no. 1 (June 2010), 39–62; Michael A. Gomez, *Exchanging Our Country Marks: The Transformation of African Identities in the Colonial and Antebellum South* (Chapel Hill: University of North Carolina Press, 1998), 117–120; and Powell, "Summoning the Ancestors," 253–280.
3. John Ernest, "Introduction," in *The Oxford Handbook of the African American Slave Narrative* (New York: Oxford University Press, 2014), 7 (quote), 2–12 (inclusive discussion).
4. Interview with Ida Blackshear Hutchinson, *Born in Slavery: Slave Narratives from the Federal Writers' Project, 1936–1938* (http://lcweb2.loc.gov/ammem/snhtml/snhome.html, accessed 31 July 2013), 374 (quotations), 369–378 (inclusive); see also Interview with Mrs. Fannie Berry, in *Born in Slavery*, 34, 43–44.
5. Interview with Ida Blackshear Hutchinson, 374; B. A. Botkin also reprints Hutchinson's narrative in *Lay Down My Burden: A Folk History of Slavery* (Chicago: University of Chicago Press, 1945), 183. As other historians have noted, WPA interviewees, such as Hutchinson, had good reasons to be less-than-forthcoming in their answers. The interviews were often conducted by strangers in the context of early twentieth century white supremacy and did not encourage fulsome discussions. As they were on other subjects, ex-slaves and their descendants may have been reticent to discuss suicide, and self-destruction was not on the list of questions given to interviewers. On the limits of the Federal Writers' Project and WPA interviews, see Norman R. Yetman, "An Introduction to the WPA Slave Narratives," *Slave Narratives From the Federal Writers' Project, 1936–1938* (http://memory.loc.gov/ammem/snhtml/snintro00.html, accessed August 2013). For an analysis of the interviews, see also Isaac, *Landon Carter's Uneasy Kingdom*, 187–232. On the lack of mention of suicide in North Carolina ex-slaves' interviews, see David Silkenat, *Moments of Despair: Suicide, Divorce, and Debt in Civil War Era North Carolina* (Chapel Hill: University of North Carolina Press, 2011), 40. For the list of questions used by the Federal Writers' Project interviewers, see Charles L. Perdue Jr., Thomas E. Barden, and Robert K. Phillips, eds., *Weevils in the Wheat: Interviews with Virginia Ex-Slaves* (Bloomington: Indiana University Press, 1976), 367–376.
6. Interview with Ida Blackshear Hutchinson, 374.
7. Interview with Ida Blackshear Hutchinson, 375.
8. "Dave's Neckliss" was originally published in *The Atlantic Monthly* 64 (October 1889), 500–508. On Chesnutt's assessments of the story and its importance, see

Joseph R. McElrath, Jr., and Robert C. Leitz III, eds., *To Be an Author: Letters of Charles W. Chesnutt* (Princeton, N.J.: Princeton University Press, 1997), 44.

9. Literary critics are divided in their assessment of the story's power. For instance, the editors of Chesnutt's letters argue that the story is so comedic that it undercuts its seriousness; see McElrath and Leitz, *To Be an Author*, 21. Other scholars have argued that the story's power lies in its attack on white prejudice and supremacy; see for instance John N. Swift and Gigen Momoser, "'Out of the Realm of Superstition': Chesnutt's 'Dave's Neckliss' and the Curse of Ham," *American Literary Realism* 42 (Fall 2009), 1–12. For other treatments of "Dave's Neckliss," see Richard Brodhead, *Cultures of Letters: Scenes of Reading and Writing in Nineteenth-Century America* (Chicago: University of Chicago Press, 1993), 206; Eric Sundquist, *To Wake the Nations: Race in the Making of American Literature* (Cambridge, MA: Belknap, 1993), 378–383; Henry B. Wonham, *Charles W. Chesnutt: A Study of the Short Fiction* (New York: Twayne, 1998), 44–47; and Silkenat, *Moments of Despair*, 40–41.
10. The text of the "Dave's Neckliss" can be found in Charles W. Chesnutt, "Dave's Neckliss" in *Stories, Novels, and Essays*, ed. Werner Sollers (New York: Library of America, 2002), 721–733.
11. Swift and Momoser, "'Out of the Realm of Superstition,'" 2.
12. William Andrews, *The Literary Career of Charles W. Chesnutt* (Baton Rouge: Louisiana State University Press, 1980), 65–66. The ham in the story also refers in part to the "curse of Ham," a central justification in proslavery arguments, see Swift and Momoser, "'Out of the Realm of Superstition,'" 5–8.
13. Alex Haley, "Alex Haley on the Writing of *Roots*," *Roots: The Saga of an American Family*, 30th-anniversary ed. (New York: Vanguard Press, 2007), 897–899.
14. Toni Morrison, *Song of Solomon* (New York: Vintage, 1997; reprint, 2004), 323.
15. Morrison, *Song of Solomon*, xiii–xiv, 322–324.
16. Yasmil Raymond, "Maladies of Power: A Kara Walker Lexicon," in *Kara Walker: My Complement, My Enemy, My Oppressor, My Love*, ed. Philippe Vergne (Minneapolis: Walker Art Center, 2007), 354 (quotations); see also 364.
17. Ann Margaret Lim, "Mendive: Cuban National, Yoruban Soul, *Jamaica Observer* 13 December 2003 (http://www.cernudaarte.com/cgi-local/publications.cgi?categ=1&pid=121&aid=8, accessed April 2015). For the image, see http://www.cubanartnews.org/news/bookshelf-the-afro-cuban-art-of-grupo-antillano/2966, accessed 14 April 2015.
18. I am grateful to K. Dian Kriz, Susan M. Smith, and Farid L. Suárez for discussing Mendive's work with me. See also Alejandro de la Fuente, ed., *The Art of Afro-Cuba/El Arte de Afro-Cuba* (Pittsburgh: Alejandro de la Fuente and Caguayo Foundation, University of Pittsburgh Press, 2013), 265–277; J. Lorand Matory, "Free to Be a Slave: Slavery as Methapor in the Afro-Atlantic Religions," in *Africas of the Americas: Beyond the Search for Origins in the Afro-Atlantic Religions*, ed. Stephanie Palmié (Leiden: Brill, 2008), 351–380. For the meaning of slave suicide in Haiti, see Amy Wilentz, "A Zombie Is a Slave Forever," *New York Times*, 30 October 2012.
19. William Mein to Pierce Butler, 24 May 1803, folder 27, box 6, Series II: Plantation Management, Miscellaneous Correspondence 1802–1803, Butler Family Papers, Historical Society of Pennsylvania, Philadelphia. On Ebos Landing, see Gomez, *Exchanging Our Country Marks*, 117–118; Powell, "Summoning the Ancestors," 253–280; Timothy B. Powell, "Ebos Landing," June 15, 2004, *New Georgia Encyclopedia* (http://www.georgiaencyclopedia.org/nge/Article.jsp?id=h-2895&hl=y); and Malcolm

Bell Jr., *Major Butler's Legacy: Five Generations of a Slaveholding Family* (Athens: University of Georgia Press, 1987), 131–132.

20. Lawrence W. Levine, *Black Culture and Black Consciousness: Afro-American Folk Thought from Slavery to Freedom* (New York: Oxford University Press, 1977); Sterling Stuckey, *Slave Culture: Nationalist Theory and the Foundations of Black America* (New York: Oxford University Press, 1987); and Saidiya V. Hartman, *Scenes of Subjection: Terror, Slavery, and Self-Making in Nineteenth-Century America* (New York: Oxford University Press, 1997), 73.
21. Paul Singleton, GWP, 17.
22. Daniel E. Walker, "Suicidal Tendencies: African Transmigration in the History and Folklore of the Americas," *The Griot* 18 (Spring 1999), 15; Hartman, *Scenes of Subjection*, 73–78.
23. Mose Brown interview, in, GWP, 18; Carrie Hamilton interview, GWP, 28–29; Prince Sneed interview, GWP, 79; Wallace Quarterman interview, GWP, 150–151; Shad Hall interview, GWP, 169, Jim Meyers interview, GWP, 191.
24. Carrie Hamilton interview, 28–29; Wallace Quarterman interview, 151.
25. Carrie Hamilton interview, 29; B. A. Botkin, *A Treasury of Southern Folklore* (New York: Crown, 1949), 481–482. For a discussion of female slaves' ability to suckle over their shoulder, see Jennifer L. Morgan, "'Some Could Suckle over Their Shoulder': Male Travelers, Female Bodies, and the Gendering of Racial Ideology, 1500–1700," *William and Mary Quarterly* 54 (January 1997), 167–192.
26. David W. Blight, "If You Don't Tell It Like It Is, It Can Never Be as It Ought to Be," in *Slavery and Public History: The Tough Stuff of American Memory*, ed. James Oliver Horton and Lois E. Horton (New York: New Press, 2006), 26; Paul Singleton interview, 17; Wallace Quarterman interview, 150.
27. For the story of the great sale, including the details of the rain, see "American Civilization Illustrated: A Great Slave Sale," *New York Daily Tribune*, March 9, 1859, p. 5. For an overview of Pierce Butler's financial troubles and the great sale, see Bell, *Major Butler's Legacy*, 319–340. For discussions of "the weeping time," see Russell Duncan, ed., *Blue-Eyed Child of Fortune: The Civil War Letters of Colonel Robert Gould Shaw* (Athens: University of Georgia Press, 1992), 344, 348; and J. C. Furnas, *Fanny Kemble: Leading Lady of the Nineteenth-Century Stage* (New York: Dial Press, 1982), 374.
28. Hartman, *Scenes of Subjection*, 78.

STUDYING SLAVE SUICIDE

1. P. E. H. Hair, Adam Jones, and Robin Law, eds., *Barbot on Guinea: The Writings of Jean Barbot on West Africa 1678–1712*, vol. 2 (London: Hakluyt Society, 1992), 639; Testimony of Henry Hew Dalrymple, an army lieutenant on the African Coast and West Indian slaveowner, *HCSP*, vol. 73, 292, 312; Charles Ball, *Slavery in the United States: A Narrative of the Life and Adventures of Charles Ball, A Black Man* (New York: John S. Taylor, 1837), 69 (http://docsouth.unc.edu/neh/ballslavery/ball.html); Harriet Jacobs, *Incidents in the Life of a Slave Girl, Written by Herself*, ed. Jean Fagan Yellin (Cambridge, MA: Harvard University Press, 1987), 122; and Letter from Frederick Douglass, 5 September 1850, *Frederick Douglass: Selected Speeches and Writings*, ed. Philip S. Foner (Chicago: Lawrence Hill Books, 1999), 162.
2. Elizabeth Donnan, ed., *Documents Illustrative of the Slave Trade to America*, vol. 2 (Washington, DC: Carnegie Institution of Washington, 1931), 586 (section XI), 583–589 (inclusive).

3. *Born in Slavery: Slave Narratives from the Federal Writers' Project, 1936–1938*, Library of Congress (http://memory.loc.gov/ammem/snhtml/snlang.html, accessed 17 August 2014).
4. Laura F. C. Holloway, *Passed On: African American Mourning Stories: A Memorial* (Durham, NC: Duke University Press, 2003), 3.

SELECT BIBLIOGRAPHY OF PRIMARY SOURCES

CORONER'S INQUESTS

Library of Virginia, Archives and State Records Center, Richmond

Coroner's inquests are found in Bonds, Commissions, and Oaths Series or Miscellaneous Records Series for Amelia, Caroline, Charlotte, Chesterfield, Cumberland, Henrico, Louisa, Lunenberg, Mecklenberg, Page, and Prince Edward Counties. For the very earliest years of settlement, they can be found as part of county court orders; see, for instance, those for York, Surry, and Westmoreland.

State Archives of North Carolina, North Carolina Office of Archives and History, Raleigh

Coroner's inquests are found in Miscellaneous Records and Slave Records in Ashe, Bertie, Burke, Caswell, Gates, Granville, Hyde, Iredell, Mechlenberg, Pasquotank, Perquimmons, Person, Randolph, Rowan, Surry, and Tyrell Counties.

South Carolina Department of Archives and History, Columbia

South Carolina Court of General Sessions for Anderson, Fairfield, Kershaw, Laurens, Marlboro, Pinckney, Spartanburg, and Union Counties.

LEGAL, JUDICIAL, AND LEGISLATIVE RECORDS

Archives of Maryland. Edited by J. Hall Pleasants and Bernard Christian Steiner. Baltimore, MD: Maryland Historical Society, 1937.

Blackstone's Commentaries on the Laws of England. Edited by Stanley N. Katz. Chicago: University of Chicago Press, 1979.

Catterall, Helen Tunnicliff, ed. *Judicial Cases Concerning American Slavery and the Negro*. 5 vols. Washington, DC: Carnegie Institution of Washington, 1932.

Committee Reports and Papers, US House of Representatives 14th Congress, National Archives, Washington, DC.

Dalton, Michael. *The Countrey Justice: Containing the Practice of the Justices of the Peace out of their Sessions*. London, 1635.

Executive Journals of the Council of Colonial Virginia. Edited by H. R. McIlwaine, Richmond, VA: Virginia State Library, 1925–1966.

Hale, Matthew. *The History of Please of the Crown*, ed. Emlyn G. Wilson and T. Dogherty. London, 1800.

House of Commons Sessional Papers of the Eighteenth Century. Edited by Sheila Lambert. Wilmington, DE: Scholarly Resources, 1975.

House of Lords Papers, Slave Trade Papers, Houses of Parliament, Parliamentary Archives, City of Westminster, London

Journals of the House of Burgesses of Virginia. Edited by H. R. McIlwaine. Richmond, VA: Colonial Press, E. Waddey Co., 1915-.

Legislative Petitions, South Carolina Department of Archives and History, Columbia.

"Records of the Superior council of Louisiana, XXXVII," Edited by Heloise H. Cruzat. *Louisiana Historical Quarterly* 11 (1928):

Sharwood's Blackstone's Commentaries. Philadelphia, PA, 1860.

State Records of North Carolina. Collected and edited by Walter Clark. Raleigh: P. M. Hale, 1886–1907.

Statutes at Large of South Carolina. Edited by Thomas Cooper. Columbia: University of South Carolina Press, 1836, rpt. 1970.

Statutes at Large of Virginia. Edited by William Waller Hening. Richmond, VA: 1819–1823.

MANUSCRIPT SOURCES

Brown University Library, Providence, RI

Brig Sally's Account Book, 1764–1765.

Duke University, Rare Book, Manuscript, and Special Collections Library, Durham, NC.

Francis Porteus Corbin Papers

Historical Society of Pennsylvania, Philadelphia

Butler Family Papers

Library Company of Philadelphia

Du Simitiere Papers Relating to the West Indies 1748–1773

Huntington Library, San Marino, CA

Log of *Le Jeune Louis*, French Clandestine Slave Trade Collection, 1822–28

South Carolina Historical Society, Charleston

DeBerniere Family Papers

DeSaussure Papers

South Caroliniana Library, University of South Carolina, Columbia

Read Family Papers

Virginia Historical Society, Richmond

William Mayo Correspondence, Carrington Family Collections, Edmundson Family Papers, George Family Papers, George Washington Miley Papers, Sarah Scarborough Butler Henry French Papers, Massie Family Papers

Special Collections Library, University of Kentucky, Lexington

Samuel Williams Papers, 1836–1850.

William L. Clements Library, University of Michigan, Ann Arbor

Shelburne Papers

NEWSPAPERS AND PERIODICALS

Agricultural, Commercial, Industrial Progress and Resources; The American Weekly Mercury; Boston Gazette; Boston Weekly News Letter; City of Washington Gazette; Connecticut Courant; Debow's Review; Derby Mercury; The General Evening Post; Gentleman's Magazine; Lloyd's Evening Post; The London Journal; Massachusetts Magazine; Mirror of the Times and General Advertiser; The Morning Chronicle and London Advertiser; New England Weekly Journal; New Hampshire Gazette; Oxford Journal; The Patrol; Pennsylvania Evening Herald; The Royal American Magazine; South Carolina Gazette; The Times (London); *Universal Asylum and Columbian Magazine; Virginia Almanack; Virginia Gazette*

PUBLISHED PRIMARY SOURCES

Addison, Joseph. *Cato: A Tragedy and Selected Essays*. Edited by Christine Dunn Henderson and Mark E. Yellin. Indianapolis, IN: Liberty Fund, 2004.

Adventures of an African Slaver: Being a True Account of the Life of Captain Theodore Canot. Edited by Malcolm Cowley. London: George Routledge, 1928.

Amazing Grace: An Anthology of Poems About Slavery, 1660–1810. Edited by James G. Basker. New Haven, CT: Yale University Press, 2002.

Andrews, E. A. *Slavery and the Domestic Slave Trade in the United States*. Boston, 1836.

Aubrey, T., M.D., *The sea-surgeon, or the Guinea man's vade mecum*. London: printed for John Clarke at the Bible under the Royal-Exchange, 1729.

Ball, Charles. *Slavery in the United States: A Narrative of the Life and Adventures of Charles Ball, A Black Man*. New York: John S. Taylor, 1837 (http://www.docsouth.unc.edu, accessed 2 June 2013).

Barbot, Jean. *Barbot on Guinea: The Writings of Jean Barbot on West Africa 1678–1712*. 2 vols. Edited by P. E. H. Hair, Adam Jones, and Robin Law. London: Hakluyt Society, 1992.

Bassett, John S. *Slavery in North Carolina*. Baltimore, 1899.

Behn, Aphra. *Oroonoko: Or the Royal Slave. A True History* (1688). Edited by Joanna Lipking. New York: W. W. Norton, 1997.

Benzoni, Giraloma. *History of the New World*. Edited by W. H. Smyth. London: Hakluyt Society, 1857.

Bluett, Thomas. *Some Memoirs of the Life of Job, the Son of Solomon, the High Priest of Boonda*. London, 1734 (http://docsouth.unc.edu/neh/bluett/bluett.html, accessed 11 September 2012).

Born in Slavery: Slave Narratives from the Federal Writers' Project, 1936–1938 (http://lcweb2.loc.gov/ammem/snhtml/snhome.html).

Botkin, B. A. *A Treasure of Southern Folklore*. New York: Crown, 1949.

Branagan, Thomas. *Avenia or a Tragical Poem of the Oppression of the Human Species and Infringement of the Rights of Man*. Philadelphia: J. Cline, 1805.

Bremer, Fredrika. *The Homes of the New World: Impressions of America*. 2 vols. Translated by Mary Howitt. New York: Harper & Brothers Publishers, 1853.

Brown, William Wells. "Narrative of William Wells Brown," in *Slave Narratives*. Edited by William L. Andrews and Henry Louis Gates, Jr., New York: Library of America, 2000.

Byrd, William, II. *The Commonplace Book of William Byrd II of Westover*. Edited by Kevin Berland, Jan Kirsten Gilliam, and Kenneth A. Lockridge. Chapel Hill: University of North Carolina Press, 2001.

Byrd, William, II. *The History of the Dividing Line*. In Louis B. Wright, ed., *The Prose Works of William Byrd of Westover: Narratives of a Colonial Virginian*. Cambridge, MA: Belknap, 1966.

Byrd, William, II. *The Secret Diary of William Byrd II of Westover, 1709–1712*, Edited by Marion Tinling and Louis B. Wright. Richmond: Dietz Press, 1941.

Carpenter, W. M. "Observations on the Cachexia Africana or the Habit and Effects of Dirt-Eating on the Negro Race. *New Orleans Medical Journal* 1 (1845), 158–167.

Carter, Landon. *The Diary of Colonel Landon Carter of Sabine Hall, 1752 to 1778*. 2 vols. Edited by Jack P. Greene. Charlottesville: University Press of Virginia, 1965.

Carter, Robert. *The Diary and Correspondence of Robert "King" Carter of Virginia, 1701–1732*. Edited by Edmund Berkeley (http://etext.virginia.edu, accessed 6 March 2011).

"Chattel with a Soul: The Autobiography of a Moravian Slave." Edited by Daniel B. Thorpe. *Pennsylvania Magazine of History and Biography* 112 (1988), 433–451.

Chesnutt, Charles W. *Stories, Novels, and Essays*. Edited by Werner Sollers. New York: The Library of America, 2002.

Cheyne, George. *The English Malady; Or, A Treatise of Nervous Diseases of All Kinds*. London, 1733.

Clarkson, Thomas. *An Essay on the Slavery and Commerce of the Human Species*. London: Joseph Crukshank, 1785.

Collins, Dr. *Practical Rules for the Management and Medical Treatment of Negro Slaves in the Sugar Colonies*. London: J. Barfield, 1811; reprint 1971.

Conneau, Captain Theophilus. *A Slaver's Log Book or 20 Years Residence in Africa*. Edited by Howard S. Mott. London: Robert Hale Limited, 1977.

Craft, William. *Running a Thousand Miles for Freedom, or, the Escape of William and Ellen Craft from Slavery*. London, 1860.

Cragin, F. W. "Observations on Cachexia Africana or Dirt-Eating." *American Journal of the Medical Sciences* 17 (1836), 356–364.

Day, Thomas. *Fragment of an Original Letter on the Slavery of the Negroes: Written in the Year 1776*. London, 1784.

Day, Thomas, and John Bicknell. *The Dying Negro, a Poetical Epistle, supposed to be written by a black, (who lately shot himself on board a vessel in the River Thames;) to his intended Wife*. London, 1775.

Deslandes, A. F. Boreau. *Dying Merrily; or Historical and Critical Reflexions on the Conduct of Great Men Who, in their Last Moments, Mock'd Death and Died Facetiously*. Translated by T. W. London, 1745.

Documents Illustrative of the History of the Slave Trade to America. 4 vols. Edited by Elizabeth Donnan. Washington, DC: Carnegie Institute of Washington, W.F. Roberts Co., 1930–1935.

Douglass, Frederick. *Frederick Douglass: Selected Speeches and Writings*. Edited by Philip S. Foner. Chicago: Lawrence Hill Books, 1999.

Douglass, Frederick. *My Bondage and My Freedom*. Edited by Philip S. Foner. New York: Dover, 1969.

Dow, Francis. *Slave Ships and Slaving*. Salem, MA: Marine Research Society, 1927.

Drake, Daniel. "Diseases of the Negro Population." *Southern Medical and Surgical Journal* 1 (1845): 341–343; reprinted from *New Orleans Medical Journal*, 1 (May 1845): 583–584.

Equiano, Olaudah. *The Interesting Narrative of the Life of Olaudah Equiano or Gustavas Vassa, The African*. Edited by Paul Edwards. London: Dawsons, 1969.

The French Intervention in the St. John Slave Revolt of 1733–34. Translated and edited by Aimery P. Caron and Arnold R. Highfield. Charlotte Amalie, St. Thomas, Virgin Islands: Bureau of Libraries, Museums, and Archaeological Services, Department of Conservation and Cultural Affairs, 1981.

Georgia Writers' Project. *Drums and Shadows: Survival Stories among the Georgia Coastal Negroes*. Athens: University of Georgia Press, 1986.

Grainger, James. *The Sugar Cane: A Poem in Four Books*. London: Printed for R. and J. Dodsley, 1764.

Gronniosaw, James Albert Ukawsaw. A *Narrative of the Most Remarkable Particulars in the Life of James Albert Ukawsaw Gronniosaw, an African Prince, as Related by* Himself. London, 1770.

Hammond, Henry. *A Practical Catechism*. London: R Norton, 1677.

[Hayden, Lewis.] Account of Lewis Hayden. In Harriet Beecher Stowe. *A Key to Uncle Tom's Cabin*. Boston, 1854 (http://utc.iath.virginia.edu/uncletom/key/keyIII5t.html).

Heckewelder, John. *The History, Manners, and Customs of the Indian Nations*. Philadelphia: Historical Society of Philadelphia, 1819. In *Memoirs of the Historical Society of Pennsylvania*, vol. 12. New York: Arno Press, 1971.

Howe, George. "The Last Slave-Ship." *Scribner's Magazine*, vol. 8 (July 1890), 113–128.

Jacobs, Harriett A. *Incidents in the Life of a Slave Girl Written By Herself*. Edited by Jean Fagan Yellin. Cambridge, MA: Harvard University Press, 1987.

Jefferson, Thomas. *The Papers of Thomas Jefferson*. Edited by Julian P. Boyd. Princeton, NJ: Princeton University Press, 1950.

The Jesuit Relations and Allied Documents. Edited by Reuben Gold Thwaits. Computerized transcription by Tomasz Mentrak. Cleveland: Burrows Brothers, 1902 (http://puffin.creighton.edu/jesuit/relations/relations_58.html, accessed 24 February 2012).

Johnston, J. H. ed. "Antislavery Petitions Presented to the Virginia Legislature by Citizens of Various Counties." *Journal of African American History* 12 (1927), 671-673.

Keckley, Elizabeth. *Behind the Scenes, or, Thirty Years a Slave and Four Years in the White House*. New York: G. W. Carleton & Co., Publishers, 1868 (http://www.docsouth.unc.edu, accessed 15 April 2015).

"A Kind of Wild Tragedy." In *The Spectator*, no. 215. Vol. 2, 228–241. Edited by Donald F. Bond. Oxford: UK, Clarendon Press, 1965.

Knipe, Elizabeth. *Six Narrative Poems*. London, 1787.

A Lamentable Ballad of the tragical end of a gallant lord and a virtuous lady, and the untimely end of their two children, wickedly perform'd by a heathenish black-a-moor, their servant, the like never heard of before." Newcastle, 1760.

Laurens, Henry. *The Papers of Henry Laurens*. Edited by Philip M. Hamer, George C. Rogers, Jr., and Peggy J. Wehage. Columbia: University of South Carolina Press, 1970–2003.

Lawson, John. *A New Voyage to Carolina*. Edited by Hugh Talmage Lefler. Chapel Hill: University of North Carolina Press, 1967.

"Life Histories of Enslaved Africans in Barbados." Edited by Jerome S. Handler. *Slavery and Abolition* 19 (1998), 129–141.

Littleton, Edward. *Groans of the Plantations*. London: Clark, 1698.

Locke, John. *Two Treatises of Government*. Edited by Peter Laslett. New York: Cambridge University Press, 1960.

Long, Edward. *The History of Jamaica. Or, General Survey of the Antient and Modern State of that Island: With Reflections on Its Situation, Settlements, Inhabitants, Climate, Products, Commerce, Laws, and Government*. 2 vols. London: T. Lowndes, 1774.

Maxwell, James. "Pathological Inquiry Into the Nature of Cachexia Africana." *Jamaica Physical Journal* 2 (1835), 409–435.

Mitchill, Samuel L., M.D., and Edward Miller, M.D. *The Medical Repository*. New York, 1800.

Montesquieu, Charles. *Persian Letters*. 2 vols. Translated by John Ozell. London, 1722.

Montesquieu, Charles. *The Spirit of the Laws*. Translated and edited by Anne M. Choler, Basia C. Miller, and Harold Stone. Cambridge, UK: Cambridge University Press, 1989.

Northup, Solomon. *Twelve Years a Slave: Narrative of Solomon Northup, a Citizen of New-York, Kidnapped in Washington City in 1841, and Rescued in 1853*. Auburn, Buffalo, and London, 1853 (http://www.docsouth.unc.edu, accessed 13 April 2015).

Oldendorp, C. G. A. *A Caribbean Mission*. Edited by Johann Jakob Bossard. Translated by Arnold R. Highfield and Vladimir Barac. Ann Arbor, MI: Karoma Publishers, 1987.

Oldendorp, C. G. A. *History of the Mission of the Evangelical Brethren on the Caribbean Islands of St. Thomas, St. Croix, and St. John*. Edited by Johann Jakob Bossard. Translated by Arnold R. Highfield and Vladimir Barac. Ann Arbor, MI: Karoma Publishers, 1987.

Paiewonsky, Isidor. *Eyewitness Accounts of Slavery in the Danish West Indies*. New York: Fordham University Press, 1989.

Pioneers of the Black Atlantic: Five Slave Narratives from the Enlightenment, 1772–1815. Edited by Henry Louis Gates, Jr., and William L. Andrews. Washington, DC: Civitas, 1998.

Plantation and Frontier Documents 1649–1863: Illustrative of the Industrial History in the Colonial and Antebellum South. Two Volumes. Edited by Ulrich B. Phillips. Cleveland, OH: A. H. Clark and Col, 1909.

Prince, Mary. "The History of Mary Prince, a West-Indian Slave" (London, 1831). In *Six Women's Slave Narratives*. Edited by Henry Louis Gates, Jr. New York: Oxford University Press, 1988.

Ramsey, James. "An Essay on the Treatment and Conversion of African Slaves in the British Slave Colonies." London, 1784.

Raynal, Abbé. *A Philosophical and Political History of the Settlements and Trade of the Europeans in the East and West Indies*. 6 vols. Edinburgh: Mundell and Son, 1804.

Reflections on Slavery, With Recent Evidence of its Inhumanity. Occasioned by the Melancholy Death of Romain, a French Negro. Philadelphia: Robert Cochran, 1803.

Romans, Bernard. *A Concise History of East and West Florida*. New York, 1775.

The Royal African; or the Young Prince of Annamaboe. London: W. Reeve, G. Woodfall, and J. Barnes, 1750 (http://docsouth.unc.edu/neh/royal/summary.html).

Schwarz, Philip J. ed., *Gabriel's Conspiracy: A Documentary History*. Charlottesville: University of Virginia Press, 2012.

Scott, Winfield. *Memoirs of Lieut.-General Scott, LL.D, Written By Himself*. 2 vols. New York: Sheldon and Co., 1864.

Sewall, Samuel. *The Diary of Samuel Sewall, 1652–1730*. 2 vols. Edited by M. Halsey Thomas. New York: Farrar, Straus, and Giroux, 1973.

Slave Testimony: Two Centuries of Letters, Speeches, Interviews, and Autobiographies. Edited by John W. Blassingame. Baton Rouge: Louisiana State University Press, 1977.

Sloan, Hans. *A Voyage to the Islands of Madera, Barbados, Nieves, S. Christophers, and Jamaica*. 2 vols. London: Printed by B.M. for the Author, 1707–1725.

Snelgrave, William. *New Account of Some Parts of Guinea and the Slave Trade*. London, 1734.

Southerne, Thomas. *The Works of Thomas Southerne*. Edited by Robert Jordan and Harold Love. Oxford, UK: Clarendon Press, 1988.

Steward, Austin. *Twenty Two Years a Slave, and Forty Years a Freeman*. Rochester, NY: William Alling, 1857, http://docsouth.unc.edu/fpn/steward/steward.html.

Stanfield, James Field. *Observations on a Guinea Voyage. In a Series of Letters Addressed to Rev. Thomas Clarkson*. London, 1788.

Stewart, John. *A View of the Past and Present State of the Island of Jamaica With Remarks on the Moral and Physical Condition of the Slaves and on the Abolition of Slavery in the Colonies*. Edinburgh: 1823.

Sym, John. *Life's Preservative Against Self-Murder*. London: R. Flesher, 1637.

Torrey, Jesse. *A Portraiture of Domestic Slavery, in the United States, With Reflections on the Practicability of Restoring the Moral Rights of the Slave Without Impairing the Legal Rights of His Possessor*. Philadelphia: Published by the Author, 1817.

"The Two Negro Friends." *Virginia Almanack*. Williamsburg, 1775.

Weevils in the Wheat: Interviews with Virginia Ex-slaves. Edited by Charles L. Perdue Jr., Thomas E. Barden, and Robert K. Phillips. Bloomington, Indiana University Press, 1976.

Williams, Peter. *An Oration on the Abolition of the Slave Trade; Delivered in the African Church, in the City of New York, January 1, 1808*. New York: Samuel Wood, 1808.

INDEX